C0-CCL-101

DETERRENCE IN THE 1980s

Deterrence in the 1980s

Crisis and Dilemma

Edited by R. B. BYERS

ST. MARTIN'S PRESS
New York

St. Martin's Press, Inc., 175 Fifth Avenue, New York, NY 100010
Printed in Great Britain
First published in the United States of America in 1985

Library of Congress Cataloging in Publication Data
Main entry under title:

Deterrence in the 1980s.

Papers presented at the Conference on 'Deterrence in the 1980s,' held under the auspices of the York University Research Programme in Strategic Studies, Apr. 1984.
Includes index.
1. Deterrence (Strategy) – Congresses. 2. Nuclear Warfare – Congresses. 3. Warfare, Conventional – Congresses. I. Byers, R.B. II. Conference on 'Deterrence in the 1980s,' (1984: York University)
III. York University (Toronto, Ont.). Research Programme in Strategic Studies.
U162.6.D47 1985 355'.0217 85-10755
ISBN 0-312-19593-1

CONTENTS

PREFACE

The York University Research Programme in Strategic Studies conducts research in contemporary international security and arms control. This volume is part of the Programme's activities in Military Strategic Studies.

The editor would like to gratefully acknowledge the financial support of The Donner Canadian Foundation, the Canadian Department of External Affairs, and the Social Sciences and Humanities Research Council of Canada; and York University, especially McLaughlin College, for the use of facilities.

The editor would like to express his thanks and appreciation to the authors of the papers in this volume; and to the participants of the April 1984 York Deterrence Conference. Authors and participants alike took time from their busy schedules to address the subject matter of this book. I am particularly grateful for the research support provided by Michael Slack and James Macintosh of the York Programme. Lillian Kindree and Kirsten Semple spent long hours preparing the manuscript. Their patience and good cheer was of immense help. Peter Sowden of Croom Helm supported the project from the outset and I extend my hand across the Atlantic. Last, but not least, special thanks to my wife, Kathy Byers, for editorial assistance. Nevertheless, I assume responsibility for any errors - may there be few.

R.B.B.
Toronto

EDITOR'S INTRODUCTION

This volume originated with an April 1984 Conference on 'Deterrence in the 1980s' held under the auspices of the York University Research Programme in Strategic Studies. The Conference brought together forty-five scholars and government officials from Canada, Europe and the United States for the purpose of analysing the extent to which deterrence can and should remain the basis of American and Western security. The issues discussed were deemed appropriate and timely given the current 'distemper' in the West regarding the relationship between deterrence on the one hand and national and international security on the other.

The Conference participants focused their discussion on the full range of issues which have affected deterrence - political, psychological, military and ethical. Deterrence as theory, as strategy, and as policy came under close scrutiny. Not surprisingly considerable unease and dissatisfaction were expressed regarding various aspects of deterrence and its contemporary application and utility. In the words of one participant: 'Periodically, it is pummelled to the floor and then hauled to its feet again, only to absorb another cruel blow to the mid-section. Deterrence is said to be "fatally flawed" and the United States deterrent is said to be "not credible", but then deterrence is rehabilitated and the credibility of the American capability is said to be underestimated.'

Despite the problems and dilemmas posed by deterrence, most participants appeared to share the view that deterrence survives and governments are at least not to be condemned for retaining it - as long as they do so as part of a comprehensive political strategy. That is, deterrence as policy must be addressed within a broader context than just a focus on the military-strategic aspects of deterrence as strategy.

The contribution by R. B. Byers offers an assessment of why deterrence is currently under attack by focusing on the relationships between deterrence as theory and the dilemmas posed by the contemporary application of deterrence from both the military-strategic and the political-strategic perspectives. Byers advocates a return to a more clearly delineated distinction between 'deterrence' on the one hand and 'defence' on the other.

Janice Gross Stein addresses a gap between the logic of deterrence and the policy applications required to achieve successful deterrence. She notes that deterrence theory lacks guidance with respect to its political operation and has no real sense of 'context'. The Stein paper also stresses the importance of the psychological factors which impede the successful application of deterrence and argues that instances of misperception and miscalculation illustrate the need to include psychological considerations.

At the Conference, discussion focused on the difficulty of bridging the gap between <u>theory</u> and <u>policy</u>. Misgivings were expressed about the utility of deterrence theory to adequately explain, describe or prescribe successful deterrent policies. For some participants deterrence theory was deemed too far removed from the realities of both international and domestic political life to be of much assistance in explaining how deterrence operates. Not surprisingly a wide range of contrasting understandings of what deterrence 'really' means and how it 'really' works were expressed.

The contribution by George Quester offers a critical analysis of deterrence from a historical perspective taking into account pre-nuclear writings on air warfare, naval warfare and early works on nuclear deterrence. Quester then turns to a number of major problems of contemporary deterrence - second-strike forces, rationality, immorality, extended deterrence, and credibility. On balance, however, Quester concludes that deterrence has worked and will continue to work in the future.

Some participants at the Conference expressed skepticism regarding the future. The metaphorical characterisation of Quester's analysis of deterrence was that of a grandfather clock - as long as it is kept oiled, it will keep ticking. It was argued, however, that deterrence in the nuclear age required far more extensive modifications and needed to exhibit greater flexibility. This session also focused on the problems of rationality and the psychology of deterrence given the need to re-assure Western publics. Within this context the issue of morality in deterrence dominated the discussion. Participants expressed concern whether deterrence policies which threaten to punish - after the fact - millions of innocent civilians could ever be morally justifiable. It was pointed out, however, that while the American Catholic Bishops had practically rejected reliance on nuclear deterrence their more conservative European colleagues appeared more sympathetic to the requirements of deterrence despite the moral dilemmas involved.

Leon Sigal's chapter addresses the current state of superpower strategic deterrence within the context of the need to maintain stability which should take three forms - strategic stability, crisis stability, and arms race stability. These issues are assessed from the perspectives of the two major American schools of strategic thought: the stable balancers on the one hand and the nuclear war-fighters on the other hand. Sigal then turns to an analysis of the 1983 Scowcroft Report and concludes with an overview of possible Soviet reactions to current and future American strategic developments.

Conference participants pointed out that any discussion of deterrence is one-sided if Soviet views are not fully analysed. This was deemed to be essential if Western deterrence policies are to be credible given that Soviet doctrines appear at variance with those of the West. It was suggested that the Soviet Union is less concerned than is the West with extended deterrence and also prefers to emphasise the merits of an offensive strategy. While no consensus emerged, views were presented which suggested that the Soviet political leadership leans towards a stable balance school of strategy. Here the ABM Treaty, SALT II, and new Soviet nuclear systems which reduce the need to pre-empt were cited as arguments to bolster this proposition. Nevertheless, it was pointed out that the West has no clear idea what the Soviets really think about deterrence or how they perceive stability. It was recommended that the Soviets exhibit greater willingness to engage in a fuller strategic dialogue in order to overcome the types of misperceptions and misunderstandings which have arisen in the past.

President Reagan's 1983 Strategic Defense

Initiative is analysed by George Rathjens from the technical, the strategic and the political perspectives. Independent of the technical problems, Rathjens argues that the implications for deterrence - given the side-effects of SDI - would be destabilising. While SDI, as envisaged by President Reagan, may be unattainable, the impact on deterrence would be significant given considerations such as the Soviet response, the impact on offensive nuclear systems, the linkage to hardsite ABM defence, and the future of the ABM Treaty.

At the York Deterrence Conference most participants deemed SDI to be worrisome as the initiative raised more questions than it answered. Discussion at this session focused, in part, on the role and understanding of President Reagan regarding strategic developments and his knowledge of deterrence requirements. It was argued that 'Star Wars' defence appeared to offer the United States administration a solution to the difficult problems of a mutual assured destruction relationship. For the President the concept offers the prospect of placing less (or no) reliance on mutual deterrence which requires him to 'deal with the devil'. Discussion also focused on the apparent inability of the Reagan administration to appreciate the importance of 'arms race' and 'crisis' stability given the linkage between stability and deterrence. It was pointed out, however, that stability *per se* is really an American concept that has little place in Soviet strategic thought. Despite these differences there was general consensus that a full-scale, virtually perfect BMD system, relying primarily on space-based systems, would probably prove to be elusive. Progress would be slow and even rudimentary systems would prove exceedingly expensive. Concern was also expressed about the possible negative relationship between the United States' extended deterrence guarantee to Europe and full-scale ballistic missile defence.

Given the nature of the Western Alliance, deterrence-related concerns obviously have to take into account both American and European security. The papers by James Leonard, Lawrence Hagen, and Paul Buteux address various aspects of Atlantic relationships. James Leonard outlines four basic propositions which should guide Western security: the need for joint co-operative efforts; the need for equitable burden-sharing, taking into account Alliance diversity; the need for a strong defence but with reduced emphasis on nuclear weapons; and, the necessity to actively pursue arms control within a context of Alliance cohesion.

Lawrence Hagen offers an overview of the current 'disquiet' within NATO, taking into account the extent to which deterrence is being called into question as a result of the fissures which have arisen within the last few years. The retention of the credibility of extended deterrence in a state of strategic parity within the framework of flexible response is analysed. From the political-strategic perspective Hagen stresses the need to restore European confidence in the United States and recommends that musings on nuclear war-fighting scenarios cease; that the importance of European-American mutual understanding be recognised; and, that greater multilateralisation of the Western deterrence framework be pursued.

The chapter by Paul Buteux argues that NATO should not adopt a no first use policy given that possible first use is at the core of the strategy of flexible response. According to Buteux the options of enhanced conventional capabilities do not offer sufficient deterrence guarantees since linkages to the nuclear level are essential. No first use would serve to further decouple the United States and Europe and if adopted would require extensive changes in NATO doctrine, tactics and force posture. Even with NATO's adoption of 'deep strikes' a nuclear capability for extended deterrence would be required. At the same time, however, changes in NATO's conventional capabilities would allow the Alliance to place greater emphasis on no early first use.

Throughout the York Deterrence Conference, participants often referred to the dilemmas posed by the need to couple European and American security - and to do so within both a political and military framework. Not surprisingly concerns about the viability of extended deterrence were voiced on a number of occasions. Most participants shared the view that extended deterrence is in a state of crisis even though different perceptions were expressed regarding the impact of the possibility of escalation on deterrence. On the one hand it was argued that the possibility of escalation 'invalidated' deterrence, while on the other the possibility of escalation was considered essential for deterrence credibility. Despite these differences it was generally agreed that the strategy of flexible response, coupled with forward defence, remains valid - in part because the Soviet

Union appears unwilling to risk United States involvement in a nuclear war. Nevertheless, this meant that the possible decoupling of theatre and strategic nuclear forces presented a major challenge for the future of Western security.

The relationships between deterrence and arms control are, all too often, either ignored or down-played by policy-makers and scholars alike. Dan Caldwell's chapter indicates, however, that both deterrence as policy and differing types of arms control not only have an interactive relationship, but approaches to deterrence can affect preferences towards arms control measures and vice-versa. Thus Caldwell outlines four deterrence policies - fundamental, extended, flexible nuclear options, and nuclear war-fighting - and then assesses the affects of four types of arms control measures - confidence-building, limitations on ballistic missile defence, limitations of counterforce systems, and deep cuts - on deterrence. The paper also addresses the impact of new weapons on deterrence strategies.

Given the breakdown of the START and INF negotiations, and the lack of progress in other arms limitation fora, arms control and disarmament issues were raised on frequent occasions during the York Conference. There appeared to be a consensus that greater efforts had to be undertaken in the pursuit of meaningful and verifiable arms limitation agreements. Not unexpectedly, however, no consensus emerged on specifics. It was pointed out, nevertheless, that current - especially Western - arms control policies have often caused confusion for the military as well as being seen as cynical by the public. Building weapons to persuade the other side to reduce gives the impression that the 'West has been dressing and undressing at the same time'. This highlighted the difficult problem of using 'bargaining chips' to coerce arms control agreements with the Soviet Union - an approach which has often breathed uncontrollable life into new weapons systems programmes. The 'bargaining chip' approach indicates a close relationship between new systems, deterrence strategies and arms control.

The final four contributions to this volume assess the future of deterrence from a variety of perspectives. Robert Reford outlines the range of concerns which have arisen within the public sectors of Western society. He argues that public concerns include ones related to the number of nuclear weapons, to new deterrence policies, and to the morality of nuclear weapons. The issues raised in the Reford article were ones articulated at various stages throughout the York Conference. Ethical issues have clearly become a central aspect of the nuclear debate and these concerns have added to the difficulties of re-assurance. Most participants acknowledged the dilemmas this posed for deterrence, but no consensus emerged on how to alter deterrence policies and deterrent capabilities in a manner which would re-establish re-assurance.

De Montigny Marchand's paper serves as a reminder that for deterrence to be credible it has to be placed within the broader political-strategic context. East-West and intra-Alliance security must have political, economic, as well as military components. Similarly the internal environment within the Soviet Union must be taken into account. Marchand includes a series of security principles and guidelines which could be utilised for the conduct of East-West and Alliance relations.

At the Conference itself a consensus emerged on the importance of the political environment. The difficulty, unfortunately, was obvious to all - how to overcome the mistrust, tension and uncertainty which has pervaded Soviet-American and East-West relations since the late 1970s. Without a consistent and coherent Western set of policies vis-a-vis the East the current environment appears destined to prevail. This being the case, many participants encouraged the United States - especially President Reagan - to more actively address the need for greater normalisation in superpower relations. It was pointed out, however, that this can only occur if the Soviet Union also participates in re-establishing the dialogue.

From a military-strategic perspective General Theriault notes that no consensus exists regarding deterrence and its future. He then proceeds to outline some of the criticisms levelled against current deterrent policy and addresses a range of possible alternatives to NATO's doctrine of flexible response. General Theriault concludes that, in the absence of viable alternatives, NATO's deterrence posture will continue to rely on both nuclear and conventional capabilities. In essence NATO's strategy will not be fundamentally changed.

The majority of the participants at the Conference shared this assessment even though considerable dissatisfaction was expressed with those trends deemed to be destabilising and with the impact of new weapons and technologies - nuclear and conventional - on the viability of deterrence. As previously noted there was a diversity of views expressed concerning the impact of these trends.

Helmut Sonnenfeltd assesses the extent to which the Reagan administration's approach to deterrence is at variance with those of earlier administrations. He concludes, based on official declaratory statements, that deterrence remains a fundamental component of United States defence policy and that continuity with past administrations has been the norm.

At the York Conference this assessment was questioned. Some participants argued that United States deterrence policy has undergone substantial change, particularly with respect to nuclear war-fighting policies, while others stressed that current American policy reflected the evolution of deterrence policy since the early 1970s. Concerns were also expressed about the ability of the Reagan administration to cope with deterrence-related policies in a manner which could re-assure the publics of the West.

Given the diversity of views contained in this volume, in conjunction with those expressed at the York Deterrence Conference, it is difficult to arrive at any clear overall view about the future of deterrence. There was agreement that deterrence - as theory, as strategy, and as policy - is under attack. There was no consensus amongst scholars nor amongst policy-makers on how to resolve the deep-rooted dilemmas which are raised in this volume. Nevertheless with a continued exchange of views both within the West - and hopefully with the Soviet Union and the East - it may be possible to make strides towards some degree of consensus on how to manage East-West and intra-Alliance relations in a manner which will enhance mutual and international security.

As long as nuclear weapons remain as key components of national security policy for the superpowers, as well as for NATO and the Warsaw Pact, deterrence must be retained. The major questions, however, remain unanswered - with what policy, with what strategy, and with what capabilities?

Chapter One

DETERRENCE UNDER ATTACK: CRISIS AND DILEMMA

R.B. Byers*

Deterrence, both conceptually and operationally, has served as the foundation of Western security for more than three decades. As a consequence, there are grounds for arguing that deterrence has been successful. Despite East-West tensions and conflict, war has been avoided and deterrence should receive partial credit. Not surprisingly, therefore, Western governments remain wedded to deterrence and are unlikely to jettison it as the underlying rationale for international security.

Despite its success, deterrence has recently come under unprecedented attack. A wide range of critics, from both the left and the right, have demanded that deterrence be rejected as the basis of Western security. Deterrence has always had its critics and major reservations have been expressed for years on any number of grounds. This being the case it might be asked - why now? On what grounds has deterrence come under such attack at this point in time? The criticisms have been extensive and include the following: that deterrence no longer adequately serves the security interests of the West; that deterrence may fail; that deterrence is unethical; that deterrence fuels the arms race; that deterrence masks preparations for war - especially nuclear war; that deterrence, both conceptually and operationally, has never been accepted by the Soviet Union; that deterrence in the nuclear age can never be credible. The list goes on.

Irrespective of the validity of such criticisms, a crisis of confidence has arisen

* The author would like to thank James Macintosh of the York University Research Programme in Strategic Studies for his valuable suggestions on an earlier draft.

regarding the future of deterrence. If Western governments do not address the problems in a manner which can serve to restore greater public confidence in deterrence, the groundswell of criticisms will continue to grow. This being the case, the purpose of this paper is to assess the contemporary nature of deterrence from three perspectives - the conceptual, the military-strategic, and the political-strategic - with a view to offering specific proposals to restore greater public confidence in the future of deterrence as theory, as policy, and as strategy. Given the cruel dilemmas posed by nuclear weapons, deterrence is the only viable security option for the future - what remains in doubt is what form it should take and what military capabilities are required to support it.

Conceptual Problems and Difficulties

In the early 1960s Thomas Schelling, in his now classic work The Strategy of Conflict, observed:

> What is impressive is not how complicated the idea of deterrence has become, and how carefully it has been refined and developed, but how slow the process has been, how vague the concepts still are, and how inelegant the current theory of deterrence is.[1]

More than thirty years later the conceptual basis of deterrence remains plagued by a number of dilemmas which have contributed to the current disillusionment and concern regarding its utility.

Part of the difficulty has been a lack of conceptual clarity and consensus concerning deterrence *qua* deterrence. For better or worse the meaning and understanding of deterrence varies considerably depending upon a wide range of circumstances and considerations. Thus deterrence has multiple uses: sometimes it signifies theory; sometimes it is a synonym for defence; often it represents a general type of defence policy; at times the term refers to a strategy or to the practical application of a strategy such as deterrence by punishment or deterrence by denial; more frequently deterrence is deemed to be a particular ideal type of strategy such as 'assured destruction' or 'war-fighting'; sometimes the term is utilised to characterise a model of reality - for example, the Soviet-American strategic nuclear relationship is a deterrence relationship. As long as deterrence, in the abstract, can be and is applied to a wide range of military-strategic and/or political-strategic concerns and situations, conceptual confusion is likely to be the order of the day.[2] This situation has arisen, in part, because the conceptual basis of deterrence has been made to conform to the security prescriptions of the beholder. Deterrence has come to mean 'all things to all men'.

Given the current distemper over the operational aspects of deterrence it should be incumbent upon scholars - and, more particularly, upon the responsible government leaders and officials - to attempt to achieve a greater degree of conceptual consensus when discussing and assessing deterrence and its requirements for national and international security. This would not necessarily resolve the current dilemmas, but it could, hopefully, place the deterrence debate in a somewhat more appropriate context than is presently the case.

An attempt to develop greater conceptual consensus does not require the development of a new definitional framework - as helpful as this might be to academic and governmental careers. Analysts and governments should be encouraged to explicitly accept Glenn Snyder's 1961 proposition that 'deterrence means <u>discouraging</u> the enemy from taking military action by posing for him a prospect of cost and risk outweighing his prospective gain.'[3] In other words the underlying and fundamental tenet is one of persuasion or dissuasion based on the threat of retaliation. Conceptually this is as true in the 1980s as it was in the 1950s.

Recognition of this principle appears, for example, to have been understood by members of the 1983 Scowcroft Commission when the final report noted that deterrence is 'a condition in which a strategic power is <u>dissuaded from attack</u> because he believes the potential victim could retaliate effectively'.[4] Despite criticisms and observations to the contrary, the Reagan administration continues - as have past American administrations - to declare allegiance to this traditional definition of deterrence, at least in terms of declaratory policy. Caspar Weinberger's <u>Annual Report to the Congress: Fiscal Year 1985</u> notes that the United States continues 'to seek nuclear and conventional capabilities sufficient to convince any potential aggressor that the costs of aggression would exceed any potential gains that he might achieve'.[5]

Deterrence Under Attack

Given this definitional context it is absolutely essential to retain the necessary distinction between the threat of force and the use of force. This was fully appreciated by Thomas Schelling when he pointed out that 'a useful distinction can be made between the application of force and the threat of force. Deterrence is concerned with the exploitation of potential force. It is concerned with persuading a potential enemy that he should in his own interest avoid certain courses of activity.'[6] Similarly Patrick Morgan has argued that 'if the essence of deterrence is threat to inhibit attack, then we can separate it, in principle, from other forms of coercive behavior and still other uses of armed force.'[7] Unfortunately this fundamental point has often been forgotten and/or purposely overlooked as scholars and government officials have attempted to apply the conceptual basis of deterrence to a far broader range of policy situations than should be the case. This point cannot be stressed too strongly - deterrence involves the threat to use force in order to forestall its use. If force is employed deterrence has failed.

If this proposition is accepted, then it is necessary to remind ourselves of the difference between deterrence on the one hand and defence on the other. To return to Glenn Snyder: 'the essential theoretical problem in the field of national security policy is to clarify and distinguish between the two central concepts of deterrence and defense.' Snyder noted that:

> defense means reducing our own prospective costs and risks in the event that deterrence fails. Deterrence works on the enemy's intentions; the deterrent value of military forces is their effect in reducing the likelihood of enemy military moves. Defense reduces the enemy's capability to damage or deprive us; the defense value of military forces is their effect in mitigating the adverse consequences for us of possible enemy moves, whether such consequences are counted as losses of territory or war damage.[8]

Major conceptual and operational dilemmas have, however, arisen as a result of the blurring between the concepts of deterrence and defence. Part of the difficulty, of course, is that deterrence and defence are intrinsically interrelated. For deterrence to be credible, an effective military capability must exist. Without sufficient military power an enemy will not be deterred - or at least the prospects for deterrence failure are enhanced. Nevertheless, to claim that defence values constitute the basis of deterrence or vice versa is to distort the linkages between the two and to ignore the essential theoretical differences between the concepts.

The conceptual problem has become complicated as the result of the operationalisation of deterrence. Since the early 1950s deterrence has been the foundation of Western and American security policy. For example, Weinberger's 1984 Report to Congress clearly states that 'deterrence remains the cornerstone of our defense policy.'[9] While the Soviet case is less explicit there are grounds to argue that the political leadership in the Soviet Union accepts the principles of deterrence as guiding East-West security relations.[10]

In terms of East-West relations, deterrence - as policy - has been applied to both the bilateral (Soviet-American) and to the multilateral (NATO-Warsaw Pact) setting. Given the types of military capabilities deemed necessary to enhance deterrence credibility - that is, strategic nuclear forces, Euro-strategic nuclear forces, battlefield nuclear forces, and conventional military forces - the translation of deterrence into policy has raised serious concerns with the concept *per se*. For deterrence as a concept to be effective as policy it must be operationalised in both the bilateral and the multilateral setting - thus the perceived need by the West (particularly the Europeans) for effective 'extended deterrence'.

In principle, there are no grounds to reject the underlying conceptual basis of deterrence when the definitional context is broadened to include 'extended deterrence'. That is, the major purpose of NATO's triad of military forces is to deter. For example, the October 1984 final communique of the NATO Nuclear Planning Group stated that 'while each element of the triad requires a credibility of its own, they are only effective when seen as a whole, and indeed work to complement each other. Nuclear weapons are vital for the deterrence of aggression at all levels and by their very existence, work to enhance deterrence across the entire spectrum.'[11]

As a statement of policy the position adopted by the Nuclear Planning Group is consistent with deterrence theory. The difficulty, however, is that

Deterrence Under Attack

NATO and its members - and for that matter far too many analysts - confuse the relationship between deterrence and defence. While NATO's doctrine of flexible response has been articulated as a strategy of deterrence (which it is), the doctrine also incorporates the underlying tenets of Snyder's concept of defence (which it must). Yet it should be incumbent upon NATO - as well as the United States, Canada, _et al._, - to ensure that the distinctions between deterrence and defence are clearly delineated. For example, if NATO is attacked then extended deterrence has failed and flexible response as a deterrence strategy has been unsuccessful. Yet, in a war-fighting situation, flexible response as 'defence' _may_ serve to limit damage and terminate the conflict at a lower level of hostilities than other strategies which could be adopted by the Alliance.

Given the confusion between deterrence and defence as concepts and their applications as policy, the major argument bears repeating - _deterrence is a pre-war concept while defence is both a pre-war and war-fighting concept_.

Conceptual confusion has been compounded, in part, by the inappropriate use of deterrence language. Terminology such as 'graduated deterrence' and 'intra-war deterrence' only serves to blur the crucial distinctions between deterrence and defence. Such language conveys the impression that conceptually deterrence can be applied to a war-fighting situation. The argument presented here, however, is just the opposite - deterrence failure is deterrence failure irrespective of the type of military force employed. If consensus could emerge on this fundamental proposition, considerable progress would be made towards clarifying the conceptual problems underlying deterrence theory.

The current distemper with deterrence can, in part, be laid at the conceptual doorstep. No conceptual consensus exists and deterrence terminology has been distorted through careless and thoughtless usage. Deterrence has, to some extent, become a victim of its own conceptual baggage; but these problems can be overcome by analysts and policy-makers alike if deterrence-defence distinctions are clearly articulated.

Military-Strategic Dilemmas

The major purpose of this section is to question whether military-strategic issues have contributed to the current disenchantment with deterrence. Should deterrence _qua_ deterrence shoulder the responsibility for the military-strategic developments and issues which have generated current concerns?

Historically the operationalisation of deterrence theory - in military-strategic terms - has been the cause of much debate and has posed a number of serious security dilemmas. The post-1945 history of strategic thought serves to remind us that considerable intellectual and political energy has been devoted to coping with the intricate, and often arcane, issues and dilemmas posed by nuclear weapons.[12]

The development, deployment and use of the atomic bomb preceded the utilisation of deterrence as the key policy component of American, Western (and possibly Soviet) military doctrine. Once the destructive magnitude of the bomb was understood, and once nuclear weapons became an integral part of the military inventory of the United States and the Soviet Union - to be followed by Britain, France and China - it should have been incumbent upon strategists (military and civilian alike) and political leaders to seek ways to ensure that nuclear weapons would never again be used. Not surprisingly, however, military planners have focused their attention on how to enhance the credibility of nuclear deterrence and on how to utilise nuclear capabilities should deterrence fail. For their part, political leaders have all too often neglected the relationships between nuclear weapons and deterrence requirements.

Nevertheless, it should be appreciated that the military and political utility of nuclear weapons has been given wide-ranging credit or discredit across the full spectrum of international politics - from preserving the peace in Europe, to resolving the Cuban missile crisis, to the desire of Third World countries to acquire nuclear weapons, to the numerous conventional wars fought under the nuclear umbrella, etc. The point to be stressed in this litany, irrespective of the utility-disutility calculus of nuclear weapons, is that the underlying precepts of deterrence theory have, on balance and over time, served to circumscribe the possibility of nuclear war - at least premeditated nuclear war.

As long as nuclear weapons exist, and as long as they are perceived to have military and political utility, then the principle of non-use - as embedded in deterrence theory - should and must be retained despite the fact that mankind has developed the military capability to destroy much of the world. But since nuclear weapons exist and Pandora's box has been opened, then the theory of deterrence appears to be the only available set of principles which can serve to guide policy-makers.

Nevertheless, the irony for deterrence posed by the development of nuclear weapons should be kept firmly in mind. Deterrence as policy - as the basis for national and international security - only came into its own in the nuclear age. Deterrence as a concept existed prior to 1945, but it was not central to national security nor did it place the same degree of emphasis on the importance of non-use of weapons.[13] In the nuclear age the primary (only?) utility of nuclear weapons is to deter attack. Nevertheless, deterrence - both as theory and as policy - is under fierce attack because of nuclear weapons.

The dilemma has been apparent since the bombings of Nagasaki and Hiroshima: how to make credible the incredible. Not surprisingly some critics ask whether deterrence as policy should be linked to a military threat which if carried out, given the mutual vulnerability of the United States and the Soviet Union along with the East and the West, would result in the devastation of both aggressor and defender. Irrespective of the scientific validity of arguments relating to the dangers of 'nuclear winter',[14] the damage from nuclear war, even in a limited exchange, to both East and West - given existing and projected nuclear capabilities - would be so extensive that no cost-gain calculus could possibly support the proposition that a nuclear war could be won. Hence President Reagan's stated view that a nuclear war could not be won and must not be fought. Despite some American assessments[15] to the contrary, the Soviet political leadership appears to agree with this position. This being the case it has been argued that in military-strategic terms deterrence policy is fundamentally flawed.

The major criticisms stem from that aspect of deterrence theory which requires the threat of use - that is, the threat of retaliation to dissuade an attack. How, in military-strategic terms, can deterrence as policy be credible given the underlying realisation that if deterrence fails everyone loses?

Unfortunately deterrence as theory only offers the policy-maker limited guidance. Neither deterrence theory nor academic attempts to offer prescriptions regarding nuclear developments have assumed a prominent role with respect to the operationalisation of nuclear capabilities (for example, the United States' Single Integrated Operational Plan) or in terms of acquisition programmes. Thus there has been a notable disjunction between deterrence as theory to guide national security policy and the reality of security policy. Policy-makers, confronted by an ever increasing nuclear arsenal, have thus tried to devise rationales in the form of various declaratory strategies. One consequence of this has been the evolution of American strategic doctrine from massive retaliation, to assured destruction, to the countervailing strategy of the Reagan administration.

Similarly NATO's doctrine of flexible response - based on forward conventional defence coupled with the prospect of nuclear first use - is officially deemed the most appropriate deterrence strategy, given Soviet and Warsaw Pact doctrine and capabilities. Yet NATO's doctrine, as does American strategic doctrine, appears to place greater emphasis on the requirements for successful defence then it does on the requirements for successful deterrence. The deterrence-defence interface - in operational terms - should be clearly delineated and if policy is to err it should err on the side of deterrence rather than on the side of defence values. If this proposition has any validity it is incumbent upon policy-makers to more clearly develop the necessary conditions for deterrence as military-strategic policy. That is, how much 'defence' and what kind of 'defence' is required to ensure deterrence credibility as policy? For example, emphasis on nuclear war-fighting doctrines and capabilities appears, to many critics, to undermine the validity of deterrence theory and to contribute to public concerns over re-assurance. Here deterrence as theory is of little assistance, even though the key security conditions have been clearly articulated by strategists.

The _sine qua non_ military requirement for credible nuclear deterrence - both for the United States and, given the basis of extended deterrence, for Europe - is the retention of a viable second-strike capability. This, of course, means denying the potential aggressor a viable first-strike capability. It should go without saying that if both sides possess a viable second-strike capability, then deterrence is mutual - a more desirable situation than unilateral deterrence if deterrence stability is deemed important.[16] On the surface this may appear as a rather banal observation given the complex and arcane nature of the strategic debate. Yet this point is often overlooked - the trees have obscured the forest.

Since the mid-1960s both superpowers have possessed a viable second-strike capability. Shifts in the strategic nuclear balance have not called this most basic capability into question; nor have Soviet-American asymmetries in the triad - ICBMs, SLBMs, and long-range bombers - threatened either side's retaliatory capability. 'Windows of vulnerability' may be deemed significant for a variety of political and technical reasons and these windows have caused unease in some circles. However, they have not threatened - and in the foreseeable future will not threaten - the viability of either side's second-strike capabilities. In this sense mutual strategic stability remains robust.

The difficulty, however, is that both the United States and the Soviet Union have proceeded to develop and deploy nuclear weapons systems which exhibit, in varying degrees, first-strike characteristics. Thus American concern over the SS-18 and Soviet concern with the MX and deployment of the Trident II D-5. Furthermore, with changes in nuclear technology, primarily increased accuracy for both land and sea-based ballistic missiles coupled with improved C^3, future systems can be perceived as genuinely threatening counterforce nuclear weapons. Both nuclear powers find themselves in a strategic situation where legitimate fears have arisen that the other is striving to develop a viable first-strike posture. While such prospects are highly unlikely the end result has been to undermine confidence in the respective second-strike capabilities of the two superpowers.

These developments - actual and potential - indicate one of the major paradoxes of the nuclear age. Many efforts to enhance credibility intended to reduce the probability of nuclear war convey the opposite impression with their focus on the war-fighting aspects of deterrence. The result has been two competing, but incommensurate tendencies: reducing the probability of war by increasing its apparent probability. This, unfortunately, has blurred the distinction between the threat of force and the possible application of force.

Deterrence Under Attack

The proposed solutions to this paradox have been addressed in detail in a variety of fora and if adopted would indicate a willingness to emphasise deterrence rather than defence values at the expense of deterrence. Greater reliance on the sea-based deterrent, the adoption of Midgetman, and the elimination of MIRVs are all proposals which would enhance deterrence stability, but not adversely affect credibility. Such proposals will only be adopted if the United States and Soviet Union can reach some understanding that nuclear deterrence should be based on credible second-strike capabilities and that the pursuit - however elusive - of a first-strike capability ought not be a military objective of either.

The capability dilemmas are compounded by trends in nuclear doctrine - that is, deterrence as strategy. Here the major question is the extent to which deterrence strategy should reflect nuclear war-fighting capabilities in order to make the threat of use credible. Have the arguments dating back to the Schlesinger era been based on the legitimate requirements for selective options as distinct from the perceived need to prevail should deterrence fail? Is a countervailing strategy required from the perspective of deterrence as theory? The short answer to this latter question is 'no', yet the former questions have posed real dilemmas.

The evolution of American deterrence strategy has probably been inevitable given the changes in nuclear technology coupled with the absence of meaningful arms limitation and the deterioration of superpower relations. Yet subtle, but important, differences appear to have emerged in American doctrine since the early 1970s. The Schlesinger doctrine was primarily an attempt to move away from massive retaliation (in the form of assured destruction) by the introduction of some limited strike options. President Carter's PD59 continued the trend of introducing greater flexibility into operational plans. The Reagan administration, however, has placed greater emphasis on the need to successfully fight a nuclear war should it be necessary. Within this context the current official view in Washington is that the Soviet Union would contemplate, under certain circumstances, fighting a nuclear war. This being the case there is a considered need to base nuclear strategy on the possibility of war-fighting and thus its translation into a countervailing strategy.

Deterrence Under Attack

At the same time, current American nuclear declaratory policy attempts to portray deterrence as the uppermost consideration. This is where the debate between stable balancers versus nuclear war-fighters assumes considerable importance.[17] Proponents of both schools wish to avoid nuclear war, both acknowledge the destructive potential of current capabilities, and both support the need for deterrence credibility. The crucial difference lies in the fact that the nuclear war-fighters place greater emphasis on defence values - that is, to prevail should deterrence fail; while the stable balancers emphasise the need to ensure non-use. Many of the critics of deterrence, especially those in the peace movement, do not perceive this important distinction between the two schools of strategic thought and the implications it has for nuclear strategy.

The various nuclear strategy arguments which have dominated the debate - punishment versus denial, countervalue versus counterforce, mutual assured destruction versus nuclear utilisation targeting - have all too often neglected the fundamental point that given the destructive potential of nuclear weapons and the cost-gain calculus of nuclear war, no nuclear strategy can ever be credible in the sense that 'victory is possible'. The difficulty has been to balance, in an appropriate manner, dissuasion aspects of deterrence strategy against defence value-related threats (a combination of countervalue and counterforce threats) in order to maximise credibility. Nevertheless, the arguments over specific strategies only deal with marginal differences and do not affect the reality of deterrence failure. When death can be estimated in the millions and when industrial and environmental destruction can end society as we know it, the utility of nuclear strategy for defence values becomes counterproductive and meaningless. For better or for worse nuclear weapons are qualitatively different from conventional weapons and to argue otherwise is to misrepresent and/or misunderstand what has taken place since 1945.

The ever-increasing danger, however, is that nuclear strategy based on defence values is congruent with attempts to ensure 'damage limitation', to acquire a 'countervailing' capability, to emphasise the need to 'prevail'. In practical terms it means a continuation of the current trends: increased accuracy, enhanced C^3, augmented numbers, etc. The outcome is to degrade, and possibly ignore, deterrence as policy for the sake of the illusory vision that nuclear war-fighting capabilities can do more than marginally enhance deterrence credibility. Deterrence credibility exists with a second-strike capability, but credible defence in the nuclear age is a *non sequitur* and should be recognised as such.[18]

The major policy implications of these arguments should be obvious. Both superpowers need to agree that nuclear weapons are for deterrent purposes only and that deterrence can be ensured by credible second-strike capabilities. Under these circumstances substantial reductions in current levels of strategic nuclear weapons could be implemented without adversely affecting the security interests of either side. The security objective would be to retain stable and mutual deterrence at the lowest possible force levels consistent with retention of a viable retaliatory nuclear capability. Pursuit of this objective would reverse the current trend of striving to achieve a defence value oriented deterrence posture and in the process move towards the conceptual basis of deterrence *qua* deterrence.

Extended deterrence poses somewhat of a different dilemma: not because the American guarantee is extended to Western Europe, not because of the loss of American strategic superiority, not because of Euro-strategic (INF) nuclear asymmetries, but because of the linkages between nuclear and conventional deterrence.

Concerns over the nature and reliability of the nuclear guarantee are primarily political-strategic rather than military-strategic in nature. The loss of strategic superiority does not invalidate the fundamental point that even with American superiority, the Soviet Union had a second-strike capability and thus nuclear deterrence became truly mutual rather than unilateral in the mid-1960s. The current NATO view that deterrence can only be credible if capabilities are matched across the entire range of nuclear systems overlooks or misunderstands the conceptual basis of deterrence as it should apply to nuclear capabilities. Deployment of GLCMs and Pershing IIs only marginally affects NATO's nuclear capability and does not hold out the promise for the effective application of defence values. The same arguments hold true for the SS-20. In other words, the core of the concern about extended deterrence should not focus on the nuclear, but rather on the nuclear-conventional linkages and the problems of possible escalation to the nuclear level should deterrence fail.

Within this context it is essential to appreciate that deterrence via conventional military forces - both conceptually and operationally - avoids the cruel dilemmas posed by nuclear deterrence. Enhanced conventional defence increases the credibility of conventional deterrence as the threat to use force remains within acceptable cost-gain calculations for the potential defender. Furthermore, deterrence failure does not have the same implications for the defender - that is, destruction of his homeland - as does nuclear deterrence. Consequently, defence values assume far more weight in deterrence-defence considerations within the non-nuclear framework. Here the use of force can be - and has been - far more frequently contemplated and thus there are sound military-strategic rationales for the pursuit of more effective conventional military capabilities.

Some new conventional capabilities (for example, high speed armour) and the application of tactics (for example, the AirLand Battle) have a counter-offensive orientation that could adversely affect crisis stability.[19] What should be clearly appreciated, however, is that the consequences of conventional defence failure remain qualitatively different from the dangers of nuclear deterrence failure. This is not to argue that the destructive potential of conventional military power should be downplayed, but rather to observe that the threat of conventional war remains credible to a degree that nuclear war can never be credible. This may be a sad indictment of the state of the world - death is death and killing is killing, irrespective of the method. Nevertheless, the Clausewitzian dictum of war as a continuation of politics by other means remains well entrenched and is a frequent occurrence in the contemporary international environment.

For the West, and particularly for the Europeans, extended deterrence represents a much more complicated set of operational security concerns than either nuclear deterrence or conventional deterrence, given the need to operationalise deterrence across the entire force spectrum. The extent to which deterrence is extended is not exclusively geo-strategic - that is, from America to Europe - but also functionally, from the nuclear to the conventional and vice versa. This latter aspect is of greater military significance.

Deterrence Under Attack

Given the nuclear-conventional linkages which flow from the doctrine of flexible response, including forward defence coupled with possible nuclear first use, the threat to use force will always be less than credible given possible cost-gain calculations. Flexible response is based, in part, on the dangers to the aggressor of escalation to the nuclear level, but should that level be reached then the same dilemmas will prevail as in the case of strategic nuclear war - at least for the Europeans and in all probability for North Americans and for the Soviets. This being the case NATO should place greater emphasis on deterrence qua deterrence rather than on defence values as a means of enhancing security.

In some respects NATO's military response to the Warsaw Pact since the late 1970s has been questionable. In the face of the Soviet SS-20 threat, NATO has tried to apply defence value considerations to the INF decision in order to overcome the loss of American strategic superiority. From a military-strategic perspective INF deployment does not enhance deterrence credibility but rather increases the incentive for the Soviet Union to pre-empt. GLCMs add little to NATO's second-strike capability and, according to critics, are perceived to be for nuclear war-fighting purposes even though they do not possess the speed to attack time-urgent targets. In effect, NATO is deploying a second-strike system which is vulnerable to a first-strike in an era where such vulnerabilities can be circumvented. Pershing IIs are a different matter as they do constitute a first-strike system, but are not being deployed in sufficient numbers for NATO to acquire a first-strike capability. Thus, despite claims by NATO officials and by Western political leaders that the Alliance's INF response is compatible with deterrence, there are grounds to be skeptical. The end result has called into question the viability of flexible response and leads to a number of policy proposals - such as no first use - which may be desirable for political-strategic reasons, but which do not enhance deterrence given NATO's existing doctrine and force posture.

There have been, on the other hand, concerted efforts since 1978 to upgrade NATO's conventional capabilities and General Bernard Rogers, as SACEUR, has pursued this objective with vigour. Enhanced conventional capabilities, while costly and controversial in their own right, serve to raise the nuclear threshold and in the process strengthen deterrence.

However, this in and of itself, will do little to resolve the security problems in Europe. Flexible response remains predicated, in part, on the military utility of escalation. Successful implementation requires escalation control across the force spectrum - which is doubtful given NATO's capabilities. It also requires an appropriate C^3I structure and process for both a crisis situation and for war-fighting decision-making. Flexible response also assumes that NATO will be able to retain the initiative regarding the level and type of response. This is highly questionable given Warsaw Pact doctrine and capabilities.

A major dilemma is that a nuclear-conventional threshold exists conceptually and even in terms of crisis decision-making, but probably would be non-existent in the face of a Warsaw Pact attack.[20] This being the case the application of deterrence as strategy to a European conflict must acknowledge that current NATO doctrine incorporates both nuclear and conventional components. The underlying principle of nuclear deterrence must in this case prevail - that is, if force is used deterrence has failed. To rely on the military utility of escalation control is too risky a strategy given the cost-gain calculus. Furthermore, such a strategy places undue emphasis on defence values at the expense of deterrence.

It may be that European security would be enhanced if NATO were, over time, to adopt a <u>strategy of equivalent response</u>. Equivalent response would be based on the principle that NATO would respond in kind in order to defend its territory against a military attack - that is, a conventional attack would be met with conventional defence, etc. The underlying military premise would be that NATO possesses sufficient capabilities to adequately respond to the possible range of Warsaw Pact attacks.

Objections to such a doctrine are immediately obvious: the Warsaw Pact has conventional military superiority; NATO lacks an equivalent chemical warfare capability; battlefield nuclear capabilities would need to be decoupled in terms of NATO tactics; nuclear-conventional decoupling could adversely affect European security; the United States and Europe could be further decoupled politically and strategically, etc.

However, the adoption of such a doctrine would have a number of advantages. First, equivalent response would re-emphasise NATO's defensive orientatation. Second, it would more clearly delineate the nuclear-conventional threshold in terms of doctrine. Third, it would allow NATO to adopt a no first use policy, but retain forward defence. Fourth, it would place the initiative in deciding on 'how much defence is enough' with the Soviet Union. Fifth, it would link further NATO deployments and modernisation of nuclear weapons with those of the Soviet Union. Sixth, it would offer greater incentive for the Soviets to show flexibility with respect to arms reductions. Seventh, it would serve to re-assure Europeans to a greater degree than does flexible response. Eighth, it would allow NATO to clarify deterrence-defence relationships in a more satisfactory manner than is currently the case.

Equivalent response would not, unfortunately, be the panacea for European security. The dilemmas posed by nuclear weapons and extended deterrence would still exist. Nevertheless, such a strategy would reduce the emphasis on nuclear weapons. For example, there would be a considerable incentive for both NATO and the Warsaw Pact to negotiate the complete withdrawal of battlefield nuclear weapons from their inventories.

A major difficulty for NATO would be the requirement to attain conventional military parity with the Warsaw Pact, but if progress could be made within the MBFR context, coupled with greater emphasis on NATO's conventional capabilities, this might be achieved over time. Since the strategy of equivalent response could serve to resolve some of the military-strategic dilemmas of deterrence, it should be given serious consideration, but within the broader political-strategic context.

Political-Strategic Issues

Soviet-American, and as a result East-West, relations have been in disarray since the late 1970s. Superpower relations have been conducted in an atmosphere of mistrust, tension, and uncertainty. No meaningful dialogue has taken place and neither the United States nor the Soviet Union has been willing to take the necessary initiatives to restore a more normalised relationship and re-commence the search for a more co-operative approach to the problems of international security.[21] The harsh rhetoric of the early 1980s has given way to more measured public statements on the part of both Soviet and American leaders; but both Moscow and

Washington demand that deeds replace words.

Historically, the superpower relationship has always exhibited, in varying degrees, elements of co-operation, competition and conflict. This reality will continue, but the key to the relationship is the relative mix of these three components over time, by region, and by issue. Since the late 1970s co-operation has been virtually non-existent as competition and potential conflict have become the order of the day. There has been a tendency on the part of both the United States and the Soviet Union to perceive the relationship in zero-sum terms.

The causes of deterioration are complex yet well known. For our purpose the major issue is the extent to which the breakdown in superpower relations has contributed to the current disenchantment with deterrence. The extent to which deterrence as policy and/or as strategy has adversely affected the political-strategic environment is also of concern. Clarification in these areas should help to place the deterrence debate in a broader and, hopefully, more appropriate context.

The deterioration of superpower and East-West relations has adversely affected the viability of deterrence from at least six perspectives. First, and most important, Western governments have, since the Cuban missile crisis, conveyed the view that deterrence in the nuclear age had to be mutual - that both East and West had a mutual interest in war avoidance and that East-West relations could be conducted in a manner to reinforce and ensure mutual survival. Despite the use of different language the Soviet political leadership has shared this position. With the breakdown in detente this assumption has been called into question as the superpowers have accused each other of seeking military superiority, of pursuing nuclear war-fighting doctrines, of acquiring nuclear war-fighting weapons, and, in certain instances, of contemplating fighting a nuclear war. Such has been the rhetoric of the early 1980s and the rhetoric has had a profound impact on public perceptions of the dangers of nuclear war. For some segments of the public the need to re-assure has become more important than the need to deter.

In part, deterrence has been called into question on the grounds that the United States and Soviet Union have become more interested in unilateral than in mutual security. Each superpower has accused the other of pursuing policies, deploying systems and advocating arms limitation proposals which would enhance its own security interests at the expense of the other. In one sense, therefore, the pursuit of security has become zero-sum in an international climate where dialogue is virtually non-existent. Deterrence *per se* is not at fault, yet deterrence as policy and as strategy has been rooted, implicitly if not explicitly, in the mutuality of the strategic relationship. This mutuality has been called into question and President Reagan's 1983 Strategic Defense Initiative typifies the underlying desire to search for unilateral security in a political climate of mistrust.

A second factor, flowing from a greater willingness to pursue unilateral security, has been the continuation of the arms race - particularly the nuclear arms race. Both superpowers have proceeded to develop and deploy new generations of nuclear and conventional weapons and to allocate greater resources to defence. By the end of the decade it is estimated that the existing Soviet-American stockpile of nuclear weapons will have surpassed 60,000 warheads. The nuclear arms race continues unabated and is justified by the need to enhance deterrence credibility (United States) and to ensure equal security (Soviet Union). Small wonder that the critics claim deterrence is a mask for the continued build up of military capabilities.

Given the evolution of strategic doctrine and the perceived need to enhance deterrence by emphasising the threat to use force (defence values) there is an obvious linkage between deterrence as policy and the nuclear arms race. With a defence value oriented deterrence strategy there will always be demands from military planners for enhanced military capabilities. This being the case arms limitation agreements should assume considerable importance as a means to balance the dissuasion and defence value components of deterrence policy. Unfortunately with the breakdown in superpower relations there has been no progress with arms limitation negotiations.

The failure of arms limitation in the 1980s is thus a third factor which has adversely affected the viability of deterrence. The lack of progress in the various fora - START, INF, MBFR, the CDE in Stockholm, the CD in Geneva and at the United Nations - reflects the underlying unwillingness of the participants to reach consensus on any meaningful and verifiable reductions across the spectrum of arms limitation issues. The extent to which the failure of arms limitation is a function of the international environment or of the complicated issues involved remains unclear.

The Reagan administration came into office obviously skeptical about the value of arms control and determined to avoid the so-called 'mistakes' of the Carter administration. The debate continues as to whether or not the United States has addressed arms control with a view to concluding agreements.[22]

In retrospect NATO's two-track decision has been questionable. INF deployments have proceeded and in all probability will be completed; but the arms control track has not produced any results. Despite arguments to the contrary, INF deployments have proceeded more for political-strategic reasons - that is, to reinforce the American security guarantee, to reflect Alliance resolve and cohesion, etc. - than for military-strategic purposes - that is, to enhance deterrence credibility. In the process of the intra-Alliance debate, however, Western publics have become more acutely aware of the dilemmas of extended deterrence and flexible response and have expressed increased fear of the dangers of nuclear war.

The INF arms negotiations should have produced a more stable Euro-strategic environment, but the end result has been just the opposite. Soviet deployments of SS-20s have resumed and now shorter-range SS-21,-22, and -23 systems are being deployed in Eastern Europe. The prospects of NATO meeting these new threats militarily appear to be non-existent.

For its part, the Soviet leadership expressed dismay with the non-ratification of SALT II and has proved unyielding at the INF table. The Soviet position, to some extent, has been based on the view that Western public opinion would induce the United States and NATO to exhibit greater flexibility at Geneva than turned out to be the case. The Soviet walkout from START and INF has, not unexpectedly, raised serious doubts concerning the priority which they attach to arms limitation. NATO's INF deployments do not, from the Soviet perspective, significantly alter the Euro-strategic balance despite their claims to the contrary. What must be more worrisome for the Soviet leadership are the Reagan administration's plans for an accelerated strategic modernisation programme and the potential implications of the Strategic Defense Initiative.

Deterrence Under Attack

The direct linkages between the failure of arms control and deterrence are difficult to ascertain. Nevertheless, arms control holds out the prospect, if pursued to its logical conclusion, of a more stable strategic, Euro-strategic, and battlefield environment where the likelihood of pre-emption is reduced. More importantly, arms limitation agreements could serve to circumscribe the nuclear and conventional war-fighting assets of both East and West. This in turn could lead to greater emphasis on deterrence _qua_ deterrence rather than on the deterrence-defence interface.

Unfortunately the lack of progress suggests that neither side is seriously interested in the operationalisation of deterrence at lower force levels, in a more stable military-strategic environment, and less emphasis on nuclear war-fighting assets. This being the case deterrence becomes an impediment to arms control. Both the United States and the Soviet Union have attempted to retain for themselves those nuclear weapons deemed most credible for their defence value purposes while trying to limit the defence value assets of the other. When arms limitation proposals are presented based on this premise the prospects for acceptance are minimal.

A fourth factor of some importance has been the tendency of both the United States and the Soviet Union to resort to the use of military force. President Carter expressed considerable surprise and dismay when the Soviet Union invaded Afghanistan. While assessments of ultimate Soviet objectives in the region vary, there are grounds to be concerned that Afghanistan represents a new era in terms of Soviet willingness to utilise force outside of Eastern Europe. The 1983 destruction of the KAL jet liner reinforced perceptions of the utility the Soviet Union attaches to military force. Similarly the American invasion of Grenada, the use of force in the Middle East and the fears of possible military intervention in Central America have raised concerns regarding the willingness of President Reagan to employ military power in the pursuit of American national interests.

The military action and behaviour of both superpowers indicate that defence values are not only held in high esteem, but that force will be utilised where deemed appropriate. When coupled with the corresponding emphasis on the means to fight an East-West war there are grounds to question the extent to which deterrence can prevail in a crisis situation. This is not to suggest that the concrete examples are analogous to an East-West conflict situation, but rather to indicate that the seeds of doubt have been planted.

A fifth consideration is the exercise of political leadership in both Moscow and Washington. Deterrence has always been criticised for its reliance on 'rationality' in decision-making.[23] Rationality underlies much of deterrence theory and strategic analysis is supposedly based on such premises. Many observers have pointed out, of course, that strategic policy-making and crisis management are open to numerous non-rational influences which undermine the assumptions of strategic analysis.[24] Nevertheless, deterrence as strategy - in terms of flexible options, countervailing, etc. - is based on assumptions which are rooted in rational actor behaviour.

Given the West's lack of understanding of Soviet decision-making, of the reasoning modes of Soviet leaders, of the exact nature of C^3 arrangements and a host of other factors including Soviet strategic doctrine, it should not be assumed that Soviet crisis management or response patterns will conform to Western assumptions and scenarios. A further complicating, yet crucial ingredient, is the state of the Soviet political leadership and their relations with the Soviet High Command. No one really knows the extent to which President Chernenko can make decisions. No one really knows how or why Soviet strategic decisions are made. The entire question of the future Soviet leadership remains smoke and mirrors. While most observers would agree that the Soviet leadership would like to avoid war with the West, crisis management and behaviour is in the realm of the unknown.

In the case of the United States the strategic decision-making role of President Reagan has been called into question on grounds of knowledge and interest. There is also, as is the case with the Soviet leadership, the age factor. When these concerns are coupled with rather off-handed statements regarding the prospects and implications of nuclear war by a political leader who seems to have little interest in nuclear doctrine and capabilities, the public has a right to be concerned. Furthermore, the actual conduct of American foreign policy has called into doubt the President's judgement - for example, United States involvement in the Middle East and in Central America.

Deterrence Under Attack

Thus a situation has arisen where the lack of superpower dialogue and understanding has been coupled with skepticism regarding the ability of political leaders to exercise the necessary qualities which would be demanded for crisis management. In the final analysis, President Reagan's finger over the nuclear button is deemed to be too shaky, while no one is sure whose finger hovers over the Soviet button. In a climate of mutual accommodation this factor would not have loomed as significant. Under current circumstances - given Soviet and American strategic doctrine and capabilities - the viability of deterrence tends to be undermined.

Lastly, it should be noted that the heated debate concerning the morality of deterrence has, to some extent, been a function of the unsettled international climate. Issues of war and morality have historically been controversial and no consensus has ever emerged within the international community regarding the morality of the use of force. What is a 'just war' to one side is generally deemed 'unjust' by the other. Deterrence in the nuclear age - whether the strategy is one of punishment or denial - holds millions of civilians as hostage, and it is difficult to envisage on what grounds and under what circumstances the failure of nuclear deterrence - and, hence, war - could be justified.

The morality of nuclear deterrence - to say nothing of nuclear war - has thus come under wide-ranging criticism.[25] Is it significant that the debate has emerged so forcefully during the 1980s? If the superpowers had been conducting their relations in a manner which indicated greater seriousness in coping with the current military-strategic dilemmas, then issues of war and morality would probably have assumed less prominence. However, when East-West relations are conducted in an atmosphere of tension and mistrust and under circumstances where misunderstandings could exacerbate the situation, it is not surprising that ethical considerations assume greater importance.

The earlier discussion of military-strategic dilemmas serves to indicate how and why deterrence as policy and as strategy contributed to the current unsettled international climate. These arguments need not be repeated, but it is important to note that much of the tension and uncertainty has been a function of the views and policies adopted by Moscow and Washington. Thus it is difficult, if not impossible, to change the international political climate unless some consensus emerges regarding military-strategic policy. The emphasis on defence values as such an important component of national and international security has thus spilled over into the political arena. This has made it more difficult for the superpowers and for the East and the West to proceed with a greater degree of normalisation in the conduct of their relations.

Deterrence *qua* deterrence is not primarily responsible; but deterrence strategy, given its defence value orientation, must bear some of the responsibility. This has, not surprisingly, led to the criticism that deterrence as policy is apolitical. Yet this is not the major problem. Deterrence always functions within a specific policy context; but, unfortunately, the current international climate tends to emphasise the underlying fragility of deterrence strategy given existing doctrines and capabilities. Thus we return to our main theme - as the emphasis on a defence value deterrence orientation increases, so too does the criticism of reliance on deterrence for security. To expect otherwise is to misinterpret and misunderstand the major security debate of the day.

But what of the future? The current military-strategic trends offer only a limited prospect for meaningful security. Greater emphasis on defence values can, at best, only affect deterrence credibility at the margins; but can add considerably to public demands for certain types of disarmament measures which, by themselves, could possibly undermine strategic stability and international security. Unilateral security is beyond the grasp of either superpower and efforts to achieve it can be counter-productive.

Are there alternatives? The attempts since the late 1960s to enhance international security by means of negotiated arms limitation agreements have failed. Even with a return to the climate of the 1970s, agreements would only produce marginal improvements in international security. Negotiations should, of course, proceed; but it is imperative that they be placed within a different political-strategic context.

Major political and diplomatic efforts should be undertaken by world leaders[26] to initiate discussions, in an appropriate international forum, with the objective of establishing an East-West security regime - the military-strategic equivalent to the Law of the Sea regime. This would require, as a first step, consensus regarding underlying security principles which should include the following:

1. The major purpose of a comprehensive East-West security regime is to enhance international security within a stable political and military environment.
2. A credible deterrent posture - nuclear and conventional - is the major function of East-West military forces.
3. Nuclear deterrence must be based on credible second-strike capabilities within a framework of overall nuclear parity and with reduced force levels.
4. Conventional deterrence must be based on military parity - manpower and equipment - in the European theatre; force posture, doctrines, and tactics must be structured primarily for defensive purposes.
5. The nuclear/non-nuclear threshold must be clearly delineated.
6. Confidence-building measures must be utilised to help avoid the dangers of surprise attack and to ensure communication in crisis situations.
7. A verification regime must be established for purposes of ensuring compliance with all regime restrictions.

An East-West security regime based on these principles would still require the retention of deterrence as the key security component and thus military-strategic dilemmas would still exist. However, deterrence would be based primarily on dissuasion and thus deterrence and re-assurance would be mutually reinforcing.

Notes

1. Thomas C. Schelling, The Strategy of Conflict, (Oxford University Press, New York, 1963 edition), p. 7.

2. For purposes of this article deterrence as theory refers to the conceptual literature on the subject matter; deterrence as policy refers to the declaratory statements by officials and leaders in North America and Europe which indicate that deterrence is the foundation of American and Western security; and, deterrence as strategy refers to the

various ways deterrence has been operationalised in terms of doctrine (employment plans) and capabilities (current and proposed).

Military-strategic perspectives address those factors and considerations which involve the operationalisation of deterrence as strategy. Political-strategic perspectives concern those factors and considerations which address deterrence as policy, including the state of the international environment, decision-making, public responses, etc.

3. Glenn H. Snyder, Deterrence and Defense: Toward a Theory of National Security, (Princeton University Press, Princeton, 1961), p. 3. Emphasis added.

4. Report of the President's Commission on Strategic Forces, (Washington, April 1983), p. 27. Emphasis added.

5. Caspar W. Weinberger, Annual Report to the Congress: Fiscal Year 1985, (Department of Defense, Washington, 1984), p. 27.

6. Schelling, The Strategy of Conflict, p. 9. Emphasis in original.

7. Patrick M. Morgan, Deterrence: A Conceptual Analysis, (Sage Publications, Beverly Hills, California, 1977), p. 27.

8. Snyder, Deterrence and Defense, pp. 3-4. Emphasis in original.

9. Weinberger, Annual Report to Congress: Fiscal Year 1985, p. 27.

10. No consensus exists in the Western literature regarding Soviet views on deterrence. For a good overview see John Baylis and Gerald Segal, editors, Soviet Strategy, (Croom Helm, London, 1981). Also see Jack L. Snyder, The Soviet Strategic Culture: Implications for Limited Nuclear Operations, (RAND Report R-2154-AF, Santa Monica, California, September 1977); Dan L. Strobe and Rebecca V. Strobe, 'Diplomacy and Defense in Soviet National Security Policy', International Security, vol. 8, no. 2, (Fall, 1983), pp. 91-116; 'A Garthoff-Pipes Debate on Soviet Strategic Doctrine', Strategic Review, vol. x, no. 4, (Fall, 1982), pp. 36-63, and Donald W. Hanson, 'Is Soviet Strategic Doctrine Superior?', International Security, vol. 7, no. 3, (Winter, 1982-83), pp. 81-83 as examples of the debate.

11. NATO Nuclear Planning Group Final Communique, (NATO Press Service, M-NPG-2 (84) 20, October 12, 1984), p. 2.

12. Lawrence Freedman, The Evolution of Nuclear Strategy, (St. Martin's Press, New York, 1981).

13. There has been a trend in the literature to view events of the pre-nuclear era in deterrence terms, but there is a notable absence of conceptual treatments of deterrence *per se* in the pre-1945 period. For a useful discussion of the application of deterrence to World War II see John J. Mearsheimer, *Conventional Deterrence*, (Cornell University Press, Ithaca, New York, 1983).

14. Carl Sagan, 'Nuclear War and Climatic Catastrophe: Some Policy Implications', *Foreign Affairs*, vol. 62, no. 2, (Winter, 1983/84), p. 257-292.

15. For example see Keith B. Payne, *Nuclear Deterrence in U.S. - Soviet Relations*, (Westview Press, Boulder, Colorado, 1982).

16. Deterrence stability exists if there is the absence of a rational motive to launch a first-strike given the probability of retaliation. See Albert Legault and George Lindsey, *The Dynamics of the Nuclear Balance*, (Cornell University Press, Ithaca, New York, 1976), pp. 166-199.

17. Leon V. Sigal, 'Rethinking the Unthinkable,' *Foreign Policy*, no. 34, (Spring, 1979), pp. 35-51. It remains unclear whether the primary intention of the nuclear war-fighters school is to genuinely enhance dissuasion or whether they would prefer the United States to attempt to obtain a capability to prevail. See Colin Gray and Keith Payne, 'Victory is Possible', *Foreign Policy*, no. 39, (Summer, 1980), pp. 14-27 and Keith Payne, 'What if we "Ride Out" a Soviet First Strike?', *The Washington Quarterly*, vol. 7, no. 4 (Fall, 1984), pp. 85-92 as examples.

18. The debate regarding 'effective' defence has intensified as a result of President Reagan's March 1983 'Star Wars' speech and the implications of the Strategic Defense Initiative. No consensus has emerged regarding the possibility of effective ballistic missile defence even though the debate has been wide ranging. For example see Sidney D. Drell, *et al*, 'Preserving the ABM Treaty: A Critique of the Reagan Strategic Defense Initiative', *International Security*, vol. 9, no. 2, (Fall, 1984), pp. 51-91.

19. NATO is attempting to acquire a highly mobile, offensive conventional capability similar in nature to that possessed by the Warsaw Pact. For an overview see Report of the European Security Study, *Strengthening Conventional Deterrence in Europe: Proposals for the 1980s*, (Macmillan Press, London, 1983).

20. R. B. Byers, 'Thresholds and Deterrence

Credibility: The European Perspective', in William Gutteridge and Trevor Taylor, editors, The Dangers of New Weapons System, (Macmillan Press, London, 1983), pp. 91-112.

21. See R. B. Byers, editor, Nuclear Strategy and the Superpowers, The Polaris Papers 3, (The Canadian Institute of Strategic Studies, Toronto, 1984).

22. Strobe Talbott, Deadly Gambits: The Reagan Administration and the Stalemate in Nuclear Arms Control, (Alfred A. Knopf, New York, 1984).

23. For example see Philip Green, Deadly Logic: The Theory of Nuclear Deterrence, (Schocken Books, New York, 1966). Morgan, Deterrence: A Conceptual Analysis also explicitly questions the rational assumptions that seem to underlie most deterrence thinking. Few analysts have adopted an explicit, critical decision-making perspective of deterrence and the psychological aspects deserve greater attention. See Janice Gross Stein and Raymond Tanter, Rational Decision-Making: Israel's Security Choices, 1967, (Ohio State University Press, Columbus, Ohio, 1980).

24. Graham Allison, Essence of Decision: Explaining the Cuban Missile Crisis, (Little, Brown & Co., Boston, 1971).

25. The Pastoral Letter of the U.S. Bishops on War and Peace, The Challenge of Peace: God's Promise and our Response, Origins, vol. 13, no. 1, (May 19, 1983). See Bruce M. Russett, 'Ethical Dilemmas of Nuclear Deterrence', International Security, vol. 8, no. 4, (Spring, 1984), pp. 36-54 and Keith B. Payne, 'The Bishops and Nuclear Weapons', Orbis, vol. 27, no. 3, (Fall, 1983), pp. 535-542 for differing perspectives.

26. The efforts of Pierre Trudeau when he was Prime Minister of Canada should be continued by other world leaders, but with greater attention paid to the relationships between nuclear arms limitation and international security. See R. B. Byers, 'Political Confidence-Building and Strategic Coherence: Trudeau's Peace Initiative', in Byers, Nuclear Strategy and the Superpowers, pp. 116-131.

Chapter Two

DETERRENCE IN THE 1980s: A POLITICAL AND CONTEXTUAL ANALYSIS

Janice Gross Stein*

Deterrence as a strategy of conflict management is now under unprecedented assault. This sustained attack is largely a phenomenon of the last decade, when public and expert opinion converged to challenge some of the fundamental assumptions of deterrence. There are important differences across the spectrum of criticism; experts and publics attend to quite different weaknesses in theory and practice. Here we argue that the major weakness of deterrence lies in its apolitical and acontextual attributes. We do so to conclude that only a broadly framed strategy of conflict management, which pays attention not only to the possibility of premeditated attack but primarily to the probability of miscalculated war, can hope to meet the intersecting challenges of this decade.

Deterrence: A Political Analysis

The formal deductive theory of deterrence is well articulated, its axiomatic logic parsimonious, its prescriptive thrust clear. Elaborated largely through deductive reasoning, the concept of deterrence reduces to the central proposition that when a challenger considers that the likely benefits of military action will outweigh its probable costs, deterrence is likely to fail. If, on the other hand, leaders estimate that the probable costs of a use of force are greater than its likely benefits, deterrence succeeds. Crucial to these estimates of a challenger is the credibility of a defender's commitment, either to punish or deny. Credibility

* I am grateful to Franklyn Griffiths, George Quester, and Leon Sigal for their helpful criticism of an earlier draft.

in turn is generally a function of a challenger's estimate of a defender's capability and resolve. At its core, then, the concept of deterrence assumes that a rational challenger weighs all elements of the deterrence equation equally and pays attention to probability, cost, and benefit in choosing whether or not to use force. The deterrence argument, au fond, is one of opportunity. In its essence, deterrence is a theory of motivation. It looks to military denial and punishment to motivate an adversary to forego military attack. Precisely because it is a theory of motivation, it cannot rest on formal logic alone, but must deal with the metaphysics of a defender's resolve and the psychopolitics of a challenger's motivation. Consequently, it is very much the abstract formalism and parsimonious logic of deterrence which has generated so much criticism among experts.

Many consider deterrence ahistorical because, in the articulation of its set of logical maxims, it ignores important differences among challengers over time. It is also apolitical in its inadequate treatment of the political context of decisions and the political environment which shapes and alters the valuation of interests. It is remiss, behavioural scientists tell us, in its failure to treat fundamental cognitive processes, processes which compromise the capacity for the rational calculation required by deterrence. The uncertainties and costs of any conceivable use of nuclear weapons are so enormous, the decision-making processes likely to be so stressful, that calculations in all probability will be driven by cognitive rather than rational processes. Finally, deterrence is inadequate as prescriptive strategy. At times it can provoke the use of force it seeks to deter. Even more to the point, proponents of deterrence tend to focus their attention exclusively on the contingency of premeditated attack and pay too little attention to the possibility of miscalculated war. Consequently, they give little consideration to alternative strategies of conflict management. Its critics allege that deterrence has become a legitimating umbrella for spiralling and indiscriminate defence expenditure and a provocative and inadequate strategy in a post-detente era.

The indictment is not trivial. To consider these charges systematically, we look first at the contradictions inherent in nuclear deterrence as a set of logical propositions relevant to the 1980s. How does deterrence work in theory? Secondly, we consider the inadequacies of deterrence as an explanation of what leaders actually do. Although there are important differences, particularly in the scale of relevant costs, we look at the contradictions between the evidence we do have on the workings of conventional deterrence and the abstract principles of deterrence theory. Third, we examine the weaknesses of deterrence as policy, as prescriptive advice on the management of conflict. Drawing on this three-fold examination of deterrence, alternative ways of conceiving the management of enduring conflict in the coming decade are explored.

The Logic of Deterrence: Contradictions in the Nuclear Age

The debate about deterrence has swelled in the last decade partly in response to the explosion of new technological capabilities and to the dangers and opportunities which military technology appears to create. The logical dilemmas of nuclear deterrence, however, antedate the imperatives of a dynamic technology. They are rooted in the realities of nuclear weapons, particularly in the mutual vulnerability of the United States and the Soviet Union. Indeed, it is appropriate to draw back from the intricacies of the current debate about the impact of new technology to belabour two rather obvious points, points from which much else follows.

First, it is the mutual vulnerability of the two 'superpowers' which gives nuclear deterrence its special characteristics and resonance. It is worth underlining yet again that neither of the two 'superpowers' can protect its civilians in a nuclear exchange, that neither can 'defend'. Uniquely in the nuclear age, a putative 'loser', if that term has meaning, can devastate a 'winner'. Consequently, nuclear capabilities are useful not primarily on the battlefield but rather to deter and, secondarily, to coerce without resort to force, to compel through diplomacy. Although strategists consider their options should deterrence fail, in the nuclear age the primary purpose must be the prevention of war. Nuclear capabilities are useful primarily as a resource rather than as an instrument; at best, they are assets in high-risk bargaining strategies. These two distinguishing characteristics - the vulnerability of the most powerful and the importance of nuclear capabilities largely as bargaining assets rather than as battlefield instruments - create contradictions inherent to the strategic relationship between the two superpowers. Although analysts of deterrence struggle with these contradictions, we argue here that there is no escape from the logical dilemmas which flow from the realities of the nuclear relationship. Only two of the most fundamental are discussed.

Because neither superpower can defend its economy, its infrastructure, its civilians, against a devastating retaliatory strike should it initiate a nuclear attack, each can protect what it values most only through co-operation with the other. Co-operation among adversaries is not new, but nuclear second-strike capabilities create an unprecedented interdependence, interdependence which is fundamentally at variance with what is perhaps the central assumption of deterrence. Deterrence takes as given a hostile adversary posed to strike at the first opportunity; it builds on the assumption of temptation. Yet, the interdependence that flows from mutual vulnerability contradicts this assumption of readiness for attack dependent only on opportunity. Indeed, most of the current analyses of the likely origins of a nuclear exchange give little credence to a calculated, premeditated attack but concentrate rather on miscalculation and the autonomous risk of escalation. The focus on readiness to attack, given the 'opportunity', is illogical in the face of second-strike capabilities; it is a relic of the pre-nuclear era. Yet, if inherent readiness to strike is no longer the most likely cause of war among nuclear powers, much of the policy debate that flows from the prevailing concept of deterrence is fundamentally misguided. Not only is it misguided, it is dangerous: if the most likely contingency in a nuclear world is miscalculated escalation which spirals out of control, then exclusive reliance on deterrence can inadvertently make war more likely. Strategists are attending to the wrong set of constraints and measures.

Closely related to this first contradiction are the almost insuperable obstacles to the design of credible commitments to retaliate, especially when deterrence is extended. And here we find a confounding paradox within the terms of reference of deterrence. Second-strike capability gives deterrence prominence because defence is impossible. Mutual vulnerability reduces the likelihood of premeditated attack because of the risk of escalation and the devastating consequences of retaliation, but simultaneously makes punishment less likely because of the catastrophic consequences of counter-retaliation. Embedded within this paradox are most of the current dilemmas of strategic policy.

The dilemmas are particularly acute for the United States because of its extensive and extended commitments to its allies. Precisely because American cities are vulnerable to a Soviet second-strike, the credibility of the threat to retaliate against a Soviet nuclear or conventional attack against allies in Europe is open to question. Its credibility is questionable because it would not be rational for American leaders to risk the destruction of their own society to punish an attack against their allies. This is especially so if a retaliatory strike would put at risk not only American cities but whatever survived in Europe. Senior American leaders now acknowledge what they have tacitly admitted for years: the credibility of the American commitment, a fundamental component of any strategy of extended deterrence, is at risk because of the mutual vulnerability of the superpowers to each other. To escape this dilemma, leaders have struggled to create new options, to give themselves flexible choices despite the inflexibility of their constraints. It is not surprising that these attempts are themselves beset by contradiction and incoherence. Moreover, they stand in no formal relationship to the logic of deterrence which is itself compromised by the realities of mutual vulnerability.

In a compelling critique of much of current American policy, Robert Jervis argues that in the effort to escape these dilemmas, leaders have developed policies that are better explained by psychological dynamics than by strategic logic.[1] Recently, for example, the American President has spoken of developing the capability to defend against a first-strike by an adversary. Most analysts of present and foreseeable technology are skeptical, however, that the capability to defend can be developed in the next two decades. And, paradoxically as some would argue, if it could, it might well enhance crisis instability by increasing the likelihood that nuclear weapons would be used in a pre-emptive or preventive attack: it is the perception of mutual vulnerability which now makes the initiation of a counterforce attack so unattractive. Indeed, it is tempting to suggest that the attempt to develop a defensive capability exemplifies a typical pattern of 'wishful thinking', a motivated - and dangerous - response to an unpleasant and inescapable policy dilemma.

More problematic, because it is better grounded in current capabilities, is the stress on 'options' to escape from the inflexibilities of the nuclear dilemma, the build-up of the capacity to initiate limited and precise nuclear strikes and of conventional capabilities. Discussion of these two broad packages has dominated much of the strategic debate of the last decade. Since they will be discussed in detail by others in this collection, the specifics will not be entered into here, but at least two general comments are relevant.

First, as Jervis so cogently argues, neither of these two broad sets of options provides any relief from nuclear dilemmas. They do not because of the ever-present risk of escalation to higher levels of violence. Escalation may come by design or inadvertently. It can be argued, for example, that the side that is 'losing' on the battlefield will be strongly motivated to move to a higher level of violence in an effort to reverse an unfavourable outcome or to compel the termination of the fighting. Alternatively, escalation can come through processes that are unpredictable and unforeseen by the leaders who initiate the fighting. Battle has its own dynamics, dynamics which are both difficult to foresee and control. It is this 'autonomous risk', as Schelling described it, which simultaneously strengthens deterrence yet vitiates the logic of much current strategic planning.

Proponents of increasing current capabilities to initiate limited and accurate nuclear strikes can counter that their principal utility is not to reinforce deterrence but rather to limit the damage should deterrence fail. Although the two are not unrelated, they are, of course, separable and distinct functions. It is as difficult, moreover, to sustain the second claim as it was the first. If escalation to the highest level of violence remains a possibility, then, when both sides are vulnerable, initiation of limited attack in response to a partial failure of deterrence is almost as dangerous as a full-scale strike. As long as the 'loser' can do devastating damage to the 'winner', as long as civilians in cities remain in hostage, then advantage on the battlefield may not be decisive and may be potentially devastating. To compound the dilemma, limited nuclear strikes require the co-operation of the adversary to keep the engagement limited. Yet Soviet military doctrine, responding largely to its own past, is explicit on this point: it categorically rejects the possibility of a limited exchange of nuclear weapons.[2] Insofar as it does, a policy of limited nuclear retaliation may be useful to improve the credibility of deterrent threats at the margin, and even this is questionable, but it is of no use in reducing the damage if deterrence fails. It is arguable that emphasis on the advantages of nuclear flexibility derives from military technology which permits increasing accuracy and precision. Here doctrine follows rather than guides technology. This 'conventionalisation' of nuclear weapons, as Jervis describes this process, provides no escape from painful policy dilemmas. At the very best, it restructures the competition in risk-taking, the bargaining process in crisis, in ways that are not at all predictable from a reading of relative military capabilities.

The renewed attention to conventional military capabilities, both to defend against conventional attack and, more recently, to retaliate and punish the attacker, suffers to a lesser degree from many of the same logical difficulties.[3] Even though hostilities would begin at a lower level of violence, superior conventional capability would not translate either into the capacity to deter escalation to a higher level or the capability to terminate the fighting on favourable terms. Nor would advantage on the local battlefield necessarily determine bargaining advantage, since the willingness to tolerate a higher level of risk would likely be a function not only of battlefield position but also of the interests at stake and the resolve of the belligerents.[4] To put the point only somewhat too starkly, military superiority on or off the battlefield cannot predict the willingness to run risks, the resolve of the participants in the struggle, or the firmness with which leaders bargain. If anything, we can speculate that the threat of the 'weaker' party to escalate to a higher level of violence would be the more credible. Nor can military superiority delimit and control the autonomous risk of escalation. And as long as escalation runs the risk of devastating the stronger as well as the weaker, the threat of escalation is a powerful bargaining asset.

At best, then, improved conventional capability would raise the costs of an attack to the challenger and signal resolve. It would improve deterrence at the margin. It is not likely to do what its proponents claim it will do - create options if deterrence fails.[5] The expectation that it will can probably be best explained again by the painful consequences of vulnerability, by the unacceptable consequences of a nuclear exchange when civilians and cities are held in hostage.

Finally, theories of nuclear deterrence tend to treat relative cost in their analyses of the calculations of a challenger and pay little attention to absolute cost. Formal construction of a challenger's decision whether or not to resort to force includes only a comparison of the likely gains of military action relative to its costs. A recent analysis of American policy in the nuclear age suggests, however, that absolute rather than relative cost may be far more important.[6] The nature and magnitude of the costs of a use of nuclear force take on meaning independently of the likely gains. Even if the probable gains were estimated as extraordinarily high, the enormous cost of the use of nuclear weapons might well invalidate such a comparison as a critical decision rule. Recent scientific speculation about the likely impact on the global weather system of the use by only one superpower of its nuclear arsenal is likely to escalate further an already high level of absolute cost.[7] Indeed, we can suggest that it is not only the uncertainty of a defender's response but the absolute cost to the challenger which reinforces nuclear deterrence. If these latest prognoses are accepted as valid by the leaders of the two nuclear giants, in the ultimate paradox, nuclear weapons may become self-deterring. Self-deterrence, which derives from consideration of absolute cost by a challenger, is largely ignored in most abstract conceptualisations of nuclear deterrence.[8]

This brief and preliminary survey of trends in the development of contemporary strategic logic suggests a number of tentative conclusions. First, mutual vulnerability in a nuclear context creates inescapable contradictions in the logic of deterrence. Much of current policy, however, is an attempt to escape these contradictions rather than to acknowledge their significance. The consequences of this 'escapist' reasoning are not unimportant. As Jervis notes, the credibility of the existing American deterrent is underestimated and the increase in credibility of an increase in capabilities is overestimated.[9] Both consequences can be dangerous in the interactive coercive bargaining that defines the superpower relationship; both can lead to serious miscalculation.

Second, and closely related, development of more powerful missiles, improvement in their accuracy (which is far more important and destabilising than nuclear yield), the development of anti-satellite capabilities and ballistic missile defence systems, and deployment of more differentiated capabilities are likely to exacerbate rather than resolve the dilemmas created by nuclear logic. Short of impregnable defence - a highly unlikely and dangerous contingency - there is no 'technological fix' to the dilemmas created by mutual vulnerability. The emphasis on technological breakthrough obscures the far more important political and psychological determinants of a deterrent relationship in a nuclear world. Even worse, it permits technology to drive doctrine and policy rather than encourage strategy to channel technology. Attention to the benefits of mutual vulnerability would suggest different kinds of technological priorities and weapons' choices. A keener appreciation of the consequences of mutual vulnerability would also permit a more sophisticated reading of the sub-text of coercive bargaining in a nuclear world, of the asymmetries above the nuclear threshold between gradations of capabilities and bargaining strength, and of the credibility of threats in a competition in risk-taking among the vulnerable. At present, deterrence reigns but rules neither strategy nor tactics.

The Elusive Workings of Deterrence: What Do We Know?

If deterrence generates important contradictions as an abstract set of principles, it runs into even greater difficulty as a set of explanatory propositions. Leaders diverge in important ways from these propositions in considering a use of force: they do not behave the way the theory of deterrence expects. A growing body of empirical studies of conventional deterrence challenges many of the critical expectations of the concept. Although the differences between nuclear and conventional deterrence are critical, particularly the estimates of absolute cost, the evidence of the breakdown of conventional deterrence is suggestive of the way leaders think. Let us discuss just a few of the counter-theoretical findings which have important implications for strategies of conflict management.

Leaders, as we noted earlier, are expected in theory to calculate the likely gains and losses of military action, weigh all parts of the deterrence equation equally, and choose to use force only when probable gains are greater than the losses. Investigation of the ways leaders have considered a use of force in practice points to considerable divergence from the norm. Most important, the empirical evidence shows that challengers considering a use of force often see no benefits from military action, but rather overwhelming loss from a perpetuation of the status quo. Under these circumstances, as Lebow argues, states tend to jump through closed windows.[10]

It is not, as abstract concepts of deterrence expect, that leaders see opportunity, but rather that they estimate the costs of inaction as intolerable. In 1973, for example, President Sadat of Egypt chose to use force not because he considered military force an attractive option. On the contrary, he anticipated considerable losses even from a limited resort to force. But he saw no 'good' option and his calculations were dominated by the extraordinarily high costs of continuing inaction, costs which were largely domestic and regional. In his consideration of alternatives, the President compared risks and chose the less damaging option.[11] This kind of calculation is not at all uncommon: to cite only the most prominent instance, Japan's leaders in 1941 chose among unattractive options and gave greater weight to the unfavourable consequences of inaction.[12] If this kind of calculation is not atypical but rather frequent[13], then the concept of deterrence as it is now articulated is seriously flawed.

What is immediately striking in both these cases is that challengers and defenders do not dispute relative military advantage or even the likely outcome of a battlefield confrontation. Challengers did not resort to force either because they estimated that they held the military advantage or because they miscalculated the military balance. On the contrary, they were generally pessimistic in their evaluation of their military capabilities. In other words, they saw no 'opportunity', no 'window of vulnerability'. What they did see, however, was a deteriorating military balance and intolerable domestic or international costs of inaction; they chose force in desperation or weakness.

The concept of deterrence as it is now formulated ignores entirely this set of calculations. It pays no attention to leaders' estimates of the costs of inaction, only to the likely costs and benefits of military action. But challengers were certain and pessimistic about the costs of inaction, even as they tended to be uncertain but pessimistic about the likely consequences of action. In treating only the military component of leaders' calculations, the concept of deterrence is profoundly apolitical, distorting in its singular emphasis on the relative military balance. We argued earlier that leaders may not jump through open windows because of the high absolute cost. The evidence shows as well that they do jump through closed windows when frustration and desperation inflate the costs of inaction relative to those of a use of force. Deterrence as a concept makes no provision for either set of calculations by a challenger. By ignoring the political context in which leaders consider a resort to force, formal theories of deterrence violate the most fundamental Clausewitzian dictum.

If formal theories of deterrence do not capture the nuances of a challenger's calculations they do equal violence to the dilemmas of a defender. It is the defender who must design and communicate a credible commitment to a challenger and signal resolve if deterrence is to succeed, yet the barriers to signalling and reception are severe. We have already looked at the obstacles to credibility which flow from the special condition of mutual vulnerability to nuclear technology. Technological barriers are compounded, however, by the political and perceptual biases which interfere with the transmission and reception of signals from one set of leaders to another.

These perceptual barriers have been the subject of extensive investigation and are by now well documented.[14] The scope for misperception by a defender is large. Leaders can misperceive the values of a challenger and consequently fail to design threats that jeopardise centrally important interests. Or, even if the threat is credible, the message can get lost in the 'noise' and consequently never receive the attention its transmitters expect that it will command. Often cultural differences between societies interfere with the decoding and interpretation of a signal, yet defenders ignore these barriers and assume that the meaning of their message is obvious. Lebow's analysis of the pre-war bargaining between Argentina and Britain documents precisely this kind of cultural bias. Argentinian leaders, coming at it from an entirely different context, gave a radically different meaning to British signals about the future of the Falklands. Britain's leaders, for their part, ignored the very different cultural and political context of the two societies and assumed that their intentions were obvious and clear.[15] A defender can also overestimate the alternatives open to a challenger and assume that its adversary can retreat, that withdrawal from the brink is an option. As we have seen, however, challengers have estimated the relative costs of inaction very highly, effectively precluding retreat as an option. Under these circumstances, the credibility of a commitment, the resolve of a defender, become almost irrelevant. These three kinds of misperception by a defender - of an adversary's values and alternatives and of the clarity of its own commitments and resolve - can each defeat a strategy of deterrence. And these are only three of the most obvious kinds of perceptual errors commonly made by leaders designing deterrent strategies.

The consequences of these kinds of perceptual errors are again not trivial. Broadly speaking, we can group almost all the important types of errors, errors with direct policy consequences, under four headings: underestimation of a challenger's capability or intentions, or overestimation of these capabilities or intentions.[16] If leaders underestimate the capabilities or misjudge the intentions of a challenger, if they are over-confident in the effectiveness of their warnings and threats, they may well be surprised, caught unaware and unprepared. They may fail to reinforce deterrence before a challenger is fully committed to military action, thus forfeiting the opportunity to avoid war. As we have seen, however, some challengers would not be deterred even by vigorous and unambiguous threats; they are responding to their own agenda and needs, to their estimate of the intolerably high costs of inaction rather than to the costs of action.

Equally grave, if a defender overestimates the hostility of a challenger's intentions, if its leaders anticipate a military challenge even though its adversary is not preparing a resort to force, their actions may provoke the very challenge they are attempting to avoid. This is especially so when offensive preparations are indistinguishable from defensive measures, when the 'security dilemma' is acute as it so often is in the contemporary international system.[17] Responding to an exaggerated estimate of their adversary's intentions or capabilities, leaders can augment their capabilities or initiate defensive action which cannot be differentiated from offensive preparation. A chain of action and reaction can easily be set in motion which culminates in a spiralling arms race at best and miscalculated escalation at worst.

In designing their deterrent strategy, leaders run different kinds of risks from different kinds of miscalculations. Overestimation can culminate in miscalculated escalation by an adversary and underestimation in surprise and defensive unpreparedness. In our century, the Kaiser and the Tzar were entrapped by the first error in 1914 and Neville Chamberlain by the second in 1938-1939. And, to compound the policy dilemma, these two kinds of errors are not independent of each other: as leaders try to avoid one, they become more vulnerable to the other.

The poor fit between the central propositions of the theory of deterrence and the empirical investigations of its practice when weapons are conventional is disturbing. The differences between nuclear and conventional deterrence are, of course, terribly important. The gap in the relevant costs alone should have a major impact on the way leaders think about a use of force. Nevertheless, the evidence we now have is alarming because it suggests that the concept of deterrence, as it is formally articulated, omits critically important dimensions of a challenger's calculations. Its singular emphasis on consideration of the relative gains and losses of military action is incomplete, apolitical, and distorting. Finally, it does not - and indeed it cannot - incorporate within its logic the cognitive processes that shape leaders' calculations; it is psychologically illiterate. If we suspect that the fit between the theory and practice of nuclear deterrence is even remotely as poor as that between conventional theory and practice, that the discrepancy between the expectations of formal theory and the calculations of challengers and defenders at the conventional level is replicated even in part at the nuclear level - and we have no way of knowing short of catastrophe - we cannot but be alarmed. Perhaps the most serious implications derive from the impact of an apolitical and psychologically illiterate concept on strategies of conflict management. A brief examination of the weaknesses of the concept of deterrence as a set of policy guidelines follows.

Deterrence as a Strategy of Conflict Management

In the history of science, the central assumptions of a theory may well be unsupported by empirical evidence, indeed, be contradicted by the available data, yet still be extraordinarily useful in generating policy prediction and prescription. The 'dismal science' of economics comes most readily to mind: although few consumers make their choices fully in conformity with the central assumption of rationality, the rationality postulate nevertheless permits economists to predict economic performance with some accuracy and to offer a set of policy recommendations with reasonable confidence in their likely outcomes. The same cannot be said for deterrence. Two central areas of policy are examined briefly.

Deterrence, building on the balance of military capabilities as the essential prerequisite of success, should be able to prescribe, at least within broad limits, the kinds of weapons development and acquisition needed to deter. Yet, there is no consensus on the military prerequisites of stable nuclear deterrence and, consequently, no agreement on the impact of changing nuclear technology. Even the most cursory examination of the research and development and the military spending of the two superpowers in the last two decades belies the expectation that theory guides policy. If anything, one would argue that a burgeoning military technology is now propelling strategic theory. This failure is especially remarkable in the nuclear age.

Nuclear deterrence rests on the special condition of the mutual vulnerability of the two greatest powers to mutual destruction. In broad outline, one would then expect that weapons systems that preserved this vulnerability, that limited the exposure of counterforce systems and protected second-strike capability, would be privileged: at least in theory, the prescription should be for 'soft cities' and 'hardened missiles'. This distinction has existed only in theory. As early as the 1960s, planners included an ever-widening range of economic and industrial targets as the object of a counter-force strike and researchers began to develop increasingly accurate and precise nuclear delivery systems which significantly augmented the 'hard-target' kill capability. A decade later, the introduction of multiple independently targeted warheads by both sides made offensive weapons increasingly vulnerable and changed the ratio of offence and defence in favour of the offence, at least in theory. Paradoxically, even though the MIRVing of missiles reduced the likelihood of successful ballistic missile defence (BMD), the growing vulnerability of counterforce systems revived interest in defensive technology, technology that, again at least in theory, can be adapted to defend cities as well as missiles. Technology is in the process of driving theory full circle.

Deterrence in theory also demands functional command, communication, and control facilities as prerequisite to effective second-strike capability. Similarly, satellite intelligence that can provide critical warning time is built into the assumptions of the concept of deterrence. Again, however, the practice does not match the theory. The improved accuracy of missiles threatens to increase the 'decapitation capability' of both sides, and the increasing militarisation of space may permit both sides to develop anti-satellite capabilities which could further hamper communication and control. In general, the heightened interest in ballistic missile defence technology, in anti-submarine warfare, in decapitation capability, in technology that can blind satellites in space, all threaten to compound the vulnerability of the counterforce capability of both by strengthening the precision and accuracy of each and by limiting warning and C^3 facilities. Proposed technological innovations threaten to undermine the effectiveness of second-strike capability and the vulnerability of civilian populations and infrastructure. President Reagan's commitment to defence is symptomatic if symbolic. Although few expect that defensive capability can be achieved, the commitment to try is visible testimony to the bankruptcy of deterrence as a guide to policy.

The specifics of these new technologies are treated in detail by others in this volume, but two general points are relevant. First, it can be argued that in the early nuclear age, there was a good fit between technology and doctrine. The very big yields of the early bombs and warheads, the bluntness of the early nuclear instruments, made for countervalue strategies and mutual vulnerability as the basis of nuclear deterrence. But as strategy became more differentiated, as it accommodated the need for 'flexibility' and 'options' to counter the challenge to credibility inherent in the consequences of large-scale retaliation, strategy ran ahead of technology. Increasingly, it required differentiated and precise military capabilities. The explosion in technological capability that followed, however, now threatens to outpace strategy and to undermine the stability of nuclear deterrence. The paradox is clear: technology developed in the attempt to escape the contradictions of the nuclear revolution now threatens to invalidate the doctrine which legitimated the exponential increase, both qualitative and quantitative, in military capabilities. In the next decade, it is likely that technology will propel strategy. The expanding elasticity of the concept of nuclear deterrence, the logical contradictions it tolerates, will legitimate almost every kind of weapons system that becomes feasible. Strategy that is silent on its technical requirements, that provides no prescriptive direction, is emasculated.

Second, and closely related, the emphasis of deterrence on military capabilities and on demonstration of resolve can skew strategies of conflict management below the nuclear level. By stressing the interdependence of commitments, the interconnectedness of interests, the concept of deterrence tends to exaggerate the stakes inherent in a given conflict and to build in an escalation dynamic.[18] It also makes compromise more difficult, since what is at issue is not a specific interest but a bargaining reputation. Finally, deterrence can also inflict self-generated wounds from a costly and inappropriate escalation of the interests at stake. President Reagan's definition of the deterrent role of the Marines deployed south of Beirut illustrates this point nicely. The President inflated the issue and defined the stakes as the credibility of the United States in its global competition with the Soviet Union, rather than as an attempt to support a weak government in crisis. When withdrawal came, it inevitably compromised American credibility and its capacity for extended deterrence; here, strategy became a self-denying prophecy. Policy-makers tend to resort to deterrence as a strategy of conflict management below as well as at the nuclear level because it promises to be relatively inexpensive in comparison to the alternatives of either compromise or defence, but the appearance of a bargain is misleading. Deterrence can be very expensive.

The Cat Has Nine Lives, Or Does It?

The indictment of deterrence as theory, as explanation, and as strategy is damning. It is so damning that increasingly its critics question the necessity of deterrence. They treat its assumptions and consequences as toxic and they are not at all persuaded that it can be appropriately detoxified.[19] Because it conflates the prevention of war from means to end, because it ignores other strategies of influence across the spectrum, because its logic is premised exclusively on the use of threat, it is fatally flawed at its core. Equally to the point, because conventional deterrence has worked under some conditions but not under others, its record simply is not good enough in the nuclear age where a single failure can spell catastrophe. In the words of a strategic analyst, deterrence has now become part of the problem rather than part of the solution.[20] Its critics call for a wholly new paradigm that integrates the political and military dimensions of national security in novel and imaginative ways.

The demand for reconceptualisation, freed from past assumptions and rigidities, is attractive but the specifics of a new paradigm are far from obvious. Because they are far from obvious, we tend to bury deterrence only to resurrect it for want of something better; like the cat, deterrence seems to have nine lives. When we resurrect deterrence, however, and allow it to dominate our strategic thinking, we do so at enormous cost. To put the point starkly insofar as we continue to rely heavily on deterrence to avoid nuclear war, we make a judgment about what kinds of crises we are likely to face in the future. This judgement is, of course, fraught with consequences.

As has been argued throughout this analysis, deterrence is designed to cope with the single contingency of premeditated war, with the determined military challenger. The analogue is to Germany of the 1930s. The alternative judgement suggests that war is likely to erupt not through premeditated action but rather through miscalculation, through escalatory processes that leapfrog out of control, through pre-emption from weakness. Here the analogy is not to the 1930s but to 1914 where threat and counter-threat provoked demonstrations of resolve, major miscalculations, and a competition in risk-taking that culminated in a war that no one intended and all misjudged. If this is the more likely contingency, then deterrence is a wholly inappropriate strategy, one which through the dynamics of threat and counter-threat runs the risk of provoking the conflagration it is designed to avoid. If a miscalculated war is more likely than a premeditated war, then deterrence is indeed part of the problem rather than the solution.

Unfortunately, strategic planners and political leaders cannot remain indifferent between these two contingencies. Ideally, they would want to work simultaneously to deter planned attack and to avoid escalation. They cannot do both at the same time, however, since the two contingencies and the appropriate strategies to deal with each are not independent of the other. If a miscalculated war erupts, we have overestimated an adversary's hostility and if a premeditated attack occurs, we have underestimated an adversary's intentions. Policy-makers stand between Scylla and Charybdis, between underestimation and overestimation of an adversary's intentions and capabilities to attack. To make matters worse, we cannot stand indefinitely without making an informed judgement about which of these two contingencies - premeditated or miscalculated war - is the more likely in this decade. We cannot avoid judgement because the strategies appropriate to reduce the likelihood of miscalculation can at times make premeditated attack more likely while deterrence can exacerbate and provoke if an adversary is apprehensive and defensive. No strategy in the nuclear age is without risk.

A great deal of expert opinion and the very limited evidence we have that is relevant suggest that a miscalculated war is the more likely. We cannot be certain, indeed these uncertainties are endemic in an anarchic international environment, but miscalculated war seems the more probable given the enormous absolute cost of the use of nuclear force and the self-deterring characteristics of nuclear weapons. Indeed, the enormity of these costs simplifies calculations for political leaders and makes a cool, rational, and deliberate choice of the use of nuclear force increasingly less likely. Far more dangerous is a gradual move up the escalatory ladder where one or another leader resorts to force from weakness or desperation. Such a decision would be fully consistent with the evidence of leaders' decisions to use conventional force, even when they know they are militarily inferior. Or, political leaders could find themselves entrapped by technology which permits and requires instantaneous and decentralised decision; launch-on-warning is this decade's equivalent of rigid mobilisation schedules in 1914.

Our analysis suggests that we must pay extraordinary attention to avoiding an unplanned and unintended war throughout this decade. It goes without saying that if this fundamental estimate is wrong, the policies that follow would often be beside the point and at times dangerous. If, however, the estimate is right, a continuing and almost exclusive reliance on deterrence as the principal strategy of conflict management could bring disaster. When deterrence competes with re-assurance, as it often does, the former must give way to the latter. Several propositions follow from this basic estimate of the most likely threat to international security in the coming decade.

First, and most obvious, identification of miscalculated war as the most likely contingency dictates broad technological parameters. Most important, the search for a technological solution to vulnerability in the nuclear age, a solution which makes an adversary even more vulnerable, is not only futile but dangerous. Even the public proclamation of the intention to develop increasingly accurate offensive weapons in conjunction with a greatly enhanced defensive capability can be extraordinarily dangerous if the principal threat is miscalculation: fear of vulnerability can itself be a powerful incentive to pre-emption. Any technological gain is more than offset by the political damage that is done. Decapitation strategies and anti-satellite technology make little sense in this context; our analysis suggests that they might well provoke rather than prevent war. In the 1980s, strategy must seek simultaneously to assure the absolute cost of the use of nuclear force, to underline the constant risk of escalation, to emphasise the dangers of competition in risk-taking. Planners must seek to preserve mutual vulnerability as the basis of political re-assurance rather than seek superiority as the basis for deterrence.

Second, political leaders as well as military planners must avoid creating a frightened, frustrated, desperate, or humiliated challenger. As Lebow concludes in a comparative investigation of deterrence, formal theory appears to stand reality on its head.[21] Deterrence assumes a constant level of hostility and expects that a challenger awaits only opportunity. A great deal of the evidence that we have suggests, however, that a challenger often resorts to force primarily from weakness, even though they see no opportunity. The implications of the evidence are strong and obvious: a defender must pay as much attention to its adversary's needs and vulnerabilities as it does to its ambitions and strengths if it hopes to avoid war. Since challenge may arise from weakness rather than strength, it is incumbent on a defender to attend to these weaknesses and to try, if at all possible, to ameliorate the most pressing of grievances.

Attention to an adversary's constraints would generate very different kinds of policy issues. At a minimum, for example, confidence-building measures would become important not for the technical advantage they might provide but rather for the contribution they would make to the political atmospherics and to the reduction of the opportunity for miscalculation. It should be obvious as well that an escalating rhetoric, denigration of an adversary's fundamental values, attribution of incessantly evil motives, disparagement, all these can charge the political atmosphere and create or enhance a sense of humiliation or desperation. They are, of course, consistent with deterrence which is premised on intense threat and requires public support, but they are counter-indicated if the principal concern is miscalculated war. To put the point most directly, they work to provoke war.

It would be appropriate as well to raise the question of where, on what kinds of issues, conciliation and concession might be appropriate to change the political atmosphere in which larger issues are considered. The political context of an adversarial relationship is critical: it sets the tone and texture which shade the meaning and interpretation of often ambiguous military action. Miscalculation of military intention is far more likely to occur in a charged political environment than in a more relaxed political climate which juxtaposes positive dimensions with enduring conflict.

All these propositions are consistent with a plea for a broader political-strategic calculus which abandons single contingency analysis - the premeditated war of deterrence - as its central premise and moves to assess the spectrum of political, economic, and psychological as well as military incentives to action and inaction. We must go beyond elegant but misleading models of an adversary's motives to encompass the variegated factors which propel an adversary's behaviour. Although such an analysis will be far more difficult to do, differentiated and richer explanations will prove far more rewarding.

Finally, I would urge that we look not only to strategic thinkers but to political leaders to communicate their vision not of what they want to avoid, but of what they want to achieve. In a complex multi-dimensional relationship between nuclear powers who can destroy each other, who are locked in intense competition even as they are acutely interdependent, what are appropriate goals? How might the relationship best be conceived? Are there ways of highlighting a shared and vulnerable commonality that can be conserved and preserved only within a paradigm that both permits and delimits conflict? How can political re-assurance be used effectively to reduce the shared risk of a confrontation that escalates out of control, without at the same time projecting irresolution? How can understanding of mutual weaknesses as well as strengths best be promoted? What are appropriate arenas of co-operation as well as competition? How can a strategy that builds on the dualism inherent in a nuclear relationship be orchestrated and supported? In the nuclear age, even more so than in earlier historical periods, we must pay attention to positive as well as to negative goals and relate a panoply of techniques to the multiple purposes we pursue simultaneously.

The difficulty, of course, lies not with the prescription of a nuanced and mixed strategy that reflects political as well as military imperatives, but rather with its specifics. Its design will require the talents of the imaginative and the skilled. The evidence we now have before us shows, however, that exclusive reliance on one strategy alone, one that may be focused on the less rather than the more probable catastrophe, is fraught with danger. This is especially so when deterrence is narrowly interpreted within a military context. In the 1980s, we ignore the evidence at our peril.

Notes

1. Robert Jervis, The Illogic of American Nuclear Strategy (Cornell University Press, Ithaca, 1984).

2. Dennis Ross, 'Rethinking Soviet Strategic Policy', Journal of Strategic Studies I, May 1978, and Jack Snyder, The Soviet Strategic Culture: Implications for Limited Nuclear Operations, (Rand, R-2154-AF, Santa Monica, September 1977).

3. Samuel P. Huntington, 'Conventional Deterrence and Conventional Retaliation in Europe', International Security, vol. 8, no. 3 (Winter, 1983-84), pp. 32-56.

4. For an abstract discussion of 'critical risk' as a threshold in competitive risk taking, see Daniel Ellsberg, 'The Crude Analysis of Strategic Choices', American Economic Review, LI, pp. 472-478, and Glenn Snyder and Paul Diesing, Conflict Among Nations (Princeton University Press, Princeton, 1977).

5. Huntington is careful to discuss an increase in conventional capability as an increase in the capacity to deter, not as an option should deterrence fail. This is a critically important distinction, for much of the discussion of conventional capabilities focuses on the contingency of deterrence failure.

6. Richard Ned Lebow, 'Windows of Opportunity: Do States Jump Through Them?' International Security, vol. 9, no. 1, (Summer, 1984), pp. 147-186.

7. The effect of nuclear war on world climate is discussed in Carl Sagan, 'Nuclear War and Climatic Catastrophe', Foreign Affairs vol. 62, no. 2, (Winter, 1983/84), pp. 257-292.

8. See Robert Jervis 'Deterrence and Perception', International Security, vol. 7, no. 3, (Winter 1982-83), pp. 3-31, for an interesting discussion of self-deterrence when force is conventional.

9. Jervis, The Illogic of American Nuclear Strategy.

10. Richard Ned Lebow, 'Conclusions', in Robert Jervis, Richard Ned Lebow and Janice Gross Stein, Psychology and Deterrence (The Johns Hopkins University Press, Baltimore, 1985).

11. Janice Gross Stein, 'Calculation, Miscalculation, and Conventional Deterrence I: The View From Cairo', in Jervis, Lebow, and Stein, Psychology and Deterrence.

12. Lebow finds a similar pattern in Argentinian decision-making before the invasion of the Malvinas. Argentina's military leaders chose among unattractive options and gave greatest weight to the domestic political consequences of inaction. See his 'Miscalculation in the South Atlantic: the Origins of the Falklands War', in Jervis, Lebow and Stein, Psychology and Deterrence.

13. See Richard Ned Lebow, Between Peace and War (The Johns Hopkins University Press, Baltimore, 1981).

14. See Robert Jervis, Perception and Misperception in International Relations (Princeton University Press, Princeton, 1976); Charles Lockhart, 'Flexibility and Commitment in International Conflicts', International Studies Quarterly, vol. 22, no. 4, (1978) pp. 545-558, and Richard Ned Lebow, 'Conclusions' in Jervis, Lebow and Stein, Psychology and Deterrence.

15. Lebow, 'Miscalculation in the South Atlantic'.

16. For a discussion of the linkage between different kinds of misperception and war, see Jack S. Levy, 'Misperception and the Causes of War: Theoretical Linkages and Analytical Problems', World Politics, vol. XXXVI, no. 1, (October, 1983), pp. 76-99.

17. For an analysis of the impact of different kinds of security dilemmas, see Jack Snyder, 'Perceptions of the Security Dilemma in 1914', in Jervis, Lebow, and Stein, Psychology and Deterrence.

18. For an examination of the escalatory impact of interconnected interests, see Janice Gross Stein and Raymond Tanter, Rational Decision Making: Israel's Security Choices 1967, (Ohio State University Press, Columbus, Ohio, 1980).

19. I am indebted to Franklyn Griffiths of the University of Toronto for this analogy.

20. Michael McCGwire, 'The Dilemmas and Delusions of Deterrence', in Gwyn Prins, (ed.) The Choice: Nuclear Weapons versus Security, Random House, New York, 1984).

21. Lebow, 'Conclusions', in Jervis, Lebow and Stein, Psychology and Deterrence.

Chapter Three

THE STRATEGY OF DETERRENCE: IS THE CONCEPT CREDIBLE?

George H. Quester

Is deterrence credible as a concept? Is deterrence something that can survive into the future, or has it outlived its moral, psychological and political acceptability? These are ways of phrasing the question which seems to be bothering people so much around the world in the 1980s. As the competition in nuclear arms procurement shows no sign of abating, people who might have been relatively content with mutual deterrence, not wanting to dwell upon its mechanisms so very much, are now forced to think about it, and are often enough upset by what they see.

Can we conclude that deterrence has worked? How can one ever prove that the threat of nuclear destruction prevented any enemy attack, when the prospective enemy (the Soviet Union) is so secretive about all of its decision processes, when we will never be able to read any meaningful Soviet documents or diaries, or logs of Politburo meetings? Some alarmed skeptics would lead us into a discussion of psychological constructs, citing theories or definitions of 'rationality'. If 'deterrence presupposes rationality', what do we do with most studies of individual or mass psychology, which suggest that we are all rather lacking in this respect?

Yet a very different reaction to 'deterrence' has all along been one of 'ho hum', 'much ado about nothing'. Is deterrence something so very new - a different approach to international security since 1945 - or is it merely old stuff - something that we have used much longer - with anyone touting its alleged novelty merely displaying an ignorance of history? Some of those who see 'nothing new' are trying to ease our concerns. But others would use this argument to amplify our concerns, noting how arms races often became wars in earlier decades, noting some striking similarities between the outbreaks of a World War I and a World War III.

The Newness of Deterrence

As Glenn Snyder pointed out very clearly some two decades ago, there is indeed a major difference between what might have amounted to deterrence in an earlier age and what it became after World War II. The difference is illustrated, in his terms, by the distinction between 'deterrence by denial' and 'deterrence by punishment'.[1] Peace has, of course, been maintained often enough in the past because potential aggressors were dissuaded (deterred) by a reckoning of the likely consequences if they attacked, as (with only a modicum of 'rationality' being presupposed) they had responded to this reckoning by holding their forces back. The reckoning in earlier times was, however, normally that of 'who would win' if someone launched a war. If one simply loses soldiers and equipment by attack, failing to gain any territory thereby, perhaps even losing some territory, there is no point in launching the attack. Perhaps the other side is too strong; should the other side therefore launch the attack? Perhaps there is an advantage for the defence (the side which does not move forward to attack) so that either side would lose soldiers and tanks (and prestige) by attacking.

A fear of destruction of one's own cities thus did not play much of a role in deterring military adventures in the old days. To be sure, cities sometimes were devastated as by the Huns or the Mongols, but this was only the fate of the losers in battle, not any dissuading factor for those who could win. The winner on the battlefield *ipso facto* thereby maintained a safety for his women and children. All that one had to fear - all that normally could work as a 'deterrent' - was the prospect of defeat on the battlefield, the prospect of being denied the gains one was seeking (and perhaps, in a badly executed military adventure, even losing some of what one had begun with).

Contemporary deterrence is instead something based much more on the suffering that can at the last gasp be imposed on the winner, as a victory on the battlefield would no longer assure a victor against the punishment and destruction of his cities. The punishments inflicted here would thus not be simply the normal wear and tear of combat.

Rather these punishments violate the normal ethics and laws of combat, by making civilians targets along with the men in uniform. The deterring retaliation is heavily a move of spite and revenge, intended to be painful and mean, thus intended by its very prospect to preclude aggressions even where victory on the battlefield would have gone to the aggressor. This is a new approach to warfare - new enough to seem 'untested', jarring to our traditions and moral sensibilities, and perhaps therefore, not fully 'credible'.

It is easy enough to sketch out some of the prerequisite physical changes which made such deterrence by punishment possible. First there had to be a third-dimensional means of delivery, so that the stout forward-moving line of one's victorious infantry or victorious fleet no longer could shield one's home front. The airplane and the missile obviously offered this, as does the submarine, and the submarine combined with the missile. (When we look for earlier analogies to deterrence by punishment, we may occasionally also find them already in the fogginess and the porousness of battle lines at sea, as punitive commerce raiders might slip by even a preponderant navy, to harass the home front of those who had counted on victory.)

The second prerequisite for deterrence by punishment was that there be a form of destructive power so compact that this third-dimensional delivery approach would become unignorable, even for a foreign power which otherwise would have gone to the limit in pursuing total victory. The atomic bomb may have definitely offered what was necessary here; and if the A-bomb was not quite awesome enough, the thermonuclear hydrogen bomb surely is.

Forerunners in Air Warfare

If we wish to compile a set of early analogs to contemporary deterrence by punishment, our list will not be very long. Many readers might indeed have assumed that deterrence reasoning could only date from the introduction of nuclear weapons in 1945, or even later from the introduction of thermonuclear weapons after 1952. Yet, the discussions after World War I about the strategic possibilities of air warfare are a little richer in this regard than we might normally realise.[2]

In the years between World War I and World War II, it was typically projected that an ordinary explosive or poison gas attack delivered by airplane or submarine might already suffice for this ultimately painful deterrent role. Such protections were clearly premature, but they nonetheless amounted to premises for what could be interesting forerunners of our contemporary theories about mutual assured destruction. For example, note the expectations of Giulio Douhet:

> In general, aerial offensives will be directed against such targets as peacetime industrial and commercial establishments; important buildings, private and public; transportation arteries and centers; and certain designated areas of civilian population as well. To destroy these targets three kinds of bombs are needed - explosive, incendiary, and poison gas - apportioned as the situation may require. The explosives will demolish the target, the incendiaries set fire to it, and the poison-gas bombs prevent fire fighters from extinguishing the fires.[3]

Among such analysts who won a public reputation for their early discussions of air power, it is remarkable how most of them then came very close to outlining and understanding the modern concept of deterrence, but did not quite make the connection. Writers like Giulio Douhet and J.F.C. Fuller presented versions of future air attacks on cities which certainly read a lot like the actual fire-bombings of Hamburg or Dresden or Tokyo in World War II, or even the atomic bombings of Hiroshima and Nagasaki. Yet, their descriptions of 'knockout blows' here normally leave such air attacks in the category of counterforce or countercapability strikes, designed to win the war, designed to eliminate the enemy's ability to fight, rather than eliminating his will to fight by the mere prospect of airborne retaliation.

Stressing the penetration capability of the aerial bomber, such theorists again and again concluded that the bomber would always get through. Yet they normally then perceived this confrontation as a simple race of who would get his bombers through first. However, logic might also dictate that the losing side would still be able to get <u>his</u> bombers through as well, and would wreak a terrible retaliatory havoc on the winner's cities, and thus perhaps to deter anyone from despatching his bombers in the first place.

Douhet thus sketched out all the premises, but

did not push through to the conclusion of contemporary deterrence theory. Perhaps he was held back, as many military professionals have been over the decades, by a need to pretend some compliance with the traditional canons of proper targeting philosophy, by which civilians are never aimed at as a countervalue spite target, but are struck only accidentally when they are close to some legitimate military target.

> To simplify the situation, then, let us admit that both independent Air Forces could begin operations simultaneously. We have already seen that the fundamental concept governing aerial warfare is to be resigned to the damage the enemy may inflict upon us, while utilizing every means at our disposal to inflict even heavier damage upon him. An Independent Air Force must therefore be completely free of any preoccupation with the actions of the enemy force. Its sole concern should be to do the enemy the greatest possible amount of surface damage in the shortest possible time, which depends upon the available air forces and the choice of enemy targets.[4]

J.F.C. Fuller similarly imputed horrendous capabilities to aircraft using poison gas and to submarines landing tanks at some remote coast where they would quickly make their way inland, again using poison gas (the functional equivalent of today's SLBM submarines firing missiles at our land base, after having escaped all detection at sea).

> I believe that, in future warfare, great cities, such as London, will be attacked from the air, and that a fleet of 500 aeroplanes each carrying 500 ten-pound bombs of, let us suppose, mustard gas, might cause 200,000 minor casualties and throw the whole city into panic within half an hour of their arrival. Picture, if you can, what the result will be: London for several days will be one vast raving Bedlam, the hospitals will be stormed, traffic will cease, the homeless will shriek for help, the city will be in pandemonium....
>
> If we meditate for a moment on the above possibilities, rendered practical by wedding tank to submarine, two facts will strike us forcibly; these are:

> (i) The secrecy and celerity of the operation.
> (ii) The vulnerability of the civil target.
>
> If to these two weapons we add the aeroplane, this secrecy and this vulnerability becomes enormously enhanced. Consequently, we may well ask ourselves, as Fontenoy courtesies have become completely out of date, will not formal declarations of war follow suit. Bearing in mind that the main tactical problem in war is to hit without being hit, is it common-sense to expect a nation, reduced to fight for its life, a nation which possibly possesses scientific weapons of tremendous power, and the development of the power of which demands surprise in its positive form - an unexpected and terrific blow, moral or physical, according to the theory of warfare held - to place its adversary on guard by saying: "On August 4 I am going to hit you." What is far more probable is that the enemy will say nothing at all, or: "On August 4 I will agree to your terms," and then launch a surprise attack on the 3rd.[5]

The destruction such forces could inflict on London would be quite horrible, but Fuller again never rounded in the possibility that the British Navy might have its own submarines at sea, carrying tanks equipped with poison gas, and its own aircraft similarly capable of striking back to inflict the same horrible destruction on the enemy's cities. What Fuller feared was that the enemy attack could stun and incapacitate the British government and military command, as well as imposing terrible suffering on the British people. Yet what good would it do a French or German government to stun the British command, if the existing aerial and submarine units could impose a comparable suffering on Paris or Berlin?

If then one wishes an example of where this connection indeed got made, between aerial bombardment vehicles and mutual deterrence - deterrence by punishment - one can turn to the prolific writings of J.M. Spaight, a British strategic writer of the inter-war years who never commanded an audience as large as Douhet or Fuller or Liddell Hart, but who indeed predicted that aerial bombardment might be held back on each side in future wars, as a deterrent to the other side's launching of such bombardment:

> The very magnitude of the disaster that is possible may prove to be a restraining influence. Because the riposte is certain, because it cannot be parried, a belligerent will think twice and again before he initiates a mode of warfare the final outcome of which is incalculable. The deterrent influence may, indeed, be greater than that. It may tend to prevent not only raids on cities but resort to war in any shape or form. No one can tell what will happen if war does come. Its momentum may carry it to lengths not intended before it began to gather speed. Wars have a way of deteriorating in their course.
>
> Omne ignotum pro magnifico. At present air attack is regarded as a menace, a withheld thunderbolt, an impending calamity. All nations fear it. For that very reason it should be a deterrent influence against war.[6]

Having thus actually opened the 'deterrent' vocabulary in his argument, Spaight in effect foresaw a pattern of restraints very like what we have experienced since World War II, whereby the worst bombing capability of each side deters the other side from using its worst bombing capability and also deters it from a great deal more.

Since the deterrence will usually not be totally effective on each side however, something like contemporary 'limited war' emerges - a limited war which is indeed the conceptual twin brother of deterrence, since limits on what weapons get used are now accepted for fear of what the other side could do - and is not yet doing - rather than for any of the other traditional reasons for limits. For a nice inter-war illustration of this kind of argument, we can turn to a piece published anonymously under the name of 'Ajax', offering a prediction of limited wars in the future - a prediction which held for less than a year of World War II, but which certainly has been confirmed in practice many times since, with the adversary being Soviet rather than German or Italian:

> ...It is more than probable that if either Germany or Italy were ready for a colony-snatching adventure, or a trade war supported by arms, they would carry on with the enterprise using only such military means as conform to established civilized warlike custom

> and tacitly defy us to bomb them at home. If this happened the author feels very sure that Britain would have to keep her "strategic bombers" at home and the people who would decide this would not be the British War Cabinet but the British people.[7]

As for the actual implementation of such deterrence and limited war theory, we must also note the decisions made by the British Royal Air Force and its civilian superiors at the onset of World War II in 1939. Convinced (somewhat prematurely and erroneously) that the Luftwaffe would be able to inflict horrendous damage on London and Paris, the British and French governments held back their own air forces as war was declared, striking at only the very most explicitly military targets. While Hitler's Luftwaffe was imposing substantial devastation on targets in Poland during the German invasion of that country, he claimed that this was directed only at 'tactical' targets, close to advancing German ground forces; Hitler had indeed also reined in the Luftwaffe with regard to any attacks on British and French cities, for the German dictator was very fearful of how his people might react to being bombed. Had this pattern persisted (based on the exaggerated premises developed between the wars on how much damage could be inflicted in an aerial attack with ordinary high-explosive bombs - poison gas was not to be used in the European campaigns of World War II) we would now be dating our discussion of deterrence theory back to 1939, rather than to 1945 or later. In a process of escalation after the fall of France in 1940 however, the two sides slid into a maximum effort at crippling or intimidating each other by air attack, efforts which (at least until the introduction of nuclear weapons at Hiroshima and Nagasaki) are typically remembered as a failure by most strategic analysts.

Forerunners in Naval Warfare

As noted, a part of the reason why the 'credibility' of deterrence is questioned is that it is new - something lacking much historical test. And another part is that it is of such dubious morality, intended somehow to prevent wars by threatening those on the other side who would have been relatively innocent in any decision to launch a war.

Yet, both in terms of historical experience and

the slippery slopes of targeting moralities there is a little bit more to examine besides the history of thinking about air warfare. The sea has also often offered ways of getting back at the enemy's civilian sector, as the ability of navies to harass commerce and bombard coasts generated some non-trivial countervalue options. A very nice theoretical opening of these issues can be found in the arguments of the British historian Sir Julian Corbett, writing at the beginning of the twentieth century after the first works of Mahan had appeared, but before the outbreak of World War I. Corbett contended that Mahan's emphasis on counterforce uses of a fleet was overdrawn, and that the countervalue punishment role of naval power might ultimately be as important, or more important, than driving the enemy fleet from the seas.

> It ignores the fundamental fact that battles are only the means of enabling you to do that which really brings wars to an end - that is, to exert pressure on the citizens and their collective life. "After shattering the hostile main army," says Von der Goltz, "we still have the forcing of a peace as a separate and, in certain circumstances, a more difficult task... to make the enemy's country feel the burdens of war with such weight that the desire for peace will prevail. This is the point in which Napoleon failed.... It may be necessary to seize the harbours, commercial centres, important lines of traffic, fortifications and arsenals, in other words, all important property necessary to the existence of the people and army."
>
> If, then, we are deprived of the right to use analogous means at sea, the object for which we fight battles almost ceases to exist. Defeat the enemy's fleets as we may, he will be but little the worse. We shall have opened the way for invasion, but any of the great continental Powers can laugh at our attempts to invade single-handed. If we cannot reap the harvest of our success by deadening his national activities at sea, the only legitimate means of pressure within our strength will be denied us.[8]

Corbett's argument, that Britain should retain freedom of action for its fleet crippling the commerce of an adversary, in effect set the stage for British policy during World War I, and interestingly opens up much of the moral debate about air attacks as well. In World War I, the British stopped all ships going to Germany, not just those carrying explicitly military goods, but also those carrying food or anything else.

To satisfy the morality of neutrals or of British fighting men, this was always officially labelled a counterforce operation rather than countervalue, intended (even in the case of food) to reduce Germany's <u>ability</u> to fight, rather than specifically to punish the Germans by imposing on them malnutrition and diminished resistance to disease. Much the same was the official rationale for the United States submarine attacks of World War II, which obstructed the arrival of <u>all</u> ships going back to Japan, not just those carrying soldiers or weapons; to cut off food would be to reduce Japanese military <u>capabilities</u>, and only incidentally to make life miserable for Japanese civilians.

The same kind of double-think was, of course, applied to the aerial bombardments carried through in World War II. Critics of the final use of atomic weapons against Japan (Hiroshima was officially a 'military target'), or of the massive conventional firebombings of Tokyo, have suggested that Japan was about to surrender in any event, so that such destructive aerial assaults were unnecessary brutality.[9] When asked to explain how they conclude that the Japanese government would have surrendered anyway, however, such critics typically then cite 'the naval blockade'. Since the blockade was of this same dual nature - officially intended to weaken Japan militarily - only unofficially torturing the Japanese civilian population to reduce the government's willingness to continue the war, we would then seem simply to be comparing the moralities of two kinds of hypocrisy, two kinds of countervalue torture. If Japanese civilian life had not been suffering, if civilian homes had not been bombed, and if civilian cargo ships had been allowed to come in under neutral flag, it is more questionable whether Tokyo would ever have surrendered. If the war had thus been fought honourably and cleanly, the Japanese would not have surrendered until beaten on the battlefields of their own islands, a terribly costly process for the Allies.

As an illustration of a possibly still earlier version of such naval 'deterrence by punishment', we might then ask how one would explain the securing of Canada against United States invasion for the years from the War of 1812 to the beginning of the twentieth century. The favourite British plan (analogous to the favourite plan of many Americans today for the defence of NATO against Soviet attack) was that the Canadians should generate a larger militia capability and otherwise prepare to defend themselves effectively against any United States invasion (i.e. a policy of deterrence by denial).[10] Since the Canadians (like the NATO countries) typically did not generate the forces required for this, the ultimate assurance against a United States invasion was rather the retaliation the British fleet could have inflicted on the United States cities along the Atlantic seaboard. The burning out of Boston or New York or Washington or Baltimore would not have prevented an advance of the Union Army intent on 'liberating Canada'; but it would have imposed enough pain and destruction to make the military adventure a bad bargain from the perspective of Washington, and the Fourth of July speeches calling for the absorption of Canada thus never led to any military move north.

Such an ability to burn out the Atlantic coastal cities of the United States, as with the contemporary ability to fire thermonuclear missiles at cities, was thus something qualitatively different from what prevailed in the days of Mongols. It is not so different in the level of destructiveness because the depredations of Mongol or Viking armies, or the armies of the Thirty Years War, may have been comparable to what we would have to suffer today. It is qualitatively different rather because the military victor is also exposed to this kind of attack and suffering in the revenge inflicted by the side whose troops or fleets had lost the battles. 'Don't you dare beat me on the battlefield, because I will get even in a way that makes you sorry you won' is the modern message in what we now normally refer to as 'deterrence', and it does not have much of an equivalent to earlier days.

The Slow Development of Nuclear Deterrence Reasoning

In the immediate aftermath of the atomic bombing of Hiroshima and Nagasaki, followed by the surprisingly sudden Japanese surrender, it was to take some time for serious analysts to sort out any consensus interpretation of the impact of such weapons on the international system. Indeed, no such consensus may yet exist, even some four decades later.

As in the earlier more general analysis of air power by Douhet and others, one could have chosen to stress the counterforce impact of such weapons, or their countervalue impact. In terms of crippling an enemy's military capability - thus settling quickly who the 'winner' of any war was to be - nuclear weapons delivered by aircraft might work far more rapidly and decisively than any of the weapons or plans of the past, surpassing even the most smoothly functioning Schlieffen Plan, indeed taking the point out of any industrial and troop mobilisations after war was declared. This side of the possibilities of nuclear weapons was consistent with traditional thinking about the purpose of weapons and about what was a professional and moral approach to thinking about the use of weapons. It was the line of emphasis presented in a book by William L. Borden published in 1946, There Will Be No Time.[11]

A somewhat different conclusion would have come in stressing the countervalue damage that could be inflicted by nuclear weapons - the damage they would inflict on cities and on all of civilisation regardless of who 'won', since the victor most probably would be unable to keep the losers from imposing such damage on his cities. This interpretation, premised on what we now would call assured second-strike retaliation or mutual assured destruction, was much more the launching of contemporary notions of deterrence. It was an analysis outlined by Bernard Brodie in chapters of his book of 1946, The Absolute Weapon.

> If the aggressor state must fear retaliation, it will know that even if it is the victor it will suffer a degree of physical destruction incomparably greater than that suffered by any defeated nation of history, incomparably greater, that is, than that suffered by Germany in the recent war. Under those circumstances no victory, even if guaranteed in advance - which it never is - would be worth the price. The threat of retaliation does not have to be 100 per cent certain; it is sufficient if there is a good chance of it, or if there is belief that there is a good chance of it. The prediction is more important than the fact.[12]

As long as only the United States possessed nuclear weapons, of course, such issues of second-strike retaliation could not play any role. The Japanese had no way of retaliating for Hiroshima and Nagasaki and the United States had thus gone ahead to use its atomic weapons, officially claiming that these nuclear attacks were intended to cripple the Japanese ability to continue fighting the war, and actually also hoping (very probably correctly) that these new bombs would eliminate the Japanese willingness to fight, inducing Tokyo instead to surrender.

Any hope that this monopoly would persist - that it would take the Soviet Union many years to produce nuclear weapons of its own - were dashed, however, as the first Soviet nuclear detonation was detected in 1949. A National Security Council study (NSC-68) was commissioned by President Harry S. Truman to consider the implications of the Soviet detonation. The study was itself not to be declassified for public perusal until 1975, but various accounts of its analysis and conclusions leaked to the public earlier at the end of the 1950s - accounts emerging along with a flood of academic analysis on arms control and deterrence.[13] The NSC-68 study addressed - yet only in a somewhat blurry fashion - the possibility that the two nuclear forces might now deter each other, with neither side using its nuclear weapons until the other did, but with the Soviets then being free to pursue nickle-and-dime aggressions using purely conventional forces.[14] But the study also devoted a fair amount of attention to the counterforce possibility that nuclear weapons might be used by either side to try to win a victory by crippling the other side militarily.

This NSC-68 study was indeed not quite as crisp in its analysis as it was credited. Many of the academic authors dissecting the issues of limited war and mutual deterrence by the beginning of the 1960s assumed that NSC-68 had already preceded them on the same analytical pathway within the government, but this was true in only very general terms.

What should one make, then, of this slowness of the strategic analytical community to assign priority to the deterring significance of the countervalue retaliation which a nuclear force could inflict? Some of this was simple wishful thinking, escaping how awful war would now be. Some of it was sheer momentum from the past. Another part stemmed from the 'cry wolf' of the similar countervalue predictions which had been made in the 1920s and

1930s, only to be disproven, as bombing during during World War II did not force Britain or Germany to surrender. After the Bikini test of nuclear weapons in 1946, there was even a general reaction that nuclear weapons were less awesome than had been thought, as a fair number of ships remained afloat (albeit radioactive and uninhabitable), as a bathing suit was named after the atoll, - a monument to the seriousness with which the nuclear test had been received.[15]

Another part of this delay in regarding the atomic bomb as 'the absolute weapon' stemmed from the traditional professional outlook of the military, who are still not conditioned to thinking of their weapons as earmarked for attacks on civilian homes, except where this is ancillary to an attack on a 'military target'. Basing everything on preparation for spiteful retaliation resembled the felonies indicted at war crimes trials.

Rounding out this resistance to accepting any revolutionary implications of mutual deterrence, Soviet spokesmen now generally persisted in claiming that nuclear weapons were not important (at least for as long as the Soviet Union had none of its own, and even for a while longer), and that aerial bombardment in general was pointless; the World War II destruction of Hiroshima and Dresden was portrayed as purposeless brutality by American leaders, with such destruction of population centres presumably being incapable of changing anyone's feelings about persisting in a war, or beginning a war.

Second-Strike Forces and Deterrence

All such doubts about the awesomeness of nuclear retaliation amounted, in the analysis of the prerequisites of deterrence, to what we would today worry about as the sufficiency of 'assured second-strike retaliation'.

There are several major kinds of worry about nuclear deterrence - worries that have persisted since 1950, worries which probably will never go away. The most basic of these is the fear that our second-strike might not suffice to punish the other side's first-strike, leaving the other side undeterred, and thus tempted to launch a World War III in the prospect of winning it. What if the force launching a sneak attack catches most of the nuclear forces of its victim on the ground? Can the surviving forces inflict enough retaliation on second-strike to make the aggressor sorry? This has been the American worry at the time of various 'bomber gaps' and 'missile gaps', and is one version of the worry today about a 'window of vulnerability'. It is a worry which is compounded when Soviet statements about civil defence and nuclear war still in part seem to shrug off the damage United States retaliation would inflict. Are the Soviet leaders callous enough to shrug off repetitions of Dresden and Hiroshima inflicted on their cities? If the major theme is to be just as much 'there will be no time', as 'the absolute weapon', then it will be difficult to be sure that one has an absolute enough weapon - a sure enough deterrent.

Albert Wohlstetter radiated a great deal of this concern in his Foreign Affairs article of 1959 on 'The Delicate Balance of Terror'.[16] The article repeated concerns which had been outlined several years earlier in a RAND Corporation classified study for the United States Air Force on the possible vulnerability of Strategic Air Command bombers to Soviet bombers equipped with nuclear weapons.

Two different kinds of factors thus interlace to determine whether this first problem of nuclear deterrence - the problem of the survivability of sufficient retaliatory forces - can be solved. First, we need to be convinced that the horror of nuclear destruction is real enough, a patently obvious proposition for many of us, but a proposition which has been questioned sufficient times - explicitly or implicitly - to remain bothersomely unsettled. Second, we must be sure that the counterforce first-strike of the attacker could not wear down the countervalue second-strike of the retaliating power to get below the threshold of what is needed to deter. Deterrence is in trouble, to repeat, if either side can do to the other what the Mongols did to their enemies: inflict devastation without suffering unacceptable devastation in return.

With regard to this second factor, the possible prowess of counterforce attacks, we have seen the threat rise and fall and rise again over the years since 1949. In the years when manned bombers were the only means of delivering nuclear weapons, it was distinctly possible, as noted by Wohlstetter and others, that a single enemy bomber could destroy a large number of our bombers on the ground. Even if the penetrating bomber were lost (i.e. was unable to fly a round-trip mission), the force-exchange ratios would dictate that the side striking would do much better than the side being struck, perhaps so much better that it might get off scot-free - or acceptably low - in terms of retaliation. 'There will be no time' thus would become a more relevant phrase than 'the absolute weapon' again, as the gestalt of the confrontation was that of bomber crews racing to get their aircraft off the ground before an enemy attack caught them.

In the second phase of the nuclear arms confrontation, where each side had nuclear-tipped missiles on board submarines and in underground silos, the apparent advantage of striking first very much receded as it appeared that the submarines carrying missiles would be undetectable and untargetable, while the concrete layers protecting such land-based ICBMs as Minuteman would shield their missiles against anything except a very direct hit. It would thus typically require the expenditure of more than one ICBM to destroy one ICBM on the other side, perhaps as many as three fired for every one destroyed; as a result, it would be military folly for someone to race to launch his missiles in a crisis, and there would be no plausible way to escape the retaliation that might come against one's cities.

The third phase is the one we unfortunately seem to be entering for the 1980s, indeed perhaps explaining a great deal of the current anxiety about the nuclear arms confrontation, as the accuracies of missiles have been very much improved and as multiple warheads have been developed for the payloads of these missiles. If any matching breakthroughs were to be made in anti-submarine warfare (ASW), this pattern of restoring an advantage to striking first would be dismally complete. With multiple warheads and good accuracies, it will take considerably fewer than 1000 missiles launched from either side to destroy as many as a thousand on the other side. Militarily, the side which is first to launch its missiles would have a considerable advantage.

Whether the second-strike retaliation against cities could be reduced enough to make this ever worthwhile is much less certain. Compared to the worries of the 1950s about whether assured destruction would be sufficient to deter, the destruction that would be inflicted, even on the victor in any nuclear war of the 1980s or 1990s, promises to be still quite unbearably horrendous. We would prefer the strategic balance of the 1960s, perhaps, which needed less explaining and less examination. But one certainly prefers the stability of the current nuclear confrontation to that of the middle or later 1950s.[17]

Rationality and Deterrence

Nuclear deterrence is thus in trouble if either side can strike and escape meaningful retaliation by the other. Nuclear deterrence is also in trouble if either side retaliates before there is anything to retaliate for, if it uses up the leverage of the nuclear devastation it can threaten, by having already inflicted such devastation. Nuclear deterrence amounts to a mutual hostage relationship between the population centres of the United States and the Soviet Union. Anyone familiar with the workings of a more normal hostage situation knows that the kidnapper or blackmailer loses all his bargaining power if the hostage is killed.

But what if one of the nuclear weapons arsenals comes into the control of someone who capriciously decides to inflict nuclear destruction anyhow? Nuclear deterrence is often labelled as depending on 'rationality', which can lead to some relatively foolish criticisms of the credibility of the deterrence concept, if too broad or too loose a definition of rationality is plugged into the proposition. All that one means by 'rationality', in the sentence 'deterrence depends on rationality', is that the people in control of nuclear arsenals must be averse to seeing their own cities and people attacked with such weapons, and must be elementarily aware of the link by which their attacking other populations with nuclear weapons would lead to nuclear retaliatory attacks on their own cities. If someone were to become so out of tune with reality as to miss this elementary link, or if someone were to become indifferent to nuclear devastation (perhaps even welcoming foreign nuclear attacks on the cities he governed), then the 'rationality' we need for our purposes here would surely not exist, and deterrence again would surely have failed.[18]

The Immorality of Deterrence

As a third issue for our list, to be added to the problems discussed so far of assured retaliatory force survivability and rationality, we also have to come to grips with the sheer immorality of the deterrence approach; if we have been achieving a peace by deterrence, this has been grounded heavily on the deliberate or inadvertent damage that would be inflicted on innocent civilians.[19]

For reasons of traditional civilian morality and also because of the professional military standards already noted, which so often cause strategic planners to think about counterforce rather than countervalue uses of weapons, this continues to be an unsettling line of thought. It is analogous to trying to reduce the number of murders, by punishing the wife and children of the murderer when the criminal himself has escaped the police (or when he was already under the death sentence for another murder, and thus had exhausted his personal susceptibility to being dissuaded by prospect of punishment). Any of us would scoff at such a proposal in the domestic arrangments of life, regarding it as a throwback to the worst of the Dark Ages. Yet the prevention of war and aggression in the years since 1950 has depended on something comparably inhumane.

The normal justification of deterrence is, of course, the unprovable (but very plausible and probable) proposition that it works, that the number of conventional wars that would have been fought in Europe and elsewhere since 1945, with American and Russian sponsors locked in combat, would have been greater if nuclear weapons had never been invented. Looking back on the impact of nuclear weapons, we most probably now have to welcome this impact, because it freed up resources that would otherwise have had to go into 'deterrence by denial', preparations for a conventional defence of Western Europe. Such a conventional defence might have made impossible the 'economic miracle' in West Germany, and the economic growth elsewhere around the NATO area, which has made life so much richer than before.

Looking ahead to the future of nuclear weapons, of course, we may have to be much less sure that we would welcome their impact. That something 'worked' in the past is no assurance that it will work in the future. New weapons keep being invented and deployed, upsetting any general conclusion that things will work just as in the past. 'New' strategic concepts get put forward on 'war-fighting', etc. although one drift of this article should be that most of these concepts are not really very new.

West Europeans and Americans will be continuously worried in the future about the comparison of two contingencies. If war has not yet broken out, what is one's favourite choice? A continued reliance on nuclear weapons for deterrence may be the right answer. But what if war nonetheless breaks out, what if deterrence has failed? Then many or most of us might decidedly regret our reliance on nuclear weapons, indeed would lament the fact that nuclear weapons had ever been developed in the first place.

Those Americans and West Europeans who are now agitated about a reliance on nuclear deterrence may thus be concerned about a greater likelihood of nuclear war in the future. Alternatively, they may simply be going through a moment of truth about the moral nature of deterrence, having finally been forced to think about an arrangement that has been in place for several decades.

Even if deterrence is accepted on the argument that the alternatives are equally bad from a moral or practical standpoint, there is at least one other negative possibility in the way that nuclear arsenals have been so much configured for mutual assured destruction. If we aspire to a loosening up of the Soviet Union, to a real detente with a normalisation of relations and a reduction of mutual acrimony and suspicion, it is at least possible that the missiles each side continually aims at the other's cities amount to permanent obstacles to this, a political poisoning of the system not so unrelated to the blatant immorality of this indirect approach to peace.

All of us, on either side of the line, must now attach a contingency rider to any long-term plans we make, whether it be on what career field to enter or how many children to have, or where to choose a house or apartment. When contemplating the future, all our problems may look solvable enough, with a message of 'things seem to be working out', but also with a qualifier then 'that is, as long as there is not a nuclear war'. Seeing each other as the possible source of the most complete devastation of all normal civilian life, Americans could develop an irreducible hostility toward Russians, and vice versa; this might be something that would never go away, as long as mutual assured destruction was the price of peace and freedom.

Extending Deterrence

The fourth worry on this list may be the most serious of them all, and is perhaps where the issue of the credibility of deterrence is most often brought into discussion. It is a concern which has been with us ever since the Soviet Union was detected as having become the second nuclear weapons state in 1949. In face of a Soviet nuclear weapons stockpile, could such American weapons be applied to keep Soviet forces from entering Western Europe?

It might seem reasonably credible that a country possessing nuclear weapons could deter someone else's nuclear attack on itself, and that it probably can deter conventional invasions and occupations of its homeland as well. If Japan had possessed nuclear weapons in 1945, there might have been no nuclear attack on Hiroshima or Nagasaki, and no final demand for unconditional surrender with an occupation of Tokyo. Washington was occupied and burned by the British in 1814, and Moscow was occupied by the French in 1812, but neither of these cities is fair game for occupation by the winner of any grand conventional battles any more, and neither is London nor Paris nor Beijing.

But if nuclear deterrence can thus shield the capital and territory of the country possessing such weapons, by the prospect of a 'deterrence by punishment', even where a 'deterrence by denial' could not have worked, can such deterrence by punishment be extended to shield any friends and allies of the nuclear weapons state? The most abstractly logical and clear answer might be negative, since it would be folly for the United States to retaliate against Soviet cities after only a Soviet conventional invasion of West Germany, or after a Soviet nuclear attack only on Bruxelles, since all of the cities of the United States had not yet been attacked, still being alive and well as hostages for American behaviour.[20] And similarly for a Soviet nuclear response, if only Hanoi were hit with nuclear weapons, or if only Hungary were penetrated by a liberating force from NATO?

Such abstract logic is far too tidy here, however, for there have been many ways for either of the superpowers to breathe some life into the credibility of their extensions of nuclear deterrence (the extensions of 'the nuclear umbrella') including the deployment forward of nuclear weapons, the deployment forward of conventional troops from the nuclear weapons state, the issuing of public statements, and the signing of formal treaties of alliance.

Our worst worry about extended nuclear deterrence is thus not to be stated simply as 'Nuclear escalation on behalf of an ally will be incredible, and therefore the other side will be able to attack with only his conventional forces, picking up one piece of territory after another'. This has been one, but only one, of our serious concerns for three decades now, and was part of the fears elaborated in the NSC-68 study in 1949. A still worse worry might rather be that an attacker thought the opposing superpower was bluffing with any threats of escalation to all-out nuclear war if a place like West Germany (or East Germany in reverse) was invaded, and then this turned out not to be a bluff; both sides would then be plunged into a nuclear World War III which neither had wanted.

The Soviets know that there is a non-trivial risk (for reasons that may not be rational, but still are effective - 'the threat that leaves something to chance', in the words of Thomas Schelling)[21] that the United States would thus indeed escalate into a nuclear war - a war destroying Soviet cities and American cities and very much else, if Western Europe were to be invaded by the forces of the Warsaw Pact. For this reason, if not for some others as well, there has been no such invasion across the Elbe.

It may be impossible to prove that 'deterrence has worked', for lack of any scientific test or reliable evidence of what Moscow would have done if nuclear weapons had not existed. Nonetheless, given all the political conflicts and conventional military preparations, a 1944 analyst (knowing about everything that was to come, except the development of nuclear weapons) could hardly have been expected to predict that no wars would be fought for the next four decades in the middle of Europe.

More relevant for policy than the issue of 'has deterrence worked?' is the question of 'can deterrence continue to work?' for the shielding of Western Europe. Could it be, now that the Soviet nuclear force totals have grown to match or surpass those of the United States, that an extension of nuclear deterrence to shield NATO will no longer be possible?

Such concerns are sometimes linked to a concept of 'escalation dominance', as if the presence or absence of such an advantage to the United States and its allies will make all the difference for whether 'nuclear umbrella' threats are credible.[22]

'Escalation dominance' has at least two distinct meanings which are too often confused. First, even for those advocating a conventional defence for places like Western Europe (i.e.

advocating a 'deterrence by denial'), something nuclear will be seen as prerequisite for any such moderated and limited approach: the preparation of sufficient Western nuclear forces, strategic or theatre, so that the Soviets never saw an advantage for themselves in escalating to the nuclear level. It would be cruelly ironic if NATO forces mounted a stout conventional defence against a Soviet advance, without either side using nuclear weapons, and the Soviets then employed their nuclear weapons as a way of salvaging some kind of victory to redeem their original investment in the attack.

A second, considerably different, sense of 'escalation dominance' also calls for greater Western nuclear force preparations - strategic and in the theatre - but with a view less to deterring Soviet nuclear escalation, and more to making Western nuclear escalation look plausible and credible (because it looked as if it would pay off in terms of battlefield victory). One of the reasons that an American nuclear response on behalf of nations like West Germany has been credible, despite the arguments about the vulnerability of American cities, has been all along that we could become so entranced by plausible considerations of counter-force victory that we would not have time to be immobilised by considerations of suffering. 'Escalation dominance' would in this second sense thus mean that we could be expected to try to snatch victory from the jaws of a conventional defeat, by escalating to nuclear weapons if the Soviet tank advance could not be checked otherwise. If it was foolish for Americans to escalate in quest of victory, this would make less difference, as long as Americans were known to believe such foolishness.[23] The impact of all this prognostication on Moscow decision-makers would have to be the same; an invasion of the NATO area would lead to nuclear escalation, and no invasion thus would occur.

'Escalation dominance' in the first sense is thus to be sought by any American strategists who are convinced of this inutility of nuclear deterrence for shielding Western Europe or South Korea, but who would acknowledge a need to make sure that the Soviets did not themselves elect to escalate to the use of nuclear weapons, whenever a successful conventional defence of these places, or some other untoward events from Moscow's point of view, had occurred.

'Escalation dominance' in the second sense would be part of an effort to maintain the credibility of a United States first use of nuclear weapons but not a threat of immediate nuclear escalation. Rather escalation could occur after a 'pause', after a conventional defence had proved impracticable. Thus NATOs adherence to the murky but possibly still effective policy of 'no early first use'.

Each of these approaches would thus entail some striving for conventional defensive capabilities, to turn back a Soviet tank attack without immediately moving to a use of nuclear weapons which would very possibly become all-out. The earlier sense of 'escalation dominance' hopes for a total posture of no first use; however, the second sense of 'escalation dominance' decidedly does not. Each of these approaches might also be plausibly endangered if Soviet nuclear stockpiles, theatre and strategic, grow in size, and if improvements in the American nuclear arsenal were not sufficient to cancel out the impact of this growth.

Pessimists about United States protection of European allies will claim that the erosion of 'escalation dominance' (in the second sense - by which the United States might be viewed as wanting to escalate because of its military advantages in doing so) may take all the credibility and the contributions to deterrence out of United States invasion threats.

Yet there have been many other explanations of why the United States would move to the use of nuclear weapons if Western Europe was being overrun, beside any suppositions of military advantage that underlie a theory of escalation dominance. The logic of escalation dominance has indeed been under attack for more than two decades. Mindless and irrational considerations of impact on the battlefield, of 'winning the war that the Russians had started', might indeed persuade an American President to release the tactical and other nuclear weapons ear marked for NATO, rather than accepting a conventional defeat. But this would fly in the face of the risk that such nuclear weapons could not be limited to the battlefield, so that Moscow and New York and Leningrad and Washington would then be destroyed (where otherwise they might have been spared). There has also all along been the risk that such weapons might still not favour the defence, might in the end actually make a Soviet conquest of Western Europe (a Western Europe now devastated and radioactive) that much easier.

If there has been a life to the credibility of

American nuclear escalation, it has not at any time since 1949 been because escalation has made perfect sense for the United States. Rather it has been because traditional fixations on the phenomenon of 'victory' might still capture the attention and imagination of the United States leader, despite all the rational considerations of United States national interest working to the contrary, and/or because a Soviet leadership would at least have to take the possibility of such American thinking into account.

Even if the input of 'escalation dominance' is thus logically imperfect (but nonetheless very possibly quite effective in shielding Europe), we could identify several other linkages to nuclear escalation which (however irrationally and illogically) also strengthen the deterrence of a Soviet invasion (conventional or nuclear) of Europe.

First of all, the mere deployment of nuclear weapons into the potential combat zone *ipso facto* tends to make their use more likely, however much the rule books say that such weapons could not be used without higher (perhaps Presidential) authority, however effective various kinds of locks and Permissive Action Links (PAL) are reported to be. A Soviet planner contemplating an advance across West Germany to Frankfurt cannot be certain that all the United States 'theatre' or 'tactical' nuclear weapons might not be used. Might not some captain of artillery, about to be surrounded by an advancing Soviet tank column, elect to fire off his nuclear rounds, rather than face the ultimate disgrace of letting his ammunition be captured by the enemy? Might this not lead to an escalation including the destruction of Soviet cities and of all the world? Even if it did not, might it not destroy enough of West Germany to make the capture of Frankfurt pointless?

It should be noted and stressed, for any discussion of deterrence, that almost no one presumes that the Soviets look forward to the nuclear destruction of Western Europe. Far more worrisome and plausible is that Moscow would look forward to the imposition of Communism and Soviet control on an intact Western Europe. To revert to a very crude analogy, Western Europe does not have to worry about murder as much as about rape. It is simply too attractive, on account of its economic prowess, to the Communist world. Historically, a defence against rape was that the victim would kill herself and her attacker, thus preserving her honour, thus perhaps dissuading (deterring) her attacker.

The normal first reaction of young West Europeans, as illustrated in the West German 'Greens' today, and illustrated in the 1950s Social Democrats' reaction to the deployment of tactical nuclear weapons, amid the 'Carte Blanche' Exercise, is to be appalled at the destruction that would be brought down on West Germany and the Benelux countries in any use of the atomic warheads stationed there. A normal second reaction, upon some reflection, is instead to become resigned to this, and indeed to welcome it, on the logic that 'It keeps the Soviets from invading in the first place.'[24] Why would the Soviets invade an area just to make it radioactive, and in the bargain to bring an uncontainable nuclear devastation down on their home and country?

Aside from the forward deployment of nuclear forces, the likelihood of escalation and deterrence has similarly been reinforced by the deployment of American troops to places like West Germany and South Korea. If these young men and women are killed in battle, there is no assurance that the anger of their parents and fellow citizens back in the United States will be contained or that nuclear escalation will not follow.

Similarly effective at reinforcing nuclear deterrence have been statements of commitment, as in Presidential speeches and press conferences, and as in Mutual Defense Treaties. When the United States makes a formal treaty commitment, it (being a nation of legalistic and law-abiding people) may feel very much bound to keep that commitment, even where practical logic would lean against the pursuance of such commitments once nuclear escalation was involved. When an American President gives a speech with lines like 'Ich bin ein Berliner' and 'We will defend your cities with our cities', a planner in the Politburo will have to think a while longer about seizing portions of Western Europe by some limited war attack confined to the use only of conventional weapons. This would be a war in which abstract logic would have suggested that American nuclear weapons can have no prior deterrent effect, but 'the threats that leave something to chance' still play a large role.

Credibility and National Interests

One can think of a variety of reasons why the United

States might feel strongly committed to any particular piece of territory in the world, so strongly that it could even, despite the risks to its own safety, be credible in threatening nuclear escalation. The reasons can be both materially selfish and more generously altruistic.

Beginning at the selfish side, we might care very much about the natural resources obtainable from a particular region - the oil of the Middle East being an example now very often on our minds - the strategic metals of southern Africa also often being cited.

Similarly, we can care about the geographic position of a particular territory. One in the past felt more secure defending one's home in someone else's frontyard or backyard. If various areas of the world fall under Moscow's control, it becomes that much easier for the Politburo to direct various kinds of military threats against the United States itself. It is easier to defend France if Germany is still not under Communist rule. It is easier to defend Britain if France has not been occupied. It is easier to defend the United States if Europe and Central America are not under Moscow's domination.

A little more psychologically, the precedent of having failed to defend any particular area may weaken the defence of other areas, as their populations will draw the lesson that the United States is not to be counted upon. Giving up on a territory that has been successfully defended in the past, for example South Korea, might be viewed as a demonstration of declining strength over time. What we were able to do in the past, we are not able to do any more, and the swing parties of the world tend to take their clue from this.

Finally, there are places that we will defend, not because of their raw materials, or their geographic position, or even because of the dangers of precedent, but simply because we identify with the people, and would feel deep grief if they were added to the list of peoples under Communist domination. West Berlin might be just one very nice example of a more general phenomenon here. When President Kennedy thus said 'Ich bin ein Berliner', he was merely adding a notch to the more general category of 'fifty-first state'. Just as the United States is presumably prepared to escalate to nuclear warfare if any of its own fifty states are invaded, it is plausibly inclined to treat some other portions of the world as almost equally precious to itself, therefore again extending nuclear deterrence, where a less strong vicarious identification with others would have made this logically impossible.

Not every place in the world could hope to win this kind of identification, of course. One can hardly imagine such an American commitment to Chad, and we know that it did not exist for Vietnam, but it seems just as clear that such a commitment does exist for Canada and for Britain, and probably for much of the world that is democratically governed and on the path of advanced industrial development. It exists for these areas not because of any particular selfish American interest in them, but simply because of our altruistic involvement, our concern for the welfare of the people living there, for their own sake.

There is no simple way to translate such <u>explanations</u> of the American commitment in any foreign area into <u>strengths</u> of commitment. It is still not beyond belief that the United States might escalate to the use of nuclear weapons for any of the reasons listed, because the resources of the territory being attacked were too precious, or because its physical location was too menacing to us at home, or because the precedent that would be set in a surrender would be too damaging, or because we cared almost as much about the people involved as we cared about our own people. If so, the hope is that the Soviets would never challenge the strength of American commitment here, never have to discover that we meant what we had threatened.

It must be remembered, of course, that all such categories of explanation can hold as well for the Soviet Union, and the likelihood that it might escalate to the use of nuclear weapons. The worst fear of all would come when the two sides simultaneously became committed to the same piece of territory, each threatening nuclear escalation if the other did not back off, each guessing that the other was bluffing.

For other corners of the world, it is more probable that the United States could not credibly threaten such escalation, because it could not credibly claim to care so much, for any of the above reasons, about the area being contested. Here we are more surely exposed to the possibility of limited wars and conventional attacks, if the normal kind of 'deterrence by denial' does not get established. Here, conversely, the risk of nuclear war goes down for both sides.

With regard to the credibility that the United

The Strategy of Deterrence

States might escalate to the use of nuclear weapons, in defence of a particular area and/or in retaliation for an attack on that area, we might in the end discern at least four categories, simply for describing what the status quo situation is in the 1980s:

1. There are areas which are vulnerable in terms of conventional military capabilities, and which (for various reasons) we feel strongly enough attached to, such that such escalation would be credible; the list here probably consists of Western Europe, South Korea, and perhaps the Persian Gulf.
2. There are areas for which we would also feel strong enough attachment to make such escalation credible, but for which no plausible conventional threat exists, so that 'the question never comes up'. On this list we would find Great Britain, Australia, Japan, New Zealand, Canada, Ireland, and some others.

   As a very special case, again where 'the question does not come up', would be the continental United States itself. What if the Soviet Marines seized Rhode Island? Would we not go to nuclear first use, even if the Soviets had stayed entirely conventional? This is entirely hypothetical, since the Soviet Marines are not capable of this.
3. There are areas which are conventionally threatened, but where we would not escalate to the use of nuclear weapons. We thus have a de facto 'no first use' policy, for countries such as Chad, Thailand and South Vietnam.
4. There are places not conventionally threatened, for which we would also not escalate, although 'the question never comes up.'

It may well be that categories 3 and 4 take up most of the globe, with category 2 also then taking up another large area, leaving two or three valuable peninsulas sticking out from Eurasia as the real sources of difficulty.

Credibility and the Strategic Balance

We might return now to the credibility of extended

nuclear deterrence as it relates to changes in the general strategic situation over time, trying once more to decipher how much the protection of NATO has really depended on 'escalation dominance', or any other kind of dominance. When looking at the stages of the comparison between Soviet and American nuclear forces, we might note as many as five possible steps:

1. United States monopoly, as existed from 1945 to 1949, with the United States being able to inflict nuclear devastation on others, and the Soviet Union (or any other state) being unable to inflict such destruction in retaliation on the United States;
2. United States nuclear 'superiority', with the Soviet Union being able to deliver nuclear warheads to a fair number of American cities, but the United States being definitely able to inflict far greater destruction on the Soviet Union, and very likely to 'win' such an all-out war, in terms of who had any forces left, or ability to wage war at the end;
3. 'parity', in the sense that the force totals on the two sides become so comparable that it is difficult to conclude which is the greater or stronger, and it is similarly difficult to predict whose war-fighting capabilities would survive at the end;
4. Soviet 'superiority', with the United States being able to deliver nuclear warheads to a fair number of Soviet cities, but the Soviet Union being definitely able to inflict far greater destruction on the United States, and very likely to 'win' such an all-out war, in terms of who had any force left, or ability to wage war at the end;
5. Soviet monopoly, with the Soviet Union able to inflict nuclear devastation on the United States, and the United States being unable to inflict such destruction in retaliation on the Soviet Union.

A few comments have to be made at the outset in looking at this overview. First, despite the seemingly logical progression of the swing of the pendulum, there is really nothing about the progression from stage 1 to stages 2, 3, and 4 that could lead anyone in Moscow, or anywhere else, to count on getting to stage 5. The mind is playing tricks when anyone comes to see such a Soviet monopoly coming, in the apparent symmetry of what has been argued to be a transition from American superiority to parity to Soviet superiority; but one basically 'can't get there from here'. (It should also be noted that it is indeed debatable whether 'Soviet superiority' is the correct way to describe the current situation, or even the imminent situation).

Second, in terms of strategic logic, the crucial transition is probably between stage 1 (United States monopoly) and the three 'stages' that follow (just as it would be crucial between these three stages and a stage 5 - Soviet monopoly). Everything in the world, in terms of the strategic logic of deterrence, depends on whether or not nuclear weapons can strike Washington and New York (which has been a fact of life since 1949), or can strike Moscow and Leningrad (which will remain a fact of life for all the future that we can foresee).

If the logical and rational credibility of American extensions of deterrence were to have been challenged, this basically would have had to come in the first transition which would have plunged the people of the United States into the role of hostages - the transition from American monopoly to American 'superiority'. As enunciated in NSC-68, and in the writings of Henry Kissinger and Pierre Gallois and countless others, the entire logic of nuclear deterrence is that a nuclear military superiority cannot be cashed in on, unless it can be carried through in a manner which substantially shields one's own civilians against attack. The success of extending deterrence has thus come in getting past this logic, not because physical reality gave the United States a continued upper hand, but because of all the psychological ploys listed above which made American commitments credible nonetheless.

The American nuclear monopoly in actual practice was used to force Tokyo to stop moving its forces forward to China (and indeed to surrender itself to occupation), and to force the Soviet Union to withdraw from Iran and to forego any advance into Western Europe. After 1949, however, everything about the use of American nuclear power has depended on something other than monopoly, something taking the vulnerability of New York and other cities into account, something nonetheless working. If it could be carried off after 1949, there is no inherent reason why it cannot be carried off as well after 1989. Unless the Soviets succeed in shielding Moscow and other Soviet cities against American nuclear attack after 1999, this kind of extension of deterrence, conceding all its worries and all its problems, should be able to persist into the next century or two as well.

Those who would see an important difference between the three middle stages 2, 3, and 4 ('United States superiority', 'parity', or 'Soviet superiority') will claim that Western Europe has been opened to Soviet advances as we have moved from stage 2 through 3 to 4. Yet, if this is so, why was Eastern Europe not wide open to free world advance when the United States was 'superior'? As noted by many authors in the 1950s even the most rudimentary Soviet ability for nuclear retaliation was more than enough to keep us from offering military assistance to the East Germans or Hungarians, or to others seeking to terminate the imposition of Communist rule in their lands. Even the most rudimentary United States capability for nuclear retaliation may conversely be enough to keep Soviet tanks from rolling further west.

The practical reality of deterrence is thus that each of the nuclear-equipped sides has a good chance of retaining its possessions, as long as it cares enough about these territories, as long as it would take a major military action by the other side - on the order of a tank attack - to change the status quo. If Western Europe were ever to become as prone to guerrilla or terrorist attacks as El Salvador or Vietnam, then our ability to shield the NATO countries by the threat of nuclear escalation would be terminated, for reasons having next to nothing to do with the over arching nuclear balance, or 'escalation dominance'. If Eastern Europe were similarly to become as ripe as Angola and Afghanistan for anti-Soviet guerrilla operations, Moscow would similarly not be able to base its hold on the Warsaw Pact countries on threats of nuclear escalation.

The Trends

As a closing comment, what trends emerge with respect to nuclear deterrence and issues of credibility?

With regard to the survivability of the forces required to maintain the prospect of retaliation in each direction, we are worse off than in the 1960s and 1970s, but we are surely also better off than we were in the later years of the 1950s. Nothing in today's speculation about a 'window of vulnerability' comes close to matching what were the most fearful American predictions about a possible 'missile gap', when a Soviet monopoly of ICBMs might catch all United States bombers on the ground, allowing Moscow to launch a World War III in which victory could be real, in which no significant countervalue retaliation would be inflicted on the Soviet Union. Moving away from multiple-warhead missiles would surely be a step in the better direction, as would emphasising the survivability of our own missiles, rather than enhancing the accuracy of such missiles so as to make them more effective against the silos sheltering the adversary's missiles.

Aiming missiles accurately is consistent with our traditional morality for it allows an honourable targeting approach of aiming only at the enemy's military targets and ability to fight, rather than at his civilians and his will to fight. But such accuracy and morality is devastatingly inconsistent with the system of mutual deterrence.

With regard to the rationality and responsibility of the people whose fingers are on the trigger, one consequence of our prolonged ordeal with nuclear deterrence is that the need for this has become increasingly apparent. Each of the powers is moving toward better controls and safeguards here, and the world is accepting the need for curtailing the spread of nuclear weapons to more countries. Every additional country possessing such weapons would obviously make the risk of what we would style 'irrational' behaviour that much greater. But it is not just nuclear weapons states like the United States and the Soviet Union that have become aware of the dangers of further proliferation; most of the world now quietly accepts the same logic - that deterrence is better left in the hands of a few forces checking and deterring each other.

On our third issue, that of basic morality, we are now seeing an increasing public sensitivity about the deterrence reliance on countervalue retaliation, in part because the sheer destructive power of the two major nuclear arsenals continue to grow. But 'overkill is overkill', such that what was more than enough to deter in the 1970s may not really have gone through any meaningful change as we acquire still more in the 1980s. At the least, the redundancy of all this countervalue capability makes counterforce strike all the less thinkable.

The sheer volume of the retaliatory destruction already in place was interestingly illustrated in the conclusions of the Nuclear Winter study publicised in 1983.[25] The study argues that all of life on earth might be threatened by the ecological consequences in a major use of even just one of the superpower's arsenals, thus almost concluding that nuclear attacks could be self-deterring, as one suffers unacceptable 'second-strike' damage from the collateral effects of one's own first-strike (even if not a single nuclear warhead of the other side survives the first attack and is used in retaliation).

This staggering situation could be interpreted quickly enough to be appalling. Upon reflection, as with all the other double-edged aspects of nuclear deterrence, it may be calming and re-assuring. Who would want to try to exploit the other side's 'window of vulnerability', if he was going to freeze himself and his own population to death in the process of such a 'splendid first-strike'?

Those who lament the overkill of something like nuclear winter must always remember and be a little on guard against the traditional morality they are bringing to this lament - a morality which also is the source of some of our questions on the conceptual credibility of deterrence. Such a morality is what reinforces the weapons developers who reach for the accuracies which threaten mutual deterrence.

We have already discussed the trends alleged to be affecting the fourth of our problems - whether nuclear deterrence can continue to be extended to shield countries as valuable as those of Western Europe. On the very debatable proposition that a Soviet move into 'parity', or beyond 'parity' to 'superiority' undermines this nuclear umbrella, two very different kinds of proposals have been advanced. One is to abandon all efforts at deterrence by punishment, and expend substantial energy and sums instead on the enhancement of conventional defences. This was perhaps already the secret aspiration of Secretary of Defense Robert McNamara in the early 1960s, and he now has joined several other prominent Americans to endorse this kind of approach openly in an important <u>Foreign Affairs</u> article some two decades later.[26]

The second approach would be to expend funds and energy enhancing the American nuclear stockpile - strategic and theatre - to bring the confrontation back toward what could be called 'parity' or 'American superiority', on the assumption that this is somehow needed to restore the credibility of nuclear escalation in support of Western Europe.

As suggested above, it is possible that neither approach is needed. And it is possible, after this burst of intense reflection on the nature and problems of deterrence is behind us, that we will all conclude once again that we are best off leaving well enough alone, that 'deterrence by punishment' has worked for decades even as things stand, and that nothing in the current trends is going to change the way it works.

Notes

1. Glenn Snyder, Deterrence and Defense, (Princeton University Press, Princeton, 1961), pp. 14-16.
2. For a longer discussion of the earlier examples by this author, see George H. Quester, Deterrence Before Hiroshima (John Wiley, New York, 1966).
3. Giulio Douhet, The Command of the Air (Coward-McCann, New York, 1941), p. 20.
4. Ibid., p. 59.
5. J.F.C. Fuller, The Reformation of War (E.P. Dutton, New York, 1923), pp. 150; 184.
6. J.M. Spaight, Air Power in the Next War (Geoffrey Bles, London, 1938), p. 126.
7. 'Ajax', Air Strategy for Britons (George Allen and Unwin, London, 1939), pp. 61-62.
8. Sir Julian Corbett, Some Principles of Maritime Strategy (Conway Maritime Press, 1911 London, pp. 94.95.
9. For an example, see Gar Alperovitz, Atomic Diplomacy (Simon and Schuster, New York, 1965), pp. 94-95.
10. An extended discussion of British strategic thinking on the protection of Canada can be found in Kenneth Bourne, Britain and the Balance of Power in North America (University of California Press, Berkeley, 1967).
11. William L. Borden, There Will Be No Time (MacMillan, New York, 1946).
12. Bernard Brodie (ed.), The Absolute Weapon (Harcourt Brace, New York, 1946), p. 74.
13. For a valuable extrapolation on the

strategic logic of NSC-68, before it was published, see Warner R. Schilling, Paul Y. Hammond, and Glenn H. Synder, Strategy, Politics and Defense Budgets (Columbia University Press, New York, 1962), pp. 267-378.

14. The declassified text of NSC-68 was published in Naval War College Review, vol. 27, no. 6 (May-June, 1975), pp. 51-158.

15. On the public's reaction to the Bikini test, see Gregg Herken, The Winning Weapon (Alfred A. Knopf, New York, 1980), pp. 224-226.

16. Albert Wohlstetter, 'The Delicate Balance of Terror', Foreign Affairs, vol. 37, no. 2 (January, 1959), pp. 211-234.

17. For a valuable overview of the earlier ins and outs of strategic crisis stability, see Michael Mandelbaum, The Nuclear Question (Cambridge University Press, New York, 1976).

18. See Philip Green, Deadly Logic (Ohio State University Press, Columbus, 1968) for an extended and critical discussion of the problems of rationality as they affect nuclear deterrence.

19. For a good exchange on the issues of morality, see 'Excerpts from the Third Draft of Bishops' Pastoral Letter on War and Peace', Science, Technology and Human Values, vol. 26, no. 44 (Summer, 1983), pp. 14-22 and Albert Wohlstetter, 'Bishops, Statesmen, and Other Strategists on the Bombing of the Innocents', Commentary, vol. 75, no. 6 (June, 1983), pp. 15-35.

20. For early versions of the argument that extended nuclear deterrence will be logically incredible, see Henry A. Kissinger, Nuclear Weapons and Foreign Policy (Harper and Row, New York, 1957), and Pierre Gallois, The Balance of Terror (Houghton-Mifflin, Boston, 1961).

21. See Thomas C. Schelling, The Strategy of Conflict (Harvard University Press, Cambridge, 1960), pp. 182-203.

22. For a statement along the lines of this argument, see Henry A. Kissinger, 'Strategy and the American Alliance', Survival, vol. XXIV, no. 5 (September/October, 1982), pp. 194-200.

23. For a skeptical discussion of whether tactical (theatre) nuclear weapons can actually do any of the things they are advertised as doing, see Robert S. McNamara, 'The Military Role of Nuclear Weapons', Foreign Affairs, vol. 62, no. 1 (Fall, 1983), pp. 59-80. It remains possible that their unadvertised contribution, of leading to escalation to all-out war, is still a very worthwhile

contribution.

24. For an elaborated explanation of West German contentment with some reliance on threats of nuclear escalation, see Karl Kaiser, Georg Leber, Alois Mertes, and Franz-Josef Schulze, 'Nuclear Weapons and the Preservation of Peace', Foreign Affairs, vol. 60, no. 5 (Summer, 1982), pp. 1157-1170.

25. Carl Sagan, 'Nuclear War and Climatic Catastrophe', Foreign Affairs, vol. 62, no. 2 (Winter, 1983/84), pp. 257-292.

26. McGeorge Bundy, George F. Kennan, Robert S. McNamara and Gerard Smith, 'Nuclear Weapons and the Atlantic Alliance', Foreign Affairs, vol. 60, no. 4 (Spring, 1982), pp. 753-768.

Chapter Four

STABLE DETERRENCE OR NUCLEAR WAR-FIGHTING: ALL UNCLEAR ON THE NUCLEAR FRONT

Leon V. Sigal*

The logic of deterrence, when it is not maddeningly opaque, can seem deceptively simple. For instance, to equate more nuclear weapons with more deterrence is often considered a truism, but it lacks the virtue of being true. The implicit assumption that the greater the prospective costs of war the more a state will be deterred from starting one is a legacy of pre-nuclear thought. Once the Soviet Union as well as the United States acquired nuclear weapons and the means of delivering them at intercontinental range, it became difficult to raise the cost of war for one side without doing so for the other. In this situation of nuclear interdependence, deterrence no longer means increasing the cost of war to the enemy but rather manipulating the shared risk of a war neither side wants.

Since the advent of nuclear interdependence, strategists have become preoccupied with deterring premeditated aggression. Yet the threats posed by deterrents may not suffice to prevent war; indeed, they may provoke it. In August 1914, for instance, the alliance obligations undertaken to deter war helped bring it about, and the mobilisation ordered as a precaution against aggression prompted pre-emption. In December 1941 the United States believed it was deterring a war by building up a sizeable fleet at Pearl Harbor. Japan, however, considered war with the United States inevitable, and the United States build-up spurred it to war sooner rather than later, when the Empire might have been relatively worse off militarily. Under

* The views expressed are those of the author and should not be ascribed to the trustees or staff of the Brookings Institution or of Wesleyan University.

conditions of nuclear interdependence, as in a conventional balance of power, the possibility of pre-emptive or preventive war co-exists with that of premeditated war. War can result not only from a failure of deterrence but also from its instability.

Stable deterrence need not be a contradiction in terms. In a fundamental sense, deterrence and stability are mutually compatible. The aim in deterrence is to convince a potential adversary that the risk of seeking political objectives by military means is prohibitively high. If two potential adversaries deter each other from deliberately resorting to military force, then a modicum of stability, however precarious, prevails in the military relationship between them. Yet military stability has always imposed more demanding requirements on armed forces than just deterrence of premeditated war. Although nuclear weapons have altered the material basis for deterrence, military stability continues to take three distinct but related forms: strategic stability, crisis stability, and arms race stability.

When both sides are secure in the knowledge that each has a second-strike capability - sufficient numbers of survivable nuclear weapons to threaten unacceptable damage to the other side even after suffering a nuclear attack - strategic stability, or mutual deterrence, exists.

Even if both sides have enough survivable warheads for a second-strike and know they do, either may still worry that a sizeable proportion of its nuclear forces may be vulnerable to attack. In a crisis in which nuclear war seems imminent, the side worried about vulnerability might see some advantage in pre-emptive attack. If either side sees itself in such a predicament, both sides are less secure for fear of pre-emption. Moreover, once nuclear war seems unavoidable, each side has some incentive to attack first in order to try to limit the damage it will suffer when the inevitable happens. When neither side has reason to fear a pre-emptive strike in a crisis, crisis stability exists.

Each side may continue to test or deploy new weapons under conditions of strategic or crisis stability. Yet some weapons developments may threaten to undermine strategic or crisis stability. If so, they may give rise to concern that deterrence is likely to fail in the future or, worse yet, that nuclear war with the other side is inevitable. Arms race stability prevails when neither side is concerned that its opponent is trying to build weapons that endanger either strategic or crisis stability. Arms race stability damps down mutual fears of aggressive intentions that lead to interpretations of the other side's acts as provocative and undermine attempts at mutual political accommodation.

Strategic stability deters either side from undertaking premeditated war. Crisis stability reduces the chances of pre-emptive war. Arms race stability minimises incentives for preventive war.

Stable deterrence has become possible in the nuclear era in a way that it was not in previous international systems: survivable nuclear forces and command and control would enable the two superpowers to achieve both strategic and crisis stability at the same time. Yet stable deterrence at the intercontinental level does not ensure stable deterrence at the theatre nuclear or conventional level. Even though the two superpowers are deterred from deliberately waging nuclear war with one another, what prevents the Soviet Union from using nuclear weapons against America's allies in NATO or from threatening to do so? By the late 1950s, nuclear interdependence between the superpowers had led to concern about America's ability to extend the protection of its nuclear deterrent to its allies in Europe. And even if extended deterrence sufficed to prevent nuclear attack or nuclear blackmail in Western Europe, what deterred the Warsaw Pact from launching a conventional attack there? Nuclear stability, it seemed, might not preclude conventional instability.

Under conditions of nuclear interdependence between the superpowers, four possible approaches to ensuring stable deterrence at the theatre or regional level have been considered. One was to have European states acquire their own nuclear weapons, but that possibility, open to Great Britain and France, was not available to West Germany. West German acquisition of its own nuclear force would undermine the post-war political settlement in Europe and jeopardise East-West, intra-European, and intra-German relations. By virtue of its military integration with NATO, West Germany has denied itself not only a nuclear potential of its own, but also a capacity to wage war on its own. Indeed, one of NATO's <u>raisons d'etre</u> is to reconcile Western Europe's dominant power to the historically anomalous status of military self-denial. A second possibility for ensuring stable deterrence in the region was a Western European nuclear force, and British or French forces could conceivably evolve in that direction. Such a force, however, would imply a degree of political community currently absent in the rest of Western Europe. A third approach was somehow to enhance the credibility of United States nuclear weapons for extending deterrence to Europe, either by adding to the number of nuclear weapons in the European theatre or by augmenting United States strategic nuclear forces. A fourth was to strengthen NATO's conventional defences, relying on them and the risk of escalation to nuclear war to deter attack from the East. It is the last two approaches that have posed most starkly for NATO planners the trade-offs between deterrence and stability.

Extending nuclear deterrence to Europe means, by long-standing NATO policy, contemplating first use of nuclear weapons. At issue is how to do so credibly under conditions of nuclear interdependence. Some strategists - the stable balancers - feel that first use need only remain a possibility. So long as that possibility exists, they argue, it introduces enough risk into Soviet military calculations to deter them from a deliberate attack on Europe. Other strategists - the nuclear war-fighters - insist that first use must be a near certainty, not just a possibility. Only by making nuclear war seem inevitable, they feel, can NATO be sure of deterring the Soviet Union. What then is to be done about the prospect of Soviet nuclear retaliation for NATO first use? This prospect leads nuclear war-fighters to two somewhat contradictory conclusions, each of them problematic. One is to prepare to wage limited nuclear war; the other is to prepare to limit damage to the United States in the event that the war does not stay limited. Yet limiting damage imposes a far more demanding requirement than does first use: it requires a disarming first-strike to destroy as many Soviet nuclear weapons as possible and some way of protecting the American people and industrial capacity from Soviet weapons that survive that first-strike. The means to accomplish these tasks do not seem attainable under present technological conditions. And even if they were attainable they would not be desirable because of the grave risks they pose for stability.

What distinguishes the stable balancers from the nuclear war-fighters is not a greater or lesser willingness to engage in nuclear war if need be or a desire to have options short of all-out nuclear attack on enemy population centres. Both schools of strategists accept the need to prepare for nuclear war and to have weapons, force postures, and targeting plans capable of attacking targets other than cities. Where the two schools part company is in their degree of readiness to jeopardise stability - all three forms of it - for the sake of extended deterrence.

Buttressing United States nuclear capabilities to make extended deterrence somehow seem more credible carries a heightened risk of instability. At the intercontinental level, acquiring a sufficient number of accurate warheads on MX and Trident II missiles, along with Minuteman IIIs, to threaten at least in theory the entire Soviet land-based missile force would contribute little to extended deterrence, but it would make crisis stability precarious by giving Soviet leaders considerable inducement to launch a pre-emptive attack if United States first use appeared imminent. So, too, would the deployment of anti-satellite weapons and Pershing IIs to supplement other means of disrupting Soviet command, control and communications (C^3). Acquiring ballistic missile defences and embarking on civil defence programmes might limit damage in the event of Soviet retaliation and thereby increase somewhat the credibility of United States first use, but such designs, if ever realised, would endanger all three forms of military stability between the super-powers. Were they capable of protecting a sizeable portion of the American populace, which seems unlikely, they would undermine the mutuality of deterrence that is at the heart of strategic stability by denying the Soviet Union a second-strike capability. Anticipating this, and uncertain how workable these programmes might prove, Soviet leaders might be tempted to start a pre-emptive or preventive war.

Not all the efforts to enhance extended deterrence are directed at the intercontinental or theatre level; some involve battlefield weapons in Western Europe. A few nuclear war-fighters hope to impress the Warsaw Pact with the automaticity of NATO's nuclear response through predelegation of nuclear authority to field commanders. They are prepared to entertain a higher risk of inadvertent nuclear war in hopes of making the threat of deliberate nuclear first use somewhat more certain of execution. Others have sought, as yet unsuccessfully, to deploy American enhanced-radiation weapons, short-range nuclear artillery shells designed to reduce collateral damage and thereby seem more usable in the crowded confines of Europe. But ERWs, like those nuclear artillery shells they would replace, would be stored in a few sites near the front, vulnerable to being overrun and to being pre-empted, by conventional as well as nuclear means.

Stable balancers oppose these efforts as counterproductive because they decrease stability without adding much to deterrence. While some have been willing to countenance a modest increase in long-range theatre nuclear forces in Europe as symbolic assurance to allies concerned about the credibility of NATO's nuclear deterrent, they have stressed the primacy of redressing NATO's conventional disadvantages. Under nuclear interdependence, they argue, a balance of conventional forces is essential to deter limited threats to peace in Europe. Their focus on the conventional balance allows them by and large to reconcile the competing demands of deterrence and stability. The more robust NATO's conventional defence, they argue, the greater the risk that a conventional war might escalate to the nuclear level, and it is this risk of escalation that deters any war in the first place. Escalation might seem far less plausible if NATO were to suffer conventional collapse at the outset of hostilities.

Since the late 1970s, the debate between strategists who want to maintain the doctrine of stable deterrence and those who advocate a shift to nuclear war-fighting has intensified. The outcome of this debate will help determine the number and character of America's nuclear forces, as well as its nuclear targeting and operations. More important, it could increase or decrease the likelihood of nuclear war.

Nuclear war-fighters argue that nuclear weapons, like all previous advances in military technology, are usable and, indeed, likely to be used; that limited nuclear war is possible and winnable; and that a Soviet attack on Western Europe can be deterred only by the certainty that the United States will use nuclear weapons, which is assured only by having nuclear options for every conceivable contingency.

Stable balancers disagree, believing that nuclear weapons mark a distinct breakpoint both in the historical evolution of warfare and in the current continuum of military capability; that first use of nuclear weapons will lead to reciprocal escalation, eventually spiraling into general war; and that a Soviet attack on America's allies in Europe is best prevented by stout conventional deterrence which inevitably carries with it some risk of escalating to the nuclear level.

Stable balancers are skeptical of war-fighters' efforts to add to existing capabilities and options for waging limited nuclear war with the Soviet Union. They recognise that nuclear weapons are so destructive, most Soviet military targets so co-located with population centres, and both sides' command and control so fragile that nuclear war will be almost impossible to limit in practice. They also reject the war-fighters' notions of 'protracted' nuclear war, if that means more than a matter of hours, or of 'prevailing', in any meaningful sense of the word.

For some thirty years after Hiroshima and Nagasaki, the doctrine of stable deterrence remained in precarious ascendency in the strategic community. Stable balancers have set the terms of the public debate. They have imposed some limits on the acquisition of weapons with particularly perverse implications for stability, most notably ballistic missile defences. But they have not kept the nuclear war-fighters in check. Stable balancers could not prevent the Air Force from devising targeting plans at odds with stable deterrence, nor could they block procurement of many more nuclear weapons, with far greater accuracy, than is desirable for stability.

With the accession of Ronald Reagan, nuclear war-fighters have gained access to the inner circles, even positions of prominence, in the American government. But have they triumphed? Without intimate knowledge of current plans and operating practices for nuclear weapons - knowledge to which few civilians in or out of government are privy - it is impossible to give a definitive answer. Nevertheless, enough information has seeped into the public domain to provide the basis for at least a tentative assessment.

The attempt to redirect America's strategic force posture according to war-fighting doctrines has run headlong into a wall of hard realities. One is that, in spite of all the loose talk about protracted nuclear war, nobody has the foggiest notion how to wage one. To be sure, most strategists favour making America's nuclear forces and C^3 more capable of riding out nuclear attack. But that is as much a cardinal principle of stable balancers' as of war-fighters' doctrines. No one, however, can have much confidence in America's ability to ensure survivability for very long under conditions of nuclear war, let alone to protect populations. For that reason, if no other, any such war once under way has little prospect of being limited short of mutual exhaustion.

A second hard reality limiting nuclear war-fighters' success is that fulfilling even minimal requirements for their doctrine puts very great demands on capabilities. Waging and limiting protracted nuclear war would require that leaders, weapons, and C^3 must survive for more than a few hours or else must be readily reconstituted; intelligence assets must remain intact to conduct post-attack damage assessments and permit retargeting of surviving weapons; economic and population centres must be spared. Furthermore, belligerents must keep in communication - not just in contact, but in a position to negotiate based on compatible conceptions of the course of the conflict and its possible resolution, and based on some capacity to make and carry out decisions and control their forces.

A third hard reality is that these demands are far in excess of what the American people seem ready to tolerate, either fiscally or practically. Public resistance to various MX basing schemes provided a re-run of the ABM controversy of a decade or so ago. The strategic force build-up and the rhetorical excess of some administration officials have provoked a sharp upsurge in anti-nuclear protest and an equally precipitous drop in public support for accelerated defence-spending. This sentiment has been amply echoed in Congressional floor debate, though not action. It has also resounded among allied publics, leading to more open questioning of the Alliance and its strategy than has been heard in years.

These realities may have instilled some caution into senior United States defence officials, who appear to be edging back to doctrinal orthodoxy in their public remarks. The 1983 posture statement of the Secretary of Defense, for instance, speaks mostly of 'flexibility' - of ensuring that United States nuclear forces 'should be capable of being used on a very limited basis as well as more massively'. This contrasts sharply to the language of the Fiscal Years 1984-88 Defense Guidance conspicuously disclosed by senior administration officials in May 1982, which stipulates, 'Should deterrence fail and strategic nuclear war with the USSR occur, the United States must prevail and be able to force the Soviet Union to seek earliest termination of hostilities on terms favorable to the United States'. Yet some of the rhetoric remains overblown, such as the President's 'Star Wars' speech calling for research and development with the 'ultimate goal of eliminating the threat posed by strategic nuclear missiles'. And behind the public rhetoric, the administration continues to push nuclear war-fighters' progammes vigorously. The requirements spelled out in the Defense Guidance, for instance, call for:

> Deployment plans that assure United States strategic nuclear forces can render ineffective the total Soviet military and political power structure through attacks on political/military leadership and associated control facilities, nuclear and conventional military forces, and industry critical to military power. These plans should also provide for limiting damage to the United States and its allies to the maximum extent possible.
>
> Forces that will maintain, throughout a protracted conflict period and afterward, the capability to inflict very high levels of damage against the industrial/economic base of the Soviet Union and her allies, so that they have a strong incentive to seek conflict termination short of an all-out attack on our cities and economic assets.
>
> United States strategic nuclear forces and supporting C^3I capable of supporting controlled nuclear counterattacks over a protracted period while maintaining a reserve of nuclear forces sufficient for trans- and post-attack on our cities and economic assets.[1]

Ballistic missile defences illustrate the limitless ambition - and the limitations - of the war-fighters' vision. The Fiscal Years 1984-88 Defense Guidance contained a requirement for such defences in the seemingly anodyne formulation, 'These plans should also provide for limiting damage to the United States and its allies to the maximum extent possible.' The phrase, 'to the maximum extent possible' suggested bureaucratic caution on this point. Nearly all who are familiar with the details doubt that comprehensive defence of the United

States is technologically feasible, especially in view of the countermeasures that the Soviet Union can take. But President Reagan, apparently influenced by extra-bureaucratic enthusiasts, threw caution to the winds, holding out the hope of protecting American cities and thereby denying the Soviet Union a capacity to strike back at the United States. Were the President's goal ever to be attained, it would undermine the mutuality of assured destruction at the heart of strategic stability and raise the prospect in Moscow that the United States was capable of undertaking a disarming first-strike and getting away with it. That prospect would be a fearsome one - and not just in Moscow. For Soviet leaders are unlikely to allow the United States to gain such a unilateral advantage without seeking to match it, or worse yet, contemplate preventive or pre-emptive war. None of these possibilities is likely to leave the United States more secure, to say nothing of its allies.

There is considerable bureaucratic skepticism whether the President's goal could ever be fulfilled. In report after report since the 'Star Wars' speech, experts have sought to redirect the American effort away from defence of populations to more limited - and in their view, more manageable - objectives. A recent report, prepared for the Future Security Strategy Study under the direction of Fred S. Hoffman, is typical. It calls for 'a flexible research and development program designed to offer early options for the deployment of intermediate systems, while proceeding toward the President's ultimate goal'. It terms this programme 'preferable to one that defers the availability of components having a shorter development lead time in order to optimize allocation of R&D resources for development of the "full system".'[2] This is polite bureaucratic language for getting the camel's nose under the tent with something more practicable than city defence.

The specific programme that the Hoffman report pushes is deployment of an anti-tactical missile (ATM) system, building on the Patriot air defence system now being deployed in Western Europe. The Hoffman report tries to square this with the President's objective by holding out the possibility that ATM components might later play a role in defending the continental United States. Furthermore the complete system may have important applications in the United States, initially to defend C^3 nodes, later as it is thickened to add to Soviet targeting uncertainties, and ultimately to serve as the lower tiers in a full multi-layered system. Yet, it insists, the United States can pursue this option 'within ABM Treaty constraints'. Perhaps, but not very far. Finally, since ATMs would be used to protect America's allies in Europe against nuclear or non-nuclear attack, they would 'reduce allied anxieties that our increased emphasis on defenses might indicate a weakening in our commitment to the defense of Europe'. Yet it is doubtful whether this option would get at the root of British or French anxieties about ABM let alone re-assure increasingly restive allied publics.

Last year's Report of the President's Commission on Strategic Forces, commonly known as the Scowcroft Commission, also indicates how much ground the nuclear war-fighters have gained in the policy battles. It bears especially close scrutiny because it marks the boundaries of currently acceptable doctrine. The Report was a political product - a last-ditch attempt to devise both a marketable rationale and a presentable package for the MX. As befits any attempt at compromise, the Commission fashioned a doctrinal position of remarkable ambiguity. No wonder it has been hailed in some quarters as a re-affirmation of doctrinal orthodoxy and in others as a veritable counter-reformation.

Stable balancers, for instance, were heartened to have the Commission restore the concept of stability to its former meaning and place in nuclear strategy and arms control. Even before 1981, the Reaganauts were demeaning 'stability' as a first step toward displacing it entirely from the criteria for force planning and for negotiating: any weapons the United States had or was planning to build, administration officials called stabilising and moved to protect at the negotiating table; any weapons the Soviet Union had or was planning to build, they called destabilising and constructed proposals for drastically reducing. The Russians predictably argued the obverse.

In contrast to the Reagan administration, the Commission's definition of stability was more forthright. It combined elements of strategic and crisis stability: 'the condition which exists when no strategic power believes it can significantly improve its situation by attacking first in a crisis or when it does not feel compelled to launch its strategic weapons in order to avoid losing them'.[3] The Commission held stability up both as the criterion for sizing and posturing American forces and as the measure of arms control.

The Commission also dismissed the public case that administration defence officials had been making for the MX. That case was predicated on strategic instability, that the increasing vulnerability of American land-based missiles might tempt the Soviet Union to launch a premeditated attack on them. As a rationale for MX, the 'window of vulnerability' was too easy to see through; the Commission shattered it. Assessing different components of America's strategic forces 'collectively and not in isolation', the Commission concluded 'that whereas it is highly desirable that a component of the strategic forces be survivable when it is viewed separately, it makes a major contribution to deterrence even if its survivability depends in substantial measure on the existence of one or the other components of the force.' By this logic the Commission could recommend basing MX in existing Minuteman silos, where it was unlikely to survive attack.

While the Commission rightly rejected the connection between ICBM vulnerability and strategic instability, it thereby ignored the real problem that ICBM vulnerability poses for crisis stability: that vulnerability still gives both sides some incentive to pre-empt, once nuclear war seems imminent. Putting MX with its ten warheads into existing vulnerable silos only makes matters worse, giving the Soviet Union more of an incentive to pre-empt. It in turn adds to the American incentive - and ability - to pre-empt in advance of Soviet pre-emption, and so on in a vicious circle. The Commission did nothing to alleviate this reciprocal fear of surprise attack in a crisis. Instead, it tried to turn that fear into an argument for deploying MX - that the resulting instability will 'encourage the Soviets to move in a stabilizing direction'. The Commission was silent about what happens if the Soviets do not accept such 'encouragement'. It also conveniently ignored existing hard-target kill capability in Minuteman IIIs, as well as Pershing IIs being deployed in Europe and the D-5 missile to be installed in Trident submarines in the next decade.

The Reagan administration's rejection of the bargaining chip argument for MX thus won Commission endorsement. The Report says nothing about putting all 200 MX missiles on the bargaining table. Instead, only the second tranche of 100 MXs is to be negotiable, according to Commission member John

Deutsch, to be swapped for cuts in Soviet SS-18s and SS-19s. The initial tranche of 100 MXs is to remain in place for the duration, a sword of Damocles hanging over the Soviets to compel them to reconfigure their strategic force posture. The Commission sees an analogy between the MX and ABM. 'The ABM Treaty of 1972', the Report says, 'came about only because the United States maintained an ongoing ABM program and indeed made a decision to make a limited deployment.' The analogy to ABM is misplaced. That decision carried the Senate with only the barest majority, a sure sign to the Soviet Union of the lack of enthusiasm for the programme. Moreover, the United States offered to trade away all of the ABM deployment, something the administration is not prepared to do with MX.

The Commission's rejection of the bargaining chip argument, a point which its defenders have tried to obscure, also seems antithetical to a key recommendation on which some stable balancers have pinned great hopes: development of a single-warhead mobile missile - Midgetman - and encouragement of Soviet movement in the same direction. Midgetman only makes sense with a drastic reduction in the number of multiple independently targetable re-entry vehicles (MIRVs) on missiles in the Soviet inventory. Otherwise, it can be defeated by barraging the areas where it would roam. Such a drastic reduction may be achievable, but only with considerable difficulty and time, and not without an American quid pro quo. This would mean an equivalent drastic cut in accurate American MIRVs, most notably, MX and D-5. If the United States refuses to put all of its MX on the table, then presumably the Soviet Union will insist on retaining at least a comparable number of accurate warheads of its own - 1000 plus counters to the Minuteman IIIs. The higher number of Soviet MIRVs drives up the number of Midgetman missiles required to be based in a mobile configuration, which will be extremely expensive to build and operate. Given the expense, it will be hard to justify Midgetman with just one warhead - and even harder to get the Soviet Union to go the single-warhead route. Without a willingness to trade away all of MX, the numbers do not add up for Midgetman.

Instead of aggravating crisis instability by recommending the deployment of 100 MXs in vulnerable silos, the Commission could have shown the way by putting all 200 MXs on the bargaining table and proceeding directly to development of a single warhead mobile ICBM without passing through this dangerous and expensive transition. The Soviet Union seems to be preparing an option to go this route themselves with recent test firings of the SS-X-25 which they call a modernised version of the single-warhead SS-13, solid-fuelled and possibly deployable in a mobile basing mode. But it is also testing an MX equivalent, the MIRVed SS-X-24.

The Commission also lends support to the nuclear war-fighters' cause by resting its case for MX on the requirements of extended deterrence under conditions of mutual vulnerability. While discounting the possibility of a Soviet threat against the United States or its allies of 'limited use of nuclear weapons against military targets' because such use would be 'likely to result in a nuclear war', the Report nonetheless insists that the threat of nuclear blackmail remains. 'In order to deter such Soviet threats', it argues, 'we must be able to put at risk those types of Soviet targets - including hardened ones such as military command bunkers and facilities, missile silos, nuclear weapons and other storage, and the rest - which the Soviet leaders have given every indication by their actions they value most, and which constitute their tools of control and power.'

This claim begs the question of how much more of a capability the United States needs for countering this threat. After all, much of the present strategic force is so targeted. Adding 1000 MX warheads to the existing Minuteman III force which has at least some prompt capability against hardened targets, plus Pershing II, with D-5 yet to come, creates a formidable force indeed - one far in excess of what is necessary to deter 'limited use of nuclear weapons against military targets' by some capability to do likewise. Prudent Soviet planners could conclude that the United States has something more in mind, with all the consequences that this conclusion would have for crisis instability. Moreover, the Commission never elucidates just how the addition of that much capability 'for controlled prompt limited attack on hard targets' would deter limited Soviet threats.

The Commission recommendations also give nuclear war-fighters a hostage, if not a hunting license, for their pursuit of a defence against ballistic missiles, the most destabilising of all potential developments. The Commission's assessment may at first seem re-assuring to stable balancers: 'applications of current technology offer no real promise of being able to defend the United States against massive nuclear attack in this century.' Yet the very next sentence gives nuclear war-fighters their opening: 'An easier task is to provide ABM defence for fixed hardened targets such as ICBM silos.' Once MX is emplaced in vulnerable Minuteman silos, it will be hostage to the war-fighters' desire for ABM. In the meantime, the Commission is content to remain silent on preserving the stabilising effects of the ABM Treaty.

On arms control the Commission left ambiguities for war-fighters to exploit as well. The Commission accepted the stable balancers' belief that stability is to be advanced by reducing the ratio of warheads to launchers. Yet the Commission blunts this point by emphasising limits on warheads and by recommending that 'over the long run' agreements 'be couched, not in terms of launchers, but in terms of equal levels of warheads of roughly equivalent yield'. War-fighters have taken this reference to 'equivalent yield' as endorsement of megatonnage as a unit of account in START. If the administration insists on equal megatonnage, or its functional equivalent, sharp cuts in Soviet MIRVed ICBMs, then it will be the long run indeed before agreement is reached.

In the meantime, the pernicious effects on the policies of America's partner in nuclear adversity, the Soviet Union, may be incalculable. Soviet leaders are unlikely to be taken in by a softening in public rhetoric. Their reactions are apt to be guided more by what we do than by what we say we are doing - more by procurements and force posture than by declaratory policy. The hardware that the United States is now buying could drive Soviet military planners further in a direction they were already heading - toward preparing for pre-emption in crisis.

Confronted by continuing NATO emphasis on the threat of first use of nuclear weapons, Soviet strategists have been preoccupied with countering that threat. In the event of a European crisis verging on war, Soviet military doctrine has a strong presumption for seizing the initiative. And should nuclear war seem imminent, Soviet doctrine calls for pre-emption - 'striking first in the last resort'[4] - and for protecting Soviet assets against enemy pre-emption. Interpreting this presumption by their own lights, nuclear war-fighters in the United States see in it a Soviet attempt to acquire the means for a deliberate disarming first-strike - as a threat to strategic stability instead of a precaution against American first use. From a Soviet perspective, American practice exposes both American pretence and Soviet vulnerability. The United States strategic build-up in the early 1960s, subsequent deployment of MIRVed launchers accompanied by promulgation of the Schlesinger doctrine of limited counterforce options in the early 1970s, and improvements in Minuteman III accuracy and the funding of MX, Trident II, and Pershing II against a backdrop of restatement of American strategic doctrine in PD-59 and the 1982 Defense Guidance in the early 1980s - all called into question the mutuality of deterrence implied in strategic stability while underscoring concern about the survivability of Soviet forces in a crisis.

The Soviet strategy of pre-empting imminent nuclear attack calls for missiles that have the accuracy to destroy nuclear forces in Europe and the United States but that are themselves not vulnerable to pre-emption. The SS-20 may not satisfy the requirements of this strategy, but it is a considerable improvement on the SS-4s and SS-5s it replaces. Its longer range allowed it to be based deeper inside the Soviet Union, out of reach of some American ICBMs as well as most GLCMs and Pershing IIs. Its mobility and improved readiness also made it less vulnerable to attack and therefore more suitable for being held in reserve as a retaliatory force. Its somewhat better accuracy and longer range made it a greater threat to all Western European nuclear installations and C^3 facilities, which are just minutes away. The fact that it was MIRVed with three warheads obviously added somewhat to Soviet target coverage but did not quadruple it as the simple calculations of some analysts suggest, since SS-4s and SS-5s were being dismantled as SS-20s were being deployed.[5] Moreover, solid fuel enables the SS-20 to maintain higher alert rates for launching a pre-emptive strike against Western Europe than did the liquid-fuelled SS-4s and SS-5s, which took hours to ready for launch. It was not, however, more capable of maintaining higher alert rates and achieving greater accuracy than Soviet SS-19 ICBMs, some of which have been and remain targeted on Europe. Thus, the SS-20 did not add much to the crisis instability already present on the continent. And the long time it took for the Soviet Union to deploy a substitute for the SS-4s and SS-5s suggests that the SS-20 was somewhat of an improvisation and not quite the threat NATO makes of it. A successor system to the SS-20 might be far more formidable because of further improvements in reliability, accuracy, and mobility.

The SS-18 and potentially the SS-19 are another matter. Some SS-18s are now capable of killing ICBMs in their silos and other American hard targets. With continued missile testing, the SS-19 will soon have the same capability. Together they add considerably to crisis instability, because, like the MX, they potentially combine hard-target kill capability with their own vulnerability to attack. The new Soviet MX equivalent, the SS-X-24, now undergoing testing will do the same unless it turns out to be capable of mobile basing. The SS-13 follow-on, the SS-X-25, and the new Typhoon SLBM suggest a Soviet response to the perils of vulnerability, but they may not ease the plight of American ICBMs and hence the prospect of crisis instability.

As the Soviet Union moves to counter the American build-up, the political environment continues to deteriorate. While some of the rhetorical excesses on both sides must be discounted as mere posturing, their effect may have been much more pernicious than either government would acknowledge. They seem to have inspired each side to magnify the worst in the other's intentions. In Washington for instance, the Soviet SS-20 deployment is understood not as modernisation of obsolescent missiles and a hedge against additional targeting requirements - in the Middle East, the Persian Gulf and the Far East as well as in Western Europe - but as an attempt at neutralising Europe through nuclear blackmail. In Moscow the American missile deployments in Europe are seen not as an attempt to shore up the credibility of NATO's doctrine of first use, but as part of a comprehensive programme to acquire the capability for a disarming first-strike. Yet neither side's interpretation is sustainable. Sober realists in Moscow are unlikely to calculate that the SS-20 threat could lead to neutralisation of Europe and the break-up of NATO, no matter how many right-wing Westerners say so - and by their insistence, inadvertently encourage this result. Similarly, prudent minds in Washington recognise that, much as some nuclear war-fighters may want to try, a disarming first-strike against forces as sizeable and diverse as the Soviet Union's is simply unattainable under present or foreseeable technological conditions. The misperceptions may be grotesque as in the Soviet response and the American reaction to the intrusion of KAL 007 into Soviet airspace, but as distorted as they may be, these mutual suspicions are driving both superpowers toward exaggerated threat assessments and gross overreactions in military programmes.

Both sides are rapidly passing a point of no return. As Tass declared after the Bundestag voted to proceed with deployments, 'The Rubicon has been crossed.'[6] New weapons now being installed and tested threaten to upset the precarious military stability that has prevailed between the superpowers for two decades. Some of these steps are irreversible; others can be halted in the next two or three years. If nothing is done to reverse the present direction, the problem of how to prevent nuclear weapons from being used - inadvertently, accidentally, or deliberately - will become all the more unmanageable. And the arms control measures of today - trying to preclude the most destabilising developments while holding down the numbers of weapons in a verifiable way - will no longer be able to contain the instability. At that point leaders on both sides will look back on the past decade with incomprehension and ask why nothing was done to prevent the nuclear predicament from becoming more awful.

Notes

1. United States, Department of Defense, Defense Guidance for Fiscal Years 1984-88, excerpted in Richard Halloran, 'Pentagon Draws Up First Strategy for Fighting a Long Nuclear War', New York Times, May 30, 1982, p. 1, and Leslie H. Gelb, 'Is the Nuclear Threat Manageable?' New York Times Magazine, March 4, 1984, p. 29.

2. Institute for Defense Analyses, Ballistic Missile Defences and U.S. National Security: Summary Report, Prepared for the Future Security Strategy Study, October 1983, Fred S. Hoffman, Study Director.

3. United States President's Commission on Strategic Forces, Report, April 1983.

4. The phrase is Malcolm Mackintosh's, quoted in John Erickson, 'The Soviet View of Deterrence: A General Survey', Survival, vol. XXIV, (November-December, 1982), pp. 242-251.

5. Raymond L. Garthoff, 'The Soviet SS-20 Decision', Survival, vol. XXV (May-June 1983), p. 115, 118n8.

6. Quoted in John F. Burns, 'Moscow

Reiterates It will Respond by Deploying Its Missiles', New York Times, November 24, 1983, p. 1.

Chapter Five

SPACE-BASED DEFENCE: THE 'STAR WARS' INITIATIVE*

George Rathjens

On March 23, 1983, at the end of an otherwise unremembered televised address to the nation, President Reagan proposed that the United States undertake a major effort to develop defences that would be effective against ballistic missiles - so effective as 'to give us the means of rendering... nuclear weapons impotent and obsolete.'[1] While he was not explicit in suggesting that he had in mind using space-based weapons or sensors to achieve this objective, the context and elaborating commentary by administration spokesmen indicated that this was the case, and the speech has since been widely referred to as the 'Star Wars' speech. Officially, the proposal is now known as the Strategic Defense Initiative (SDI).

There was widespread and varied reaction. George Reedy, a most thoughtful observer of the presidency, said, in effect, 'ho-hum', suggesting that without a call for appropriations or the creation of a new agency, the President's remarks should be regarded as just rhetoric[2]. *Business Week*, on the other hand, suggested that the speech presaged the most radical change in strategic policy since World War II.[3]

It now appears that Reedy spoke too quickly. There have since been directives promulgated and actions taken to give impetus to Reagan's proposal:

1. Two studies, directed by the President, to define the technologies necessary for defending the United States and its allies

* Published in *Environment*, vol. 26, no. 5, June 1984 under the title 'The Strategic Defense Initiative: The Imperfections of "Perfect Defense".'

from ballistic missile attack and to assess the role of defensive systems in the nation's future security strategy have recently been completed and their findings made public.
2. A new director of the programme to develop a space-based defence system has been appointed - Lt.Gen. James A. Abrahamson.
3. The administration has asked for some $25 billion to be spent on research and development over the next five years - with a request for an appropriation of $1.7 billion for the programme in the next fiscal year (see Table 1).

Business Week's projection was wrong because policy must be related in some meaningful way to capability - and there is presently no capability nor are there even ideas in prospect that offer hope of the President's objective of 100 per cent effective defence being realised.

In fact, there is so much doubt in the technical community about the feasibility of perfect defence that many supporters of both the administration and ballistic missile defence suggest that to attack the President's proposal is to attack a straw man: that the real issue is not whether the country should attempt to develop a defence that would, indeed, make nuclear weapons 'impotent and obsolete' but rather whether it should simply make a major effort to develop general ballistic missile defences (BMD), recognising that 100 per cent effectiveness is unrealistic.

The differences between these objectives are of major importance - matters not just of degree but of kind. The contrast is as between quests for improved longevity on the one hand and for eternal life on the other. As with eternal life, if one really has perfect defence as an objective, prayer is likely to be a more efficacious approach than technical development.

In the case of defence against nuclear weapons, there is an added complication. There are some who despair of *any* meaningful *general* defence - that is, defence of cities, industry, and population - but who believe nevertheless that a limited defence of selected assets, for example, missile sites, may be feasible and desirable. As will be discussed later, some of these people have seen, in the President's initiative, a vehicle for advancing their own objectives.

Table 1.1: Department of Defense Strategic Defense Initiative - FY 1985 Budget

MAJOR TECHNICAL AREAS	FY 84 APPROPRIATION IN RELATED AREAS	FY 85 PLANNED PRIOR TO PRESIDENT'S SPEECH	FY 85 SDI BUDGET
		($ millions)	
Surveillance, acquisition, tracking, and kill assessment	366.5	735.7	721
Direct energy weapons	322.5	369.1	489
Kinetic energy weapons	195.8	296.1	356
System concepts, battle management and C-3[a]	82.7	89.5	99
Survivability, weapons lethality, and support systems	23.5	36.6	112
Total	991.0	1527.0[b]	1777[c]

SOURCE: Department of Defense, 1984.

a. C-3 = Command, control and communication.
b. Percentage of real growth, after adjustment for price escalation from 1984 to 1985, is 71%.
c. Percentage of growth from FY 1985 prior to plan is 16%.

This article raises these issues so prominently and directly because judgements about whether the President's proposal makes sense, and about which approaches are to be preferred, depend critically on the objectives one has in mind, and because it is clear that there is not now a consensus among proponents of BMD on the basic objectives.

Changing Times and Beliefs

In order to understand the SDI issues, it may be helpful to recount a little history. During World War II, there were occasions when air defences exacted attrition rates of as high as 10 per cent against attacking bomber forces - even 16 per cent against one large raid - but these were the exceptions. Had losses at this level been the general rule, bomber offensives could not have been long sustained. As it was, there was more or less even competition between the offence and the defence. The defence won in the case of the Battle of Britain but lost in the strategic bombing campaign against Japan. In the case of the bombing of Germany and occupied Europe, the verdict was equivocal. While the raids were immensely destructive, they were not decisive, and perhaps not worth the cost in lives and equipment lost.

With the development of nuclear weapons, and particularly thermonuclear weapons and ballistic missiles to deliver them, everything changed. Since a single weapon could destroy a city, 10 per cent attrition hardly seemed interesting to a defender. More to the point, there developed a widespread belief, at least in the United States, that any attempt at defence would induce an offsetting, or perhaps even more-than-offsetting, adversary reaction: specifically, that it would lead to such an improvement in offensive capabilities that the damage to be expected in the event of war would not be decreased at all - and, indeed, it might even be increased because of a likely propensity of an attacker to overestimate the capabilities of a defence and to overcompensate for it.

It was widely believed that economics would favour the offence: that the 'cost-exchange ratio', the cost to the offence of offsetting any increment of defence capability, would be relatively low - certainly, less than 1:1 - assuming that the objective of the defence would be to defend the cities and population of the country against a heavy Soviet missile attack.

Space-Based Defence

This was the situation in the late 1950s when the United States and the Soviet Union began to work seriously on ballistic missile defence. The prospects did not change in any dramatic way during the next two decades, notwithstanding impressive advances in technology relevant to defence - notably in data-processing capability and in the development of interceptor missiles capable of very high acceleration and phased array (electronically steered) radars. It did not seem likely that either country could defend its population very effectively from attack by the other, given the advances in offensive technology that were occurring and in prospect.

What, if anything, has changed to justify a more optimistic outlook for the last part of the century? Are there now really promising approaches to a perfect defence against ballistic missiles, as suggested by President Reagan, or even to a very good one?

On one point there is likely to be little disagreement: if there is to be any hope of a defence that could deny the Soviets the possibility of inflicting significant damage on the United States, it will have to be based on an approach radically different from those most favoured in the 1960s and 1970s - hence, the emphasis on 'Star Wars'.

Three Defence Possibilities

To understand the defence problem, one must first have some appreciation of how long-range ballistic missiles work. A simplified description follows.

If the missile is an intercontinental ballistic missile (ICBM), heavy rockets - two or three stages - provide propulsion for about four minutes. At the end of this time, the last stage of the missile will have emerged from the atmosphere, headed towards its target, with sufficient velocity so that it can 'coast' the rest of the way - typically about 5,000 miles - in another 20 to 30 minutes. In the case of modern missiles, from three to fourteen warheads are carried on the last stage, a 'bus', and they are released individually over a period of several minutes. By changing the velocity and heading of the bus between releases, the several warheads can be delivered to different targets.

Penetration aids, including notably, 'decoys' - objects designed to simulate warheads - may also be released during this 'post-boost' phase. They, along with the warheads, will move through space unaffected by any external forces other than the Earth's gravitational field, until they re-enter the Earth's atmosphere. Drag forces will then heat the warheads, slow them down, and otherwise change their trajectories. Decoys and other objects may break up or burn up. In any case, they will be more affected than warheads by atmospheric drag. Advantage can be taken of this to distinguish them, through the use of radars and other sensors, from warheads, which is something that is likely to be difficult or impossible, depending on the capability of the sensors, prior to re-entry into the atmosphere. The point at which discrimination becomes possible will depend on the design and mass of the decoy (and of the warhead). There is an obvious trade-off problem for the offence: choosing between a relatively small number of heavy decoys, which will not be distinguishable from warheads until they are some distance into the atmosphere, or numerous, very light decoys that will be distinguishable earlier.

In the case of sea-launched ballistic missiles (SLBMs), the propulsion time, time of flight, and range have been less than for ICBMs, but as the range of SLBMs has increased from 1,200 nautical miles (nm) to over 4,500 nm, the differences in effectiveness between them and ICBMs have been much reduced.

Traditional approaches to ballistic missile defence have been based on terminal interception, that is interception within a few hundred kilometres - often, within ten kilometres - of the target. Conceptually, however, destruction of adversary missiles and/or warheads might be accomplished at any point along the trajectory. From the perspective of the 1980s, and for the purpose of this discussion, it is useful to consider the missile trajectory in three phases: the boost-phase - the part of the trajectory when the missile is in powered flight and before warhead separation occurs; mid-course - from booster burnout until re-entry; and the terminal or re-entry phase. There are both advantages and disadvantages to attempting intercept in each of these regions.

Terminal Defences

To date, terminal defence technology has been given the most emphasis and is the furthest developed. Traditional systems have involved siting nuclear-armed interceptor missiles near targets to be defended and using radars capable of tracking incoming objects, which, with appropriate data-processing, are able to distinguish between warheads and penetration aids. Either the same or different radars have been assigned the task of tracking the interceptor missiles, which, when steered to the vicinity of the attacking missile, would destroy it as the interceptor nuclear warhead explodes.

The early designs involved long-range interceptors that were so slow that they would have required a decision to intercept prior to re-entry, thus precluding effective discrimination between warheads and decoys. With the development of interceptor missiles capable of very high acceleration, it has become possible to delay intercept, thereby facilitating discrimination - but at the price of reducing the radius of intercept to a few kilometres.

As they have evolved, terminal defences offer the following conceptual advantages:

1. The technology already exists - or, in any case, the problems remaining to be worked out are relatively straightforward ones of systems design and optimisation.
2. It is at least conceptually possible to discriminate between warheads and penetration aids, thereby permitting efficient use of the defence's interceptors.
3. It allows for possibility of 'preferential defence'. The defence may elect to defend only a fraction of a set of targets, for example, of missile silos, and, with the possibility of delay in a decision to commit interceptors until it is quite clear where an adversary warhead is headed, it need not tip its hand as to which it will defend until the last minute. The offence, not knowing which targets will be defended, can be forced to 'waste' warheads, allocating them on the assumption that any target it attacks may be one of those defended.

But there are problems and disadvantages, too. If the interceptors are of short-range, as they must be to take advantage of atmospheric discrimination, many defence complexes must be deployed if a large area - say, a whole country - is to be defended, and if the attacker chooses to concentrate his attack on a few targets or regions ('preferential offence'), most of the defence capacity will be unusable. Thus, terminal defences are particularly ill-adapted to a defence of the kind President Reagan has called for: one that will essentially deny the possibility of damage to all parts of the country.

While they will be much better suited to defence of such targets as missile silos - especially if losing a fraction of them is acceptable, as is likely to be the case - it is not obvious that such defences would be a good investment. They may fail catastrophically because of radar malfunction in a nuclear-explosion environment; the cost-exchange ratio may be unfavourable; there may be less costly ways of protecting targets; or there may be relatively inexpensive ways of getting around the target vulnerability problem - for example, by investing in mobile missiles if the attack of concern is one against ICBMs.

Boost-phase Intercept

Intercept during boost phase offers not only a way around the penetration aids problem but also around that raised by MIRVs, the fractionation of missile payload into a number of independently targetable re-entry vehicles. One simply destroys the booster before the multiple warheads and/or penetration aids can be released to go their separate ways. It is an idea that is hardly new - there were a number of such proposals around 20 to 25 years ago - but one that now commands new attention because of recent technological developments and the President's March 1983 initiative.

With the possibility precluded of siting interceptors in the immediate proximity of adversary missile launch sites (at least for ICBMs, if not for SLBMs), any boost-phase defence must be based in some way on satellite systems. The simplest, and oldest, concepts have involved placing many satellites in orbits, each with an infra-red sensor that could detect the plume from an adversary booster as it emerges from the atmosphere. An interceptor missile would be directed to the booster, generally homing on the missile's infra-red signal.

Unfortunately, the interval between the emergence of a booster from the atmosphere and burnout is likely to be short - of the order of one minute - even in the case of missiles that have been developed with no concern about such defence (and it could be made to be much shorter). Assuming any reasonable velocity for interceptor missiles, there must be a satellite fairly near the booster launch site if an interceptor is to reach its target before booster burnout (and before post-boost warhead separation begins).

Any given satellite will, of course, be within range of potential adversary missile launch sites during only a fraction - possibly quite a small fraction - of its orbit. Thus, the number of satellites that must be 'on-station' to cope with a massive adversary attack at a time of the enemy's choosing is likely to be prohibitively great.

The number required could, of course, be drastically reduced if intercept could be made almost instantaneously from long range. This makes systems that rely on lasers or particle beams as kill mechanisms conceptually attractive but with such approaches come the additional problems of aiming and beam collimation. It cannot be said that these problems are insoluble, but success, if possible at all, will require major technical developments: in the case of chemically powered lasers, for example, mirrors of unprecedented size and quality; extraordinary precision in aiming; an orders-of-magnitude increase in laser brightness beyond what has been achieved; and the delivery to orbit of amounts of reactants that would exceed projected shuttle capabilities.

Moreover, there are a number of countermeasures that the adversary could implement relatively easily: reducing the burn-time of boosters so that there will be virtually no time for engagement - in fact, none at all for some variants of space-based systems; hardening boosters so that laser power requirements will be increased; and developing and deploying dummy boosters - relatively cheap vehicles that will generate signals similar to those of real boosters. And then, there are the possibilities of physical destruction of space-based defence systems by mines placed in space near the satellites, by Earth-based systems, or by adversary space-based laser systems (a much easier job than destruction of missiles).

Variants of space-based defence systems have been proposed that get around some of these problems. For example, systems have been proposed that rely on x-ray lasers driven by nuclear explosions rather than on infra-red lasers. Use of such systems would circumvent the necessity of placing enormous quantities of chemical reactants in orbit, but it carries with it other problems notably that such a satellite would self-destruct.

All of these 'Star Wars' concepts require the realisation of a number of technical developments of great difficulty. Under-Secretary of Defense for Research and Engineering Richard DeLauer has perhaps captured the flavour of this aspect of the challenge in noting that each of the several developments required is likely to be comparable to the Apollo programme. Moreover, there is the still greater challenge of integrating all the developments into a system that, of course, can never be tested in an environment like that in which it must be expected to operate.

Mid-course Engagement

There is a third possibility for defence: mid-course engagement. This is attractive in that there may be up to 30 minutes in which to conduct an engagement, compared with tens of seconds for boost-phase or terminal defence. However, given the likelihood of multiple warheads and decoys separating at the end of the boost phase and with no atmosphere to facilitate discriminating between them in mid-course, this is probably the most unattractive of the three regimes for the defence.

Decoys can be almost arbitrarily light, and therefore numerous, yet very difficult for defences to cope with. What are the possibilities? They are either producing lethal effects over very large volumes in space, or, in order to facilitate discrimination, in some way perturbing the trajectories or physical characteristics of decoys and warheads and then sensing the perturbations. As in the case of boost-phase defence (and in contrast to terminal defence), the countermeasure question has hardly been approached by proponents of mid-course systems.

If all of the problems associated with ballistic missile defence could be solved, there would still be the possibility of nuclear weapons being delivered by other means, such as by aircraft or cruise missiles. While Secretary Weinberger has suggested that those problems too could be, and would be, solved, along with the BMD problem,[4] it is not clear how this could be accomplished.

In fact, there is a strong basis in past experience with air defences that suggests that anything approaching an air-tight defence cannot be achieved. Note the record in World War II and in the Korean, Vietnamese, and Middle East Wars and the fact that, notwithstanding an enormous investment in air defences, the Soviet Union has found that even intercepting individual Korean air liners at altitudes where intercept is easiest is a time-consuming task.

Assessing the Commitment

With the prospects for defence so poor, how is the administration's commitment to the Strategic Defense Initiative to be assessed? The Congressional Office of Technology Assessment and the Union of Concerned Scientists have recently released their own analyses of Reagan's strategic defence proposal. Here it will be examined from three perspectives.

There has by now been a fair amount of discussion of the initiative, predicated on the realisation of enough success in research and development (R&D) to justify deployment of such a system. From this perspective, critics have focused mainly on the destabilising aspects of deployment, usually pointing out that if we achieve enough success in R&D, the Soviets are likely to do so as well, and that deployment by us will almost surely imply deployment by them. Thus, going ahead with a 'Star Wars' defence would be a great impetus to the arms race, with offensive forces being built up in response to defences, further improvements in defence being made in reaction to offensive improvements, and so on.

Not only would deployment of defence lead to 'arms race instability', say most of the critics; worse yet, there would be an increase in 'crisis instability'. However effective a defence system might be in coping with a massive attack - it would be far more effective in dealing with a ragged response by an adversary whose missile forces had been the subject of a disarming attack - a 'first-strike'. Each side, knowing this, would see its adversary's deployment of a ballistic missile defence as very threatening, and if there were actual deployment by both sides, there would be a reciprocally reinforcing impetus to strike first.

Critics also note that if both sides deploy such systems, they are likely to be far more effective against adversary 'Star Wars' defence systems than against ICBMs and SLBMs. Again, there would be a reciprocally reinforcing impetus to strike first, in this case against the adversary's defences.

Combine the two arguments and it does, indeed, sound pretty frightening. If A strikes first at B's defences and then just minutes later at B's missiles, B will be unable to degrade A's counterforce attack significantly, B's defences having been destroyed; as a result, most of B's land-based missiles will be destroyed in their silos. With that, any retaliatory response by B will be sufficiently degraded so that A's defences might do relatively well in coping with it. Quite an incentive to go first.

There are other arguments. Two of those most commonly raised are the almost certainly great, although at present unpredictable, costs of such a system and the fact that a Soviet system of only moderate effectiveness against United States offensive capabilities might negate Chinese, French, and British offensive capabilities, or might lead these countries to make massive expenditures to upgrade them, neither of which would be in the United States interest.

There is a certain logic to these arguments, but in my view, they are only of academic interest, particularly those relating to crisis stability. The prospects for a technically effective defence are so poor that I cannot imagine deployments in this century that would make a difference in the outcome of a nuclear exchange.

But this does not mean that the Strategic Defense Initiative should be dismissed as just another ill-founded proposal that will peter out as the impossibility of realising the President's goal becomes apparent, with there being no lasting imprint beyond a trail left as a result of having spent a few billions of dollars. There are five rather direct effects that are of considerable significance:

1. The initiative will surely induce the Soviets to make greater efforts in the same general field. Evidence of such efforts will be adduced to justify further American efforts, and so on. Thus, there is a positive feedback loop that can lead to substantial waste and concern about adversary activity in both countries.
2. To some extent, there is likely to be an effect on R&D in the area of offensive systems and perhaps even on weapons acquisition. In spite of the poor

prospects for technical success with the Strategic Defense Initiative, and that arms race instability arguments should be pretty heavily discounted, there is likely to be some anticipatory response. Proponents of ideas and/or offensive systems that can be seen as counters to a hypothetical adversary defence are likely to get a more sympathetic hearing in the resource allocation competition than if there were no SDI initiative.

3. There is likely to be some effect on efforts to develop 'hard-site' defences - terminal defences designed to degrade attacks against missile silos or 'hardened' command and control facilities - but it is probably premature to estimate the size of the effect. If there is strong congressional resistance to ballistic missile defence because of skepticism about the President's initiative, there could be limitations on defence spending.

   With other ballistic missile defence R&D efforts having been brought under the SDI umbrella, and resources syphoned off to the more far-out (in both a literal and figurative sense) work on 'Star Wars', there could be a diminution of effort on 'hard-site' defence. On the other hand, if the Congress is generous in providing support for the Strategic Defense Initiative, there could be an increase in 'hard-site' efforts - and on everything else that can be bootlegged under the SDI umbrella.

4. Notwithstanding some disclaimers by administrative spokesmen, there will clearly be pressure to modify or scrap the 1972 anti-ballistic missile treaty. Article V, Section 1 of the treaty says, 'Each Party undertakes not to develop, test, or deploy ABM systems or components which are sea-based, air-based, space-based, or mobile land-based'. While it is certainly possible to do some fundamental work on highpowered lasers, adaptive optics, etc., within the constraints of the treaty, it is obvious that if this article has any meaning at all, much that one might like to do under the SDI will be in direct conflict with the ABM treaty.[5]

Space-Based Defence

5. There are likely to be some developments of military utility as a result of 'Star Wars' work. In particular, there could be some that would contribute to the attainment of anti-satellite (ASAT) capabilities. Assuming, as most critics do, that advances by the United States would be more or less matched by the Soviet Union, this could prove, on balance, to be to the disadvantage of this country, inasmuch as the United States is, and is likely to continue to be, more dependent on satellites for reconnaissance and communications, and possibly for early warning, than is the Soviet Union.

   SDI-related interest in developing some of these technologies could be a factor in resistance to efforts to limit ASAT development and deployment by agreement between the two nations. In an April 25 appearance before the Senate Foreign Relations Committee, Reagan's science advisor, Dr. George A. Keyworth II, recommended that the United States delay, 'for the next couple of years', any new agreements on space arms control with the Soviet Union so that future United States programmes will not be 'blocked by a previous patchwork of treaty obligations'.[6]

While some research on 'Star Wars'-related technology is warranted, there has to be a serious question about going very far down the development path, considering the poor prospects for ultimate success and some of the likely consequences alluded to above. But to me, the most troublesome aspects of the President's initiative emerge when it is viewed from a third perspective: what it tells us about our decision-making processes, particularly about decision-making in the Reagan administration.

Troublesome Questions

The decision to go ahead with the initiative was made in ignorance. One has to sympathise with the President's cri de coeur about the undesirability and immorality of nuclear deterrence. There is certainly something deeply troubling about relying for survival on the rationality and good judgement of political leaders whom one had no role in selecting and about holding the lives of millions hostage for the decisions of leaders of whose behaviour they may not approve. But understandable revulsion cannot be an excuse for holding out hopes for absolute security when there is not the slightest basis for such hopes; and this is what President Reagan did when he called for an effort 'to change the course of human history' - 'to render nuclear weapons impotent and obsolete' - and then went on to say, 'I believe we can do it.'

That was just the beginning. We have since seen technical people within the administration - and knowledgeable people in the community outside - saying that a perfect defence is, of course, not possible; that defence cannot replace nuclear-based deterrence as the key to dealing with the Soviet Union, but only serve as a complement; and that offensive nuclear weapons will not be obsolete, and must be retained.

Many have said such things while supporting the President's initiative, often arguing that the pay-off they hope for is a defence that would help enhance deterrence by providing some defence for our land-based ICBMs. All this, with the Secretary of Defense having said, 'The defensive systems the President is talking about are not designed to be partial.... What we will try to do will be to develop a system that is so reliable that it will, in effect, render impotent all of these nuclear missiles.'

One is left with very troublesome questions:

> Why did the President not get competent technical advice before making his March 23 speech?
>
> Does he, and does Secretary Weinberger, understand that virtually no one in the technical community, including those in the Department of Defense and the principal advisory groups that have been established since the March 23 speech, believes the President's objectives are realistic?
>
> Do they know, and if so, do they care, that the President's initiative is generally being used, and defended, as justification for defences inconsistent with his stated objective: for 'partial' defence - including, particularly, defence of ICBM sites?
>
> What has happened to integrity in the military establishment and the technical/scientific community that permits men to

support the President's initiative when they know full well that perfect defence is an illusion?

Should there not be agreement between the President and the responsible people in the Defense Department on the programme's objectives, and, before the programme goes further, should not the Congress and the public be informed of the objectives and be given a realistic assessment of the prospects?

Should there not be some restructuring of the technical advisory process in government so that fiascos of the kind illustrated by the SDI will be less likely?

Notes

1. President's Speech on Military Spending and a New Defense, New York Times, March 24, 1983.
2. George E. Reedy, 'Space War: Why All the Flak?' Los Angeles Times, March 31, 1983.
3. 'Putting America's Defense in Orbit', Business Week, June 20, 1983.
4. Meet the Press, March 27, 1983.
5. Testifying about the SDI before a congressional committee on April 24, 1984, Lt. Gen. Abrahamson said that modification of the ABM treaty 'with Soviet agreement' would be required prior to deployment of any elements of the proposed defence system. Walter Pincus, "Star Wars" Widened', Washington Post, April 25, 1984, p. A-1.
6. 'Delay Urged in Space-Weapons Talks,' Washington Post, April 26, 1984, p. A-1. When asked by Committee Chairman Sen. Charles H. Percy whether Keyworth's desire to avoid treaty entanglements 'is the real reason why the administration refuses to undertake' anti-satellite-weapons negotiations with the Russians, Keyworth said that the principal argument was the difficulty in verifying any treaty.

Chapter Six

AMERICAN AND EUROPEAN SECURITY IN THE 1980s

James Leonard

American and European security should be based on four propositions:

1. There can be no durable security for the Alliance except through joint efforts, including all of the allies.
2. The roles and contributions of individual countries will necessarily vary from case to case; it is important, however, that each one be seen to be doing at least a reasonable minimum.
3. Security must be based on a strong defence, and the character of that defence effort must respond to changes in our military and political environment. Specifically, in this decade the role of nuclear weapons must diminish substantially.
4. Security, and the political cohesion on which it rests, requires an active and determined effort to negotiate with the Soviets, on arms control, of course, but also on the full range of political issues.

The first of these propositions is so obviously true and universally accepted that we need not spend time on it. There is, however, one point: do not be misled by some of the noises heard from time to time in the United States. There is grumbling - about burden-sharing, about lukewarm political support, about 'trading with the enemy', etc. But there is almost no one who really takes seriously the notion of the United States 'going it alone', without Europe, or Canada, or Japan. In fact, many Americans who complain most bitterly on these points are precisely the most bitter anti-Soviet elements, and thus particularly sensitive to the jubilation which the Soviet leaders would feel if the Alliance began to look as if it were coming apart.

Suggesting that one should not exaggerate the gravity of these grumblings does not mean that the specific problems do not have to be addressed. They do. But they are more likely to be managed successfully if all concerned remain confident about the basic commitment of the other parties to the basic framework of the Alliance. If the Europeans really became convinced that the United States was turning westward, then some of them would think more seriously about turning eastward, and that is not the kind of Ostpolitik that is in anyone's interest.

The second proposition suggests that there is a need to accept variations in the roles that are played by different members of the Alliance, but also that no one should be getting what looks like a free ride. Variations in roles - in 'burden-sharing' - have been accepted from the outset. The United States was obviously able to do much more in the early years and American resentment of this was minimal. In the sixties, Europe had largely recovered, the United States got deeply involved in Vietnam, and the Mansfield Amendment came to the fore. But instead of bringing its troops home from Europe, the United States got into negotiations with the Soviets on force levels. This is one of a number of examples of why the Defense Department and the hawks should be profoundly grateful to the Arms Control and Disarmament Agency and the arms control lobby. Fifteen years after the Mansfield Amendment, and after more than a decade of unsuccessful talks in MBFR, it is hard to imagine that either a conservative or a liberal administration in Washington would substantially cut American forces in Europe unless the Soviets cut theirs, and with air-tight verification as well.

That does not mean, however, that the burden-sharing problem has gone away. There seems to be a healthy current in Europe arguing that Europe must do more, not because they feel sorry for the United States taxpayer or must placate the curmudgeons in Washington, but for the sake of their own self-respect, their own political morale, and their desire to have a larger role in important aspects of East-West security problems. That clearly is a good thing, even though the United States tax burden is not likely to be reduced. The most important benefit could be an improvement in the management of the East-West relationship. The American stewardship of that matter has sometimes been brilliant; it has never been disastrous. But in recent years, it has been plagued with problems deeply rooted in American political culture, and it will do no harm to share the responsibility more broadly.

Burden-sharing and roles can take different forms. The Canadian case is illustrative as everyone is aware that Canada's military burden, in per cent of GNP, is low. If some Canadians want to see it rise, few Americans will take issue. Americans are generally not familiar with the pros and cons. But there should be no sense of embarrassment among the Canadians over these numbers. One has only to look at the role Canada plays in development assistance and in transfer of technology to the Third World. And at the United Nations one learns about the Canadian role in peacekeeping. Since some of the most serious threats to Western security arise from the turmoil and conflict in the Third World, these Canadian activities are just as much contributions to collective security as are American battleships and aircraft carriers. In fact, since it seems politically impossible, at least in the near term, to increase substantially the percentage of United States GNP going to development assistance, it will be most helpful if friends like Canada and Japan can increase still further their share of that burden. If the United States can put six per cent of its GNP into defence, against two per cent or so for Canada, perhaps Canada could put two or three per cent of its GNP into foreign aid.

A recent report of the Trilateral Commission suggested that Japan, with its enormous balance-of-trade surplus, might play the role of capital exporter and financier of development that Britain played in the last century, to the great benefit then of both Canada and the United States. Lately we have noticed a lot of Canadian capital coming to the United States. If more of that Canadian capital could be directed south of the border - that is, south of the United States border - it might be good for everyone's security.

The third proposition acknowledges what no one really disputes: that security has to be based on a strong defence. Before turning to the nuclear aspect, where there _is_ controversy, let us ask _why_ is a strong defence needed?

The immediate answer from most people, in

Canada, in the United States, and in Western Europe, would be that the Soviets are dangerous. They are aggressive and expansionist and if they could safely do so they would move in and take over Western Europe. There is, however, another view, held by a few people in the United States security community. A strong defence is needed, not because the Soviets desperately want to invade and take over Western Europe, since that is not in fact the case, but because so many people on both sides of the Atlantic think the Soviets are bent on aggression and are deterred only by defences. Since so many think that way, it would be extraordinarily divisive to try to carry through policies based on a different assessment of Soviet intentions, even if that other assessment is wholly accurate. Moreover, such policies and the lowered defence posture that would result might just possibly put ideas into the heads of some Soviets. And finally, the disaster that could ensue if this dovish assessment of the Soviets were widely accepted and acted upon, and then proven to be wrong - that disaster would be so colossal that even extreme doves should be willing to accept the rather heavy insurance payments that defence expenditures represent. One can reasonably draw attention in this connection to the heavy 'insurance payments' made by United States' friends in Sweden, who can hardly be described as hawks.

This point is worth making because there are entirely too many voices inside the Alliance, especially in the United Kingdom, in the Netherlands, in Germany, and in Scandinavia who imply that all Americans are blood-minded Russophobes, or are completely dominated by such. Yet in fact a number of Americans who are neither of the above support a defence effort not radically different from that of the Reagan administration - a few tens of billions less here and a few billions more there, but still a very heavy burden indeed. Moreover, these doves are just as firm as our hawks in wanting to see members of the Alliance carry their fair share of that burden.

Nuclear weapons are commonly given credit for the fact that there has been no war in Europe since 1945, while scores of wars have been taking place in areas of the world where nuclear weapons are not present. That analysis is neither provable nor disprovable. There are general grounds for skepticism, since great events rarely are the result of a single cause. And analysis is particularly difficult when the event is a non-event - a dog that did not bark, a war that did not occur. But the common judgement can be allowed to stand. It may well be correct. Certainly the fact can be observed that Soviet possession of nuclear weapons has made Western statesmen extremely cautious in their handling of crises in Central Europe. Thirty years of contemporary history and thousands of pages of memoirs and analyses testify to this. There is every reason to believe that a similar spirit of caution pervades Soviet decision-making circles at tense moments.

But the structure which induces this mutual caution should be looked at closely. To call it by its right name, it is a doomsday machine. It is not quite so apocalyptic in its workings as the original Doomsday Machine of Herman Kahn - the hypothetical monster designed to ensure perfect deterrence through the clear capability of destroying all life on the planet. But it is still quite apocalyptic in its potential effects, even if 'Nuclear Winter' is left completely out of the analysis. The NATO deployment of short-range and medium-range weapons, and the corresponding Soviet deployments, have the clear consequence of placing at risk whole nations at the heart of our Western civilisation. In fact, through our careful development of the ladder of escalation - the ladder with no missing rungs - the two doomsday machines which face each other in Central Europe really place at risk the whole of Western civilisation. That is a rather apocalyptic structure, and certainly justifies the provocative label of doomsday machine or of dual doomsday machines, one on each side, closely linked to each other.

One could well argue that there are five more doomsday machines: the strategic forces of the five nuclear weapon states. Four of them are linked so closely to the two machines in Central Europe that they really form one gigantic machine with a rather close resemblance to the one that Kahn hypothesised back in 1960.

Something called a 'doomsday machine' sounds inherently evil, but what in fact is wrong with a doomsday machine if it keeps the peace? For an answer to that question, one should turn to the man who invented the concept. In On Thermonuclear War,[1] Kahn worried that his invention might appeal to some colonel but found that his worries were exaggerated. Almost everyone, especially professional military men, found the concept, in Kahn's words, 'totally unsatisfactory'. And why?

Because, Kahn explains, it could not possibly be made perfectly controllable. No machine is perfect and perfect controllability is simply not attainable. It is therefore necessary, he asserted, to 'examine the consequences of a failure'. And when one does, the consequences are not acceptable. In Kahn's carefully understated language: 'In this case, a failure kills too many people and kills them too automatically.' The entire population of the planet was, for Kahn, 'too many people' to be put at risk.

One can grumble about his tone but his analysis is impeccable. And today the nuclear dispositions of the two alliances in Central Europe are seen by many people to have precisely this same defect as Kahn's original Doomsday Machine. These nuclear dispositions deter very effectively. They deter us from fishing in the troubled waters of Eastern Europe. And they deter the Soviets from a number of things that we may suspect them of contemplating from time to time. But if deterrence fails, the consequences will be that 'too many people' are killed 'too automatically'.

This is a simple and readily understandable argument. It does not require a deep knowledge of the characteristics of nuclear weapons, or of military strategy, or international relations. This argument has been accepted by large numbers of Europeans from the most sophisticated experts and political leaders down to men and women in the street. And it has made significant inroads among United States strategic thinkers. One leading, rather conservative European statesman recently commented that we have five years, at most, to develop a new approach, or we will be in real trouble. The more closely we look at this machine we have built, the more carefully 'we examine the consequences of a failure', the less we like what we see.

What this means is that the Alliance must move - and must be seen by our publics to be moving - with 'deliberate speed' to diminish the role of nuclear weapons in our defensive strategy. It does not mean - at least to the author of this essay - that a NATO strategy of no first use must be adopted. Even less does it require that the United States should promise to the Soviets that it will never be the first to use nuclear weapons. But it does demand visible and far-reaching changes in present deployments and in the military plans relating to nuclear weapons in Europe. It is difficult to be more specific, not only because of constraints of space but because no one really knows just what changes in doctrines, in tactics, in deployments, and in weaponry should be effected in what time frame. That is a complex problem which the Alliance machinery, governments and experts outside government should address, and in fact already are addressing. But it is urgent and important to carry it forward in a way that restores the confidence of our publics in our strategy and our leaders.

This aspect of nuclear deterrence should be left at this point to approach the other end of the spectrum, addressing the question of the minimum or residual role of nuclear weapons in deterring war and defending our security. There is today and there will long remain such a minimum role, a lower bound to the changes that will be brought about through the re-examination of battlefield weapons that is already under way. A careful analysis of why there will not be, for a very long time, a zero role for nuclear weapons should be re-assuring to many people, though it will be disappointing - in fact, unacceptable - to those who insist on extreme solutions for what all should acknowledge is an extremely unsatisfactory situation. This does not mean that a 'minimum deterrent', the smallest possible force structure that will reliably deter, is being discussed. The subject is the residual or minimum role of whatever nuclear force structure exists, whether it is ten weapons or ten thousand.

This bed-rock role has two components, or if one prefers, there are two minimum roles. The first of these is to deter a first use of nuclear weapons by the Soviets. That function is common to theatre weapons from artillery shells up to Pershing IIs and on to the British and French deterrent forces and the United States strategic arsenal. One cannot really imagine that in this century things will change so radically and disarmament - unilateral or multilateral - will gather such strength and move so fast that this component of deterrence will be abandoned. That judgement, however, says almost nothing about how many nuclear weapons, deployed in what manner and where, will be considered necessary to fulfill this first minimum role.

A second role seems equally unlikely to vanish: it is a minimal form of extended deterrence - what McGeorge Bundy might call 'minimum existential extended deterrence'. It is not easy to define it accurately and in a way that avoids misunderstanding but one can try. As long as one or more members of the Alliance possess nuclear weapons (and that will be for quite a while), it is extremely unlikely that sane Soviet leaders could somehow become confident that they could inflict a crushing, humiliating, devastating defeat on even one member of the Alliance, using totally conventional means, and not run a substantial risk that the United States, or the United Kingdom, or France would come to the aid of that ally with nuclear weapons in order to prevent that defeat.

There are major uncertainties here. What exactly would constitute a 'crushing defeat'? Who would define it? Would the intervention come in time? And so forth. But these are healthy uncertainties. They leave Soviet leaders healthily uncertain, unable to say to each other with high confidence that there is no risk of a nuclear war developing from some conventional adventure which might at some moment look tempting to some of them. That would remain true even if the prescription of the Gang of Four were adopted and NATO renounced first use.[2] But it looks somewhat 'more true' (if there is such a thing) as long as NATO has not explicitly given up first use, which is why the Gang of Four is not likely to prevail. And it is true even if none of the Western nuclear powers specifically promises (or threatens) such first use on behalf of an ally or of the Alliance.

Thus there is today a 'minimum' French nuclear umbrella extended over the Federal Republic, whether France promises it (which France probably will not do) or promises not to extend it (which France certainly will not do) or develops even more elaborate, intricate, obscure, self-contradictory, and yet marvellously lucid and elegant formulations of the policies and doctrines governing the *force de frappe* (which France can be counted on to do). All of these French, British and American variants of nuclear doctrine are, seen from Moscow, simply varying degrees of uncertainty. Even a small degree of uncertainty is an utterly enormous deterrent where nuclear weapons are involved, and that uncertainty is there, utterly ineluctable, as long as the weapons exist, hence the transcendent importance of Mr. Bundy's insight into 'existential deterrence', along with the relative unimportance of whether his prescription on no first use is followed or its objectives are achieved in some less contentious manner.

One may conclude then that nuclear weapons,

whether in Europe or in the oceans or in the national territory of one of the Western nuclear powers, have and will long retain these two roles: deterring Soviet first use and discouraging a major Soviet adventure aimed at one of the members of the Alliance.

There remains the third role for nuclear weapons in Europe: to provide a remedy for shortcomings in the ability to defend Europe with conventional weapons against conventional attack. That is where most of the controversy has rightly centred and where most work needs to be done. One can only note the growing consensus that this third role must decline sharply and visibly during the remaining years of this decade and should approach the zero level, both in fact and in NATO's declaratory posture, as we go into the nineties. These battlefield weapons may not have lost their ability to deter; but in Michael Howard's terms, they have 'lost their ability to re-assure', and that is a fact to which political leaders cannot responsibly fail to respond.[3]

This essay concludes with a word on the fourth basic proposition, with particular reference to Canada. There must be an active, determined effort to negotiate problems with the Soviet Union, both those relating to military establishments and what the Palme Commission rightly called 'common security',[4] and also those political problems, whether in Europe or elsewhere, which could under unfavourable circumstances develop into crises and East-West confrontations.

Unless serious, sustained efforts are made to develop negotiated solutions - or at least mitigations - for all these problems, public opinion and leaders in a number of countries of the Alliance will lose confidence; the allies will begin to criticise and quarrel with each other; and in time the political cohesion which lies at the foundation of the Alliance will be damaged.

That has not happened yet, but it is clear that the negotiating track is not in good shape. The Soviets have behaved very badly and the administration in Washington has managed its end of the enterprise in a way which falls well short of perfection. Things are not so bad, however, in multilateral forums. No 'ice age' has descended on East-West relations in Europe.

Canada is particularly well placed to be helpful in this matter. Canadians know Americans well, their strengths and their shortcomings. A

Mexican Foreign Minister once remarked that if one had to be located next to a superpower, then his ancestors had made the right choice. Most Canadians would probably agree. The strength of Canadian friendship for the United States, combined with the vigour of Canadian independence, open up possibilities for some real contributions from Canada. Prime Minister Trudeau saw and acted on this opening and hopefully he will continue to do so as a private citizen.

There are two areas where Canada could be particularly helpful. One is the revision of NATO arrangements regarding the role of battlefield nuclear weapons. It has both a unilateral NATO side and an aspect involving the Soviets, who ought to be making adjustments in their own doomsday machine, perhaps pursuant to agreements with the United States, as suggested by the Palme Commission. As a non-European power with troops but not nuclear weapons in Europe, Canada has unusual possibilities for objective analysis and diplomatic activity. Canada is also well placed to draw attention to the contributions which arms control, in MBFR and in the CDE, can make to raising the nuclear threshold in Europe.If one looks objectively at the full range of possibilities and problems, one could well conclude that more can be done through this means, and done more rapidly and cheaply, than through most of the other approaches which are under consideration for raising this famous threshold.

The second area on which Canadians might focus involves out-of-area problems. How to reduce the dangers of East-West confrontations in Third World areas is an analytic desert and a diplomatic no-man's-land. Better structures and procedures are desperately needed and are nowhere in sight. The United Nations role clearly needs re-thinking and re-invigorating. Regional structures are woefully weak.

The fact that Canada has taken so seriously the basic problem of economic development in the Third World gives it the standing to contribute to the solution of these difficult political and security problems. If Canada will take it on, one can hardly doubt that its scholars and diplomats will find themselves fully occupied at least through the eighties and nineties, that is to say, through the eighties and nineties of the twenty-first century.

Notes

1. Cited in Freeman Dyson. Weapons and Hope, (Harper and Row Publishers, New York, 1984), pp. 34-35.

2. McGeorge Bundy, George F. Kennan, Robert S. McNamara and Gerard Smith, 'Nuclear Weapons and the Atlantic Alliance', Foreign Affairs, vol. 60, no. 4, (Spring, 1982), pp. 753-768.

3. Michael Howard, 'Reassurance and Deterrence: Western Defense in the 1980s', Foreign Affairs, vol. 61, no. 2, (Winter, 1982/83), pp. 309-324.

4. Common Security: A Blueprint for Survival. The Report of the Independent Commission on Disarmament and Security Issues, (Simon and Schuster, New York, 1982).

Chapter Seven

DISQUIET ON THE WESTERN FRONT: AN INQUIRY INTO THE CURRENT DISTEMPER

Lawrence S. Hagen

Crying wolf over the state of NATO's deterrence posture is a somewhat happy, if not glorious, pastime for those preoccupied with matters strategic. In the absence of problems - indeed crises - in Alliance security, that most secretly feared state of affairs - complete security and transatlantic bliss - would deprive many of their livelihoods : the marketing of imminent insecurity and Alliance rupture. Inventing diseases and defining cures for what is asserted to be an Alliance on the verge of yet another collapse is as familiar a part of the landscape as NATO itself, and just as old.

Yet the familiarity of this phenomenon and the frequency of such analyses should not blind us to the possibility, as Pierre Hassner has put it, that 'this time, the wolf is here!'[1] Indeed, it is amongst those most preoccupied with Alliance problems that there often exists an unstated supposition that things are not as serious as they seem, or as serious as the analysts themselves have asserted, (often for reasons of professional survival or notoriety). An obvious first order question, therefore, but one which is all too often ignored - or assumed - is the degree to which there actually exists an illness requiring treatment. This might avoid the unhealthy tendency to prescribe 'a cure that lacks a disease, a wonder drug in search of a pathology'.[2] The focus of such an inquiry lies not simply in asking whether or not the correct answers are being given to specific questions, but whether or not the right questions are being asked at all.

To this end, two connected sets of issues need to be addressed. The first relates to the nature of the alleged crisis in the Alliance nuclear posture;

the second to the required curative basis for whatever state of affairs is deemed to exist. Concerning the former, there is the simple question of whether or not, despite obvious similarities, the current 'crisis' is 'new' or 'old'. In connection with this, are we witnessing a temporary fluctuation in the normal collective psychology of a democratic alliance of states, or are we watching the working through of a series of structural trends whose effects may be truly revolutionary in their consequences? In addition, while there is little doubt that the current locus of controversy - and of proposed solutions - lies in the realm of NATO's nuclear posture, it is well worth asking whether or not this flurry of protest and analysis addresses the core problem. In other words, are the issues 'strategic', in the narrow sense, or do they reflect trends more geographical and psychological in nature? And even if they are strategic, are they <u>European</u> in cause or merely the result of global problems whose <u>effect</u> is continental?

Only when these questions are answered can one evince some confidence that the current state of affairs is a failure of tactics, of strategy or of conception or in fact, the inevitable result of disruptive and uncontrollable secular trends. And only then can one begin to define sensible criteria for a curative approach. In the absence of such an inquiry, the metaphor of the blind men and the elephant becomes apposite, as does the more serious danger that while devising cures to the ills of NATO approaches the status of a growth industry, the wrong product is being sold for the wrong reasons.

The Symptoms of Change

The first question that must be asked, therefore, is what, if anything, has changed to make this period any different from the myriad others which have led observers to note that 'the history of the Atlantic Alliance is a history of crises.'[3]

After all, differences over nuclear policy and doctrine form part of the <u>leitmotif</u> of Alliance behaviour, and indeed the process of working through these controversies has served to re-assure each side of the Atlantic of the constancy and commitment of the other. The question may be approached at two levels. First, do there exist phenomena or attitudes which in either their nature or degree are qualitatively different from previous periods of Alliance trauma? And second, what trends, if any, can be identified which might assist in explaining the emergence of such phenomena?

Concerning the first, it is undeniably the case that the degree and extent of disquiet amongst European publics has reached unprecedented proportions. While vigorous campaigns for nuclear disarmament attracted many Britons in the 1960s, the recent activism surrounding the INF deployment programme is both continental in its dimensions (excluding as always, France) and mass in its nature. It is often pointed out by those who seek to play down the significance of this movement that it is neither mass nor a movement. This misses the point. What is particularly troublesome about the current situation is not that there exists a <u>single</u> political or ideological group whose energies are focused on the nuclear question, but precisely that so <u>many</u> political, cultural, and ideological forces have converged upon this issue in a formidable display of intellectual and emotional consensus.

It is also argued by some that since European public opinion polls consistently demonstrate majority support for NATO, the degree of discontent has been exaggerated both by an over-zealous (and sympathetic) media, and by timid and politically vulnerable political leaders. This too misses the point. While support for NATO is generally strong, this is not matched by support for specific programmes and policies which historically have formed the substance of the Alliance relationship. Approval in principle but disapproval in practice is not a particularly healthy sign. Similarly, the playing down of opposition on the basis that it is not a majority view ignores a familiar phenomenon of modern pluralistic democracies: 'moral majorities' which, though little more than highly influential minorities, shape government policies, effect the wider climate of public opinion, and reflect a more generalised social angst.

This leads to a second symptom which points in the direction of the severity and novelty of the current Alliance distemper: the fracturing of the political consensus amongst political parties on NATO policy. While Alliance defence policy has never been immune to political controversy, this has always been conducted within certain broadly defined limits. The events of recent months and years have disrupted this pattern. In Britain, the Labour Party has swung to a stance of virtual neutralism and unilateralism. In the Low Countries, opposition parties have criticised Alliance policy as never before. And in Germany, most significantly, the broad political consensus on Alliance matters has been broken for the first time since the 1960s.[4] It is little consolation that governments in power, with the exception of Greece, and perhaps the Netherlands, have thus far supported NATO INF policy, when it is all too easy to foresee an alteration of this political landscape during the next series of European elections. It is equally troublesome to observe that these trends threaten to turn European support for NATO policy into a right wing phenomenon. And finally, while the INF programme may go ahead as planned (although Dutch and Belgian fidelity is by no means assured) the political effect of this process has been nothing short of remarkable: for the foreseeable future, NATO will not be able to arrive at any equivalent nuclear modernisation decision.

What seems to have evolved is a situation where there is a growing distance between European leaders and their parties and publics, as opposed to previously when differences of opinion were primarily between American leaders and their European counterparts, in a context of relatively quiescent publics. This points to a new quality in Alliance affairs: nuclear matters have become a mass concern rather than a purely intramural elite preoccupation, a trend which poses serious questions for the ability of the Alliance to 'manage' its publics, as opposed to simply accommodating different national (governmental) interests and perspectives.

A third aspect of the current situation is equally important. During the late 1950s and early 1960s while disarmament movements flourished, the mood was profoundly different from that currently in evidence. In the earlier period, approaches to such episodes as the Berlin Crises reflected a general recognition of, and confidence in, United States strategic superiority, and agreement that the Soviets were the real bullies on the block. There now exists, however, a schizophrenic attitude which simultaneously holds two logically incompatible views. The United States is seen as both unlikely to come to Europe's assistance in a context of strategic nuclear parity, and all too likely to do precisely that in an age of tailored nuclear weapons effects and widely trumpeted limited nuclear options.

This specific attitude to United States security guarantees is embedded in a broader view of the United States as a real 'threat' to world peace and Western (European) values. Societal groups which have no memory of past continental wars, and little memory of continental crises, but which possess vivid 'memories' of Vietnam reinforced by more recent American military endeavours and domestic strife and corruption, have shied away from, or even rejected, the 'American model'. This is sometimes coupled with a generalised but highly significant rejection of the economic and social ideals represented by modern Western civilisation as a whole. Rejection of nuclear weapons, in this instance, is a rejection not of nuclear weapons *per se*, but of nuclear weapons as the highest 'achievement' of modern industrial society.

Germany is, to some extent, a special case. For compounding all of the above is a widespread revulsion against Germany's violent - and submerged - past and what is seen as its smug, materialist and conservative present. This critical mood is supplemented by a romantic yearning for a new idealistic Germany on a mission of peaceful emancipation. The Soviet threat, to the extent that it is acknowledged by these groups, is neatly counterbalanced by an American 'threat', and by a generalised avoidance of any positive attitude towards, or attention to, the instruments and mechanisms of Alliance defence.

Here, once again, a schizophrenic view can be detected. The realities of security policy are either ignored or assumed away, since war is seen as a distant possibility, or a certain obsessive/compulsive attitude is manifested which sees war as virtually upon us. Indeed, as Michael Howard has observed, fear of nuclear war has become independent of the political conflict behind it. To many, the East-West conflict 'barely appears as a problem connected to the potential use of nuclear weapons'.[5] The romantic vision of a new Germany, coupled with the terror of imminent holocaust, yields a certain escapism which seeks to resolve itself through an act of collective will.

Finally, a most disturbing reflection of the depth of the current malaise, one which indicates that its cause may lie in the particular context which Europe finds itself in the 1980s, is the degree to which these trends in viewpoint and mood have *not* been matched by parallel developments in the United States. While the nuclear 'freeze' and associated movements have grown in the United States, these reflect less a rejection of the central assumptions of Western security than a more measured protest against specific, perceived excesses of the current United States administration. Perhaps just as noteworthy, however, is the degree to which the United States disarmament movement is a response to an arguably stronger movement towards United States global activism. This movement in turn, has evinced a new and perhaps unprecedented frustration with the lack of European willingness to join in America's (re-)discovered mission. Although this should not be overstated, what is significant here, as Philip Windsor observes, is that 'no longer is Europe pre-occupied with its traditional chronic discussions of whether, and in what manner, the United States would come to Europe's aid; the US is now beginning to wonder if Europe is worth defending.'[6]

These disturbing and divergent trends reflect the parallel unrealisms which characterise European and American perspectives at this critical juncture in Alliance relations. The American illusion, notes Pierre Hassner, is that one can return to the cold war of the 1950s. The European illusion is that one can return to the detente of the 1970s.[7] While Americans wonder if Europe is willing to defend _anything_, Europeans fear that America is all too willing to defend _everything_, and to do so in situations which have very little to do with Europe's real interests. This is connected to a feeling of helplessness, of lack of control, where an ungovernable and unpredictable world may lead to war not _caused_ by Europe, but _fought_ in Europe.

The Context of Change

The symptomatology just outlined serves to indicate that the deterrent distemper affecting the Alliance is both new and serious. Commentators and analysts seeking revisions in NATO doctrine are responding to - or should be responding to - these wider socio-cultural developments as much as they are to 'objective' military criteria which would suggest the wisdom or necessity of doctrinal or postural review. For it would seem clear that while there are specific East-West deterrent issues deserving of attention, the current situation is as much a West-West as it is an East-West phenomenon. To use Michael Howard's formulation, the task of Alliance planners is now, more than ever, to focus on the requirements of _re-assurance_ as well as the requirements of deterrence. Or, as Christoph

Bertram succinctly puts it, 'deterrence is only credible if it frightens the adversary more than it does one's own population.'[8]

What is important to note here is that those who would suggest that renovations to NATO's posture or doctrine do so generally from one of two very different perspectives. For some, NATO's problems are military and strategic, pure and simple. Applying a technical, tactical, or doctrinal 'fix' to the current East-West military context is necessary to enhance the credibility of the Alliance deterrent posture. The evaluative criteria applied relate to the degree to which specific solutions address known military problems within acceptable budgetary and political limits. The re-assurance component of deterrence policy is either ignored, since it is ultimately irrelevant to hard military reality, or else it is assumed to naturally fall out of successful military and strategic programmes.

This approach can be detected at various points in the 'defence-ideological' spectrum - all the way from those who seek to integrate Europe into an 'Assured Survival' posture to those who advocate such doctrinal tinkerings as 'No Early First Use' or 'No Second Use Until'. In this connection, it is not coincidental that those, such as Robert MacNamara, who sought a 'rational' solution to the doctrinal mess of the ealy 1960s now seek a doctrinal fix to the current malaise. While the precise nature of the prescriptions vary, they proceed from a similar concept of the salutary social effects of doctrinal engineering.

For others, issues of war-fighting and defence are not ignored, but seen as secondary. Faults in NATO's doctrine or posture are found not so much because they provide the Soviet Union with opportunities which can be exploited politically or militarily, but because these faults are deemed to further undo the transatlantic societal consensus which has hitherto buttressed NATO. A 'deterrent solution' is required to resolve a 're-assurance problem'. In the familiar formulation of a successful deterrence policy, 'capabilities' are to be upgraded or altered so as to bolster the (collective) 'will'. The focus is inward-looking as opposed to outward-looking.

While it is not the contention of this author that the first perspective is irrelevant, it is suggested that a successful approach requires a marriage of both perspectives. And since the second approach, that which sees the essential task as one of re-assurance, is both the least understood and the most difficult to grapple with successfully, it is to these issues that this paper now turns.

In this connection, assessing the ability of particular alterations in Alliance doctrine to cauterise the transatlantic rift over nuclear policy must be preceded by an analysis of what exactly has 'gone wrong'. What has occurred to create such concern over the political if not strategic decoupling of Europe from America, and the decoupling of European governments from large sectors of their societies?

There are, of course, real differences of assessment and of interest which might explain, in a rational manner, the divergence in viewpoints between America and Europe. Whether or not a specific military programme (the SS-20 or the SS-21/22/ and 23) is seen as representative of Soviet aggressive intent is a legitimate object of debate, as are different assessments of whether or not a specific regional conflict (Central America, Afghanistan or Grenada) should be viewed as 'local' in cause and significance or as a dangerous illustration of Soviet expansionism and of shifts in the global balance of power.

Similarly there are very real differences in objective interests between Europe and America. In the case of Poland, greater European caution can be explained by the greater economic and human interest which Europe has in maintaining East European ties. And while the United States may interpret differences over deterrence as resulting from European timidity or a lack of appreciation of deterrence 'reality', Europe has quite understandably pointed to its disaffection with the idea of becoming a war zone for the third time in this century.

There may be, however, a more fundamental process at work here, one which would support the thesis that the current malaise is not simply a repetition of previous and entirely manageable episodes of diverging Alliance analysis and tactical choice. This is the far more elusive realm of _attitudes_ and _moods_. As one observer notes:

> On a rational level, interests are more common than conflicting as between the two sides of the Atlantic, and some kind of consensus on the nature of the common threat and the best strategy to meet it should not be impossible to reach. But these very perspectives and strategies cannot help but be differently

> interpreted on the basis of deep-seated differences in attitude, themselves based on differing historical experiences, leading to differing shades in each side's feeling of security or vulnerability.[9]

This may assist in explaining why in the past, East-West crises (Cuba, Berlin, Czechoslovakia, etc.) ultimately acted to create Alliance unity, whereas now they threaten to split the Alliance. And why such crises threaten to disrupt the Alliance more than differences over detente policy and regional conflicts, which hitherto have proven far more troublesome.

What may be at work here are two trends. In the United States a new global unilateralism is emerging, while in Europe, there is a trend at work, since 1945, to ignore the imperatives of power, and to refuse at all costs to run any risks of confrontation. As Stanley Hoffmann notes 'the dramas of the 1970s have affected Europeans and Americans differently. Americans seem to want to "stop being pushed around",... West Europeans concentrate on their domestic troubles.'[10]

In a self-described uncharitable depiction of the Europeans, Hassner writes:

> Very often an apparent optimism about (Soviet intentions) hides a deeper pessimism about one's self.... One is committed to the more reassuring interpretation of Soviet policies precisely because, deep down, one feels one cannot afford to act on the implications of the more worrying one.[11]

What this implies, in practical terms, is that for Washington, detente and arms control are gifts to be given. For Europeans, they are duties to be pursued.

This divergence in attitudes explains why nuclear weapons have become so controversial and so central to West-West relations. For nuclear weapons represent, in concrete form, the nature of the dependence of Western Europe for its security on a state far away, of whom West Europeans feel they know increasingly little.

There may be some lessons here. Those who in 1979 felt a technical fix to the theatre nuclear balance would generate trust and confidence between the two sides of the Atlantic should by now realise that trust is causal and not consequential. 'Nuclear weapons require trust in the security partnership if they are to be politically acceptable; if that trust is absent, they will be seen as disturbing rather than reassuring.'[12]

Similarly, those who would seek a technical fix in reverse by, for example, a withdrawal of some number of short-range nuclear systems and/or the deployment of high tech conventional munitions, must also realise that it is not the *precise* state of the balance, or the *precise* characteristics, numbers, and location of nuclear weapons which exercises Europeans. It is the existence of nuclear weapons *per se*, located on European territory, controlled by another state, in the context of a recognised inability on the part of Europe to defend itself.

This sensitivity has been accentuated by several related trends in technology, doctrine, and arms control. The first is the oft noted emergence of parity between the superpowers. This parity heightened European concerns during the SALT II process, leading ultimately to the German request for the consideration of theatre systems in some forum and in some manner. This request was made in the name of coupling. But it was this same parity which came to heighten these concerns even further, precisely because the prayers were answered. What was once coupling came to be seen by many as decoupling. Clearly, the Alliance can no longer ignore the fact of geopolitical asymmetry and regional imbalance when the great leveller of United States strategic superiority has evaporated.

The second trend relates to doctrine and technology. As parity has evolved, both superpowers have grappled with the problem of credible threat generation through the multiplication of technological and doctrinal options at increasingly lower levels of violence. For the United States, the drift in this direction has been particularly obvious in the context of the geopolitical and regional factors referred to above. What has been developed, since the 1970s, are doctrines and technologies adopted for both strategic and regional purposes which the United States feels *must* be presented in terms which at least imply the possibility of damage limitation, threat leverage, and escalation dominance. According to this view:

> Since extended deterrence consists of a scale of political contexts of increasing importance and a related set of deterring options of increasing intensity, it is necessary at any given level to have available the technological

> capability to threaten and ultimately deprive an opponent of any gains that he might seek through unacceptable action. This is the essence of escalation dominance, and without it no credible form of extended deterrence is possible.[13]

What is most disturbing here is that while for one set of reasons the superpowers feel an increasing need to make explicit the subtle distinctions which comprise extended deterrence, particularly in the case of the United States there is a contrary requirement to simultaneously argue that such weapons should never be used. This latter point, however, is increasingly lost on a Europe attuned as never before to developments in nuclear technology, and which is unprepared to believe in United States sincerity. A central problem for the re-assuring extension of deterrence, therefore, is how to make the deterrent threat more plausible without thereby making it appear to be more threatening.[14]

This tension has been accentuated by a tendency in Europe to respond to trends in American strategic policy by retreating into simple statements asserting the permanent and seamless nature of deterrence. In consequence, America is seen by Europeans as unilaterally moving away from the historical basis of Alliance nuclear policy.

Another trend relates to developments in arms control. While in the 1960s and 1970s politicians and publics looked to arms control as a means of bringing technological and doctrinal symmetry to the superpower strategic relationship and to render it more predictable in the process, precisely the opposite has occurred. Arms control as practised during the past decade has been unable to erase, or in some cases even accommodate, the asymmetrical doctrinal, technical and geopolitical factors which both reflect and determine superpower views of the precise nature of stability and deterrence. Indeed, it has accentuated these differences through the logic and practice of bargaining, as each side tries to accommodate real imbalances in a notional balance and to reduce the advantages of the other side through the application of equal ceilings and limits. The inability of arms control to accommodate these realities resulted initially in charges of betrayal and public denouncements of attempts to seek unilateral advantage, leading ultimately to the somewhat cynical and entirely second order approach of the current United States administration to arms control.

What is the relevance of all this to the question of Alliance nuclear policy? First, as the purvue of arms control has expanded to the European theatre, indeed, perhaps entity, arms control, with its demands for equality and its underlying assumptions of nuclear sufficiency, has been unable to cope with the very different demands of escalation dominance noted earlier. It has also been unable to accommodate the very different doctrinal and geopolitical factors which characterise superpower nuclear approaches to Europe. Thus arms control is held out as a promise, as in the 1979 INF decision, and subsequently fails, with all the attendant recriminations.

This relates to a second point. For at a time when arms control is seen by Washington as secondary to the pursuit of strategic force modernisation, it is considered even more important to a Europe gripped by the nuclear angst so readily apparent. Precisely those trends in strategic and geopolitical reality which have made Washington less enamoured of arms control have rendered Europeans more attached.

A further point relates less to trends in doctrine than to trends in strategic rhetoric. There is a peculiar and disturbing symmetry between those in Europe most distressed by nuclear weapons and those in the United States, often at the other end of the political spectrum, who argue that unless significant military programmes are instituted, America faces certain strategic deficit. Those who argue that 'victory is possible' imply that unless certain steps are taken, 'defeat is certain'. This ascription of inferiority and 'high noon' around the corner displays the same exaggerated view of the fragility of deterrence as that held by those in Europe who care little for the precise mechanisms of deterrence, feeling more strongly that no form of deterrence is plausible any more.

The interaction between these viewpoints has been destructive of the fabric of extended deterrence, all the more so since it has been supplemented by statements from former Secretaries of State and Defense that the United States nuclear guarantee is incredible, and Presidential alarms about a dangerous decline in United States power. As always, Europe cares less about the precise state of the strategic balance than what the United States defines that state to be.

The calls for baroque choreographies of war

which have emanated from certain quarters in the United States point to a trend which may bode ill for the Alliance. What was once a relatively healthy but unavoidably illogical mixture of the irrational and rational has been transformed through technological change and associated rationalist thought into a Ptolemaic monster. What McGeorge Bundy has labelled the existential nature of deterrence has been submerged in a circular chase to develop doctrines which make 'sense' of evolving technology and to develop technologies which can fulfill the declared requirements of doctrine.

For extended deterrence, the problem lies in the interaction between these trends in thought and technology, on the one hand, and the emerging European frame of mind on the other. Historically, Europe has always demanded empirical proof of the United States commitment to Europe. Hence an INF force was chosen which, because of its land-based nature, is non-migratory. In a context of United States strategic superiority and relative European agreement with the American view of the world, such proof was satisfactory, although periodic re-affirmation was necessary. In a context when United States superiority has dissipated, and Europe displays little confidence in the content or constancy of United States policy, such proof can, and has, backfired. Europe demands re-assurance, but is disturbed when that re-assurance is delivered. What deterrence logic would suggest is coupling is seen by Europe as decoupling. This effect is doubled when policy and rhetoric address in an explicit and unprecedented manner the escalatory 'requirements' of deterrence, and when the United States appears to lack a coherent and strong vision of a complementary <u>political</u> strategy for co-existing with the Soviet Union. What this means is that the United States is providing the (necessary?) nuclear elements of a bolstered credibility to a Europe increasingly unwilling to believe because of an overarching perceived insecurity.

Josef Joffe, in a recent article, argues trenchantly in favour of the existing Alliance framework:

> By sparing the West Europeans the necessity of an autonomous choice in matters of defense, the US removed the systemic cause of conflict that had underlain so many of Europe's past wars.... States do not coalesce to ensure their security but, in the case of Europe, because their

> security was assured.[15]

Joffe goes on to note, however, the inevitable discomfort which such a state of affairs implies:

> When the existential crunch comes, no country is likely to risk its survival on behalf of another. Therefore, no country, if given a choice, will entrust its physical survival to another.... Nuclear weapons are thus intrinsically divisive rather than integrationist in their implications.[16]

However valid this perspective is, Joffe concludes that the current state of affairs is inevitable, that the alternatives are worse, and that NATO can continue to hold hands across the nuclear divide. While the <u>logic</u> of deterrence may imply a lack of credibility, the Soviet Union is unlikely to face the real risks of the nuclear game.

While such a sanguine assessment is plausible, it may miss the point. The task of Alliance nuclear management faces both East <u>and</u> West. And what may make sense for perfectly good historical or logical reasons may begin to stop making sense for 'illogical' and 'unhistorical' reasons. As noted earlier, the viability of flexible response is a function both of re-assurance and deterrence; success in the latter field cannot be purchased - forever - at the price of the former.

The Criteria for Change

What does the above imply for the substance and direction of future NATO doctrine and force posture? Above all else, it suggests what should <u>not</u> be done, and what will <u>not</u> work in terms of enhancing Alliance self-confidence.

First, while it is claimed by some that NATO doctrine - in the declaratory sense - does not 'make sense' and requires greater clarity, the foregoing analysis would suggest that any attempt at greater formal clarity would be folly. Although the formal structure of flexible response remains intact, excessive analytical preoccupations with escalatory scenarios, and public pronouncements by officials, in and out of office, have already conferred too much 'clarity' for the system to handle.

Striving for logical coherence and predictability in an inherently illogical and irrational deterrence context is, one would hope, a mistake the lessons of which would have been learned by all by now. If massive retaliation was dysfunctional in the 1950s, and the initial attempts by Secretary McNamara to erect a structure of explicit counterforce doctrine in the 1960s were rebuffed, surely a functional equivalent in the 1980s would be greeted even less warmly. While there may be unhappiness with flexible response, this is nothing compared to the trauma the Alliance would experience in a debate over where to <u>then</u> move.

This points to a second, closely connected conclusion. There is, simply stated, no practical alternative to flexible response. Flexible response, in any case, is not really a doctrine, but a compromise, a vacuum less significant for what it says than for what it does not say. While modifications in its <u>operational</u> content may make good military sense, these can, and must, proceed under the banner of MC 14/3. There are really only two alternatives: a return to Massive Retaliation and the adoption of a doctrine providing a clear choreography of war. The former would not be credible, and the latter would be politically unsustainable in the Alliance, in addition to being, arguably, militarily foolish. When clarity has proven so disruptive and its credibility is so questionable, moving further down this road would be suicidal.

Of course, there is one other alternative: a nuclear-free Europe which relies entirely on its own resources and escapes from the traumas of flexible response by refusing to play the nuclear game altogether. This would represent a desperate move of the most extreme variety. Unless the Alliance is willing to take the cosmic risk that the Soviet Union will always <u>choose</u> not to attack, NATO must rely on the threat of escalation. Indeed, as capabilities multiply on the Eastern side, the burden of NATO credibility increasingly falls on such a threat, as the specific sub-strategic balances worsen.

Purely declaratory addenda to flexible response might be equally misguided. The fad for no first use is particularly troublesome. A declaratory NFU declaration will not fool attentive publics unless accompanied by radical reductions in the nuclear stockpile. And such a declaration might be strategically dangerous. It is not that Moscow would be any more likely to attack as a result of a NATO Communique espousing no first use. It is rather that NATO publics would be increasingly restive with the continued presence of large numbers of nuclear weapons on their soil, and would continually exert pressure to reduce NATO's arsenal to what was the most minimum of minimum deterrent forces.

Such a declaration would also preclude any future nuclear force modernisation decisions, even if these were designed to move NATO forces on precisely the directions implied by NFU: a deterrence-only posture. Large sectors of NATO publics have great difficulty in accepting that new (and inevitably more sophisticated) weapons are anything other than dangerous weapons.

The unsatisfactory dilemma represented by NFU is, therefore, clear. A declaratory NFU could generate fears of no United States commitment to Western Europe, particularly if this were seen as an American-inspired initiative. A <u>real</u> NFU posture, on the other hand, would be tantamount to the reality of no United States commitment. It is difficult indeed to see how overall European concerns would be addressed by adopting a purely conventional posture designed to deter Soviet conventional attack without at least the possibility of escalation to levels which would directly threaten central Soviet values.

The absence of <u>any</u> rungs on the ladder between conventional defence and, say, long-range theatre nuclear forces targeted on Soviet military-industrial centres, would be intolerable to Washington. Such a posture would be obviously escalatory and 'inflexible', incredible to Moscow for the same reasons, and discomforting to Europeans aware of obvious American interests in avoiding immediate, central strategic war.

There are, however, 'intermediate' options which satisfy the criteria of strategic sense and retain the desirable and necessary aspects of extended deterrence and flexible response. The first is the withdrawal of large numbers of NATO's forward-based short-range nuclear systems. Not only do these not conform to the requirements of any sensible strategic or tactical doctrine; they invite pre-emption by both conventional and nuclear means, particularly in the context of improved Soviet strike capabilities. And through inviting pre-emption, they increase Soviet and NATO first-strike incentives and instabilities.[17]

Such a move should, however, be made bearing in mind two caveats. First, not all short-range systems should be renewed. Small numbers of properly deployed and modern weapons can serve real battle-field purposes. In addition, an option for limited battlefield response is still needed as noted above, not merely for battlefield purposes, but also for signalling and escalating functions below long-range levels. Moreover, since Europeans, especially Germans, have seen short-range systems as symbolic of the United States guarantee to Europe and to forward defence for so long, a rapid and precipitous withdrawal would be highly disconcerting.

And second, NATO must ensure that it has a viable and invulnerable nuclear capacity for second-strike use. In the absence of such a capability, there would be virtually no escalatory option below the level of strategic exchange. And such a capability, of course, would have an inherent capacity for first use, should the need arise, and would be seen as such in Moscow.

Bearing these considerations in mind, such a development would go a long way towards remedying a highly undesirable state of affairs. As Johan Holst has argued, high dependence on early use has limited the availability of repeatable responses to warning and has raised the threshold against implementation. A doctrine based on possible early use, moreover, when coupled with a posture of vulnerability, could invite pre-emption rather than convey determination.[18]

Such revisions in NATO posture should be pursued along with improvements in conventional forces. It would be folly indeed to evade NATO's nuclear reliance without at the same time increasing conventional forces. In the absence of the latter, a move towards a more deterrence-dominant nuclear posture would have the effect of shifting the burden of proof to an even less credible level of deterrent threat. Once again, however, new conventional technologies must not be seen as a panacea. (Over and above geographical considerations, as Leon Sigal points out, 'how can NATO enhance deterrence by a threat that, however more likely to be carried out, reduces potential damage to the Soviet Union?'[19])

Conventional improvements must be seen, therefore, as simply raising the nuclear threshold, not removing that threshold altogether. The reality and threat of escalation with its attendant requirements for a range (perhaps smaller) of theatre-based nuclear weapons must remain.

In addition, new conventional technologies pose particular problems of their own. It is at this point unclear if they can and will perform as advertised. Even if they do, however, a high tech battlefield could be highly escalatory in its consequences. Although logic might indicate that the threshold has been raised, the pace of battle might demonstrate that it in fact has been lowered.

In addition, there are questions as to: the ability of any C^3 structure to accommodate the data requirements of effective high technology forces; the implications of such forces for NATO's consultative process (would a deep conventional strike require consultation?); the question of Soviet attitudes to deep-strike conventional attacks (would they care if they are non-nuclear?); and the additional question of whether Soviet early warning capabilities would, in fact, be able to identify an imminent conventional attack using ambiguous technologies. If not, Soviet pre-emption or nuclear escalation might occur.[20]

Over and above these questions, however, are structural problems which afflict most West European states. Can significant, or even marginal, sustained expenditure on conventional force improvements be anticipated at a time when NATO countries are having great difficulty warding off attempts to cut existing expenditures, and when the capital expenditure components of defence budgets are at an all time high? Concerning the latter, would new capital acquisitions cut into arguably more important expenditures on training, ammunition, logistics, C^3, sealift, maintenance, and reserves?

Such concerns are not designed to cast doubts on the wisdom of any exploitation of new conventional technologies, merely to suggest that the introduction of such technologies should be approached in a sober and cautious manner, linked closely with the alterations in NATO's nuclear posture noted above. It is important to note, moreover, that the uncomfortable but inevitable dilemmas of deterrence will remain. Escalation will remain a possibility, and the desirability of maintaining a credible nuclear threat should be obvious. There is simply no alternative. Therefore, permanent divergence of interest between an independent Europe and a protecting America in questions relating to nuclear use will not go away. This would indicate that these suggested alterations in NATO posture should be regarded as sensible military modifications directed at ensuring a more effective defence and a bolstered theatre stability, rather than as a means of lifting the social-psychological cloud which exists over nuclear weapons in NATO.

Are there, however, other options, other

changes of a short and long-term nature which might address in a more effective and enduring fashion this more serious existential problem? It should be noted that in arguing the importance of perceptions (of re-assurance), one is not arguing against the importance of 'military reality'. One is merely suggesting that in order for 'military reality' to be looked at seriously by all Alliance governments and publics, perceptions have to be addressed. Based on the analysis presented in this paper, the following may serve as guidelines to what is desirable in this area.

First, a prerequisite to the development of European confidence in the firmness, flexibility and prudence of the United States is the cessation of the excessive and irresponsible musings by public figures on plausible nuclear war-fighting scenarios. While it is misguided for some to object to the reality that for deterrence to work nuclear weapons must have a demonstrable capacity for use, it is equally misguided to concentrate on that which is anathema to many Europeans: consideration of a failed deterrence system.

Second, and more importantly, it is unlikely that confidence in United States leadership in Europe will be restored in the absence of the restoration of trust in United States global behaviour. It is certainly too much to ask Europe, possessed of different interests, obligations and attitudes to mimic American priorities. It is equally unrealistic to ask America, as a superpower, to conform to the inward-looking parochialism of Western Europe. Between these two extremes, however, there is a requirement that the United States recognise that for Europe there is no choice between reliance on defence, on the one hand, and co-operation with the East, on the other. As one observer has noted: 'the lesson of the interwar period is that conciliation not backed by strength is a flawed policy; the lesson of the years before World War I is that strength without conciliation is no better.'[21] If, in European eyes, United States policy does not recognise this mixture of strategies, then the perceived risks of association with Washington will induce reluctance to incur obligations and accept programmes (including nuclear programmes) which are seen as part of a misguided global policy. Only when American policy recognises this fact is it realistic to expect that each side will recognise the legitimacy of the perspective and priorities of the other.

Third, given the inherent tensions of a strategy of extended deterrence in the context of strategic parity, it is time for NATO to recognise the desirability - and to some extent the inevitability - of diluting the tortuous logic of a bipolar deterrent structure in Europe. This implies moving cautiously but consciously towards a multilateralised Western deterrence framework. As Pierre Hassner notes, 'everyone knows that a European nuclear defence is impossible today, and everybody feels, however confusedly, that it is indispensable in the long run.'[22]

The difficulties inherent in such a transformation cannot be underestimated. Historical antipathy, natural pride and policy, and reluctance to give up the devil one knows for the devil(s) one does not are there for all to see. But real world developments and the logic of deterrence are pushing NATO in this direction, willy-nilly. Few would deny that the credibility of the United States guarantee is waning; few would also dispute the impossibility of restoring the vitality - and popularity - of extended deterrence as traditionally conceived.

Were such a transformation possible, this would free the United States from the tight mechanistic logic of extending its deterrent in an increasingly inhospitable strategic context. Matching category of weapon for category of weapon and option for option would become a reduced requirement, as the tasks are shared and deterrence re-acquires a more healthy mix of certainty and uncertainty, in the context of a mixture of force structures and centres of decision-making. Such a development might also begin to defuse the destructive scenarios of European requests for (nuclear) re-assurance, American answers, and European protest and unease as a result. Such requests would be less likely and less necessary if NATO were to move towards recognition of the existence, development and encouragement of a multilateral deterrence system.

Improvements in British and French deterrent forces are beginning to allow realistic contemplation of such a state of affairs. Qualitative and quantitative changes will be such over the next decade that it would not be unrealistic to imagine the development of certain limited nuclear options which would enhance the credibility of self protection and allow extension of the credibility to others. Whether or not this transition is managed through explicit public policy is, perhaps, irrelevant; Moscow is entirely capable of inputing intent from capability. Similarly, it is equally irrelevant whether Britain and France unify their forces or engage in joint targeting. The deterrent effect of two centres of European nuclear decision-making, as opposed to one, should, in fact, enhance credibility.

It is often asked, in the words of Josef Joffe, 'why would a country like West Germany place greater faith in the puny nuclear forces of its middle power allies across the Rhine River and the English Channel than in the massive arsenal of its Superpower ally?'[23] Yet the choice is not this stark. Reliance on Britain and France <u>and</u> the United States, within a modified structure of extended deterrence would not involve replacing one set of guarantees with another, but rather their amalgamation.

It is also objected that while there may be some strategic logic in such a development, historical memory and national pride will always stand in the way - both in terms of a German 'finger on the trigger' and German willingness to rely on London and Paris. However, just as German concerns over nuclear sharing were modified in the 1960s through the consultative mechanisms of the NPG, it is not farfetched to imagine similar procedures here, particularly in the context of an enduring United States troop presence and security commitment. Germany need not acquire a nuclear 'finger on the trigger'; nor need Britain and France sacrifice their sovereignty in the name of German security.

This development, if possible over the long term, would have another salutary effect. Arms control negotiations on the continent could begin to get away from the diplomatic and bargaining imperatives of strict parity and equality and begin to reflect the reality of strategic asymmetries and imbalances arising from doctrine and geopolitical considerations. As deterrence became more diffuse on the continent, the United States, and indeed the Alliance, could begin to get away from the perceived requirement to have arms control agreements which reflected equality at all levels when that equality is not required for either doctrine or deterrence. (This is a problem which has plagued the INF negotiations. Equality is demanded for negotiating purposes but is not necessary for deterrent purposes.) Such a transition to a multilateralised deterrence framework would also allow the troublesome issue of British and French forces to be accommodated in an acceptable arms control framework.

These 'recommendations' taken together reflect what might be called a 'two-track policy of Alliance reconstruction'. In the narrow military sphere, there are specific policies which can be undertaken to enhance NATO's deterrence credibility in Moscow. And in the broader context of restoring NATO's credibility to itself, there is a series of steps which can be taken in the diplomatic and foreign policy spheres, including a gradually altered Western deterrence framework.

In the absence of a greater European unity of effort, there is little likelihood that the United States will continue to respect its allies, or that Europe will retain its respect for the Alliance. And in the absence of greater American prudence and open mindedness in its dealings with both East and West, there is little likelihood that Europe will find the psychological strength to assume its place in an Alliance which must face the strategic challenges of the future.

In response to those who might fault this analysis for its lack of focus on the 'hard' military choices which NATO must confront, there are two points which can be made. First, in the absence of a climate of mutual re-assurance, NATO will be unable to face these hard choices over the long haul. And second, could there be anything more deterring to Moscow than a Europe which has regained its pride and purpose and an Alliance at peace with itself?

Notes

1. Pierre Hassner, 'Who Is Decoupling From Whom? or This Time, the Wolf Is Here' in Lawrence S. Hagen (ed.), The Crisis in Western Security (Croom Helm Publishers, London, 1982) pp. 168-185.

2. Fen Osler Hampson, 'Groping for Technical Panaceas: The European Conventional Balance and Nuclear Stability', International Security, vol. 8 no. 3, (Winter, 1983-84), pp. 32-56.

3. Stanley Hoffmann, 'NATO and Nuclear Weapons: Reason and Unreason', Foreign Affairs, vol. 60 no. 2, (Winter, 1981/82), p. 331.

4. See Christoph Bertram, 'Europe and America in 1983', Foreign Affairs (America and the World), vol. 62, no. 3, (1984), pp. 616-631.

5. Karl Kaiser, 'NATO Strategy Toward the End of the Century', Naval War College Review, January-

February 1984, p. 71.

6. Philip Windsor, 'On the Logic of Security and Arms Control in the NATO Alliance', in Hagen (ed.), The Crisis in Western Security, p. 38.

7. Hassner, 'Who Is Decoupling From Whom? or This Time, the Wolf Is Here', p. 173.

8. Bertram, 'Europe and America in 1983', p. 629. 9. Hassner, 'Who Is Decoupling From Whom? or This Time, the Wolf Is Here', p. 172.

10. Hoffmann, 'NATO and Nuclear Weapons: Reason and Unreason', p. 331.

11. Hassner, 'Who Is Decoupling From Whom? or This Time, the Wolf Is Here', p. 172.

12. Bertram, 'Europe and America in 1983', p. 629.

13. J.S. Finan, 'Contemporary Nuclear Deterrence: The Place of Arms Control in the Search for Escalation Dominance', D Strat Staff Note No. 83/1, Operational Research and Analysis Establishment, Department of National Defence, Ottawa, January 1983.

14. Ibid., p. 6.

15. Josef Joffe, 'Europe's American Pacifier', Foreign Policy, no. 54, Spring 1984, p. 74.

16. Ibid.

17. For a good analysis of this problem see Thomas J. Hirschfeld, 'Reducing Short-Range Nuclear Systems in Europe: An Opportunity for Stability in the Eighties', Annals, AAPSS, 469, September 1983 and John Steinbruner and Leon Sigal (eds.), Alliance Security: NATO and the No First Use Question (The Brookings Institution, Washington, D.C., 1983).

18. Johan Jorgen Holst, 'Moving Toward No First Use in Practice', in Steinbruner and Sigal (eds.), Alliance Security: NATO and the No First Use Question, p. 179.

19. Leon Sigal, 'Political Prospects for No First Use' in Ibid., p. 136.

20. For two excellent analyses of suggestions for conventional force alterations, see Hampson, 'Groping for Technical Panaceas: The European Conventional Balance and Nuclear Stability'; and Jeffrey R. Cooper and and Daniel Goure, 'Conventional Deep Strike: Non-Nuclear Deterrent, Wartime Defense, or Second-Best Option', Unpublished Paper, Jeffrey Cooper Associates, Inc., Arlington, Va, February 28, 1983.

21. Steinbruner and Sigal (eds.), Alliance Security: NATO and the No First Use Question, p. 140.

22. Hassner, "Who Is Decoupling From Whom? or This Time, the Wolf Is Here', p. 175.

23. Joffe, 'Europe's American Pacifier', p. 78.

Chapter Eight

NATO, NO FIRST USE AND CONVENTIONAL DETERRENCE

Paul Buteux

Currently another 'great debate' on NATO strategy and on the place of nuclear weapons within it is occurring. The 1979 decision to deploy new intermediate-range nuclear forces in Western Europe may be the proximate cause of this renewed interest in Alliance strategy and for its present political salience, but at another level this debate can be seen as one response to a broader series of changes in the Alliance's strategic environment. These changes have had a cumulative effect on the overall military and strategic posture of NATO, and in turn have affected the political consensus that underlies them. In brief, these changes can be listed in terms of shifts in the strategic balance and of the resulting uncertainties as to the meaning and consequences for the Alliance of strategic parity. In addition, changes in the theatre nuclear balance which have undermined any notion of NATO superiority in this area, and continuing concern about the adequacy of the Alliance's conventional forces in the light of improvements in Warsaw Pact capabilities, have combined to challenge the ability of NATO to implement its declared strategy of flexible response.

In particular, the Alliance policy of threatening in certain circumstances to initiate the use of nuclear weapons has been called into question. Flexible response, since its formal adoption by NATO in 1967, has always entailed the possible first use by the Alliance of nuclear weapons in circumstances in which the allies had failed to stem an overwhelming conventional attack. The purpose of initiating the use of nuclear weapons would be to attempt the restoration of a deteriorating military situation, and would be designed to confront an attacker with the risk of further escalation and the potential for catastrophe that crossing the nuclear threshold would entail. It is argued that the threat of first use by NATO is necessary to the threat of escalation implicit in the deterrent posture of the Alliance.

The changes in the strategic environment, and the political concerns about the implications of NATO's nuclear posture that have resurfaced in recent years, have resulted in a renewed questioning of the credibility of the strategic concept of flexible response. Doubts have been expressed as to whether there are any circumstances in which it would be in the interests of any of the NATO allies for the Alliance to deliberately cross the nuclear threshold in the event of war. Anything but the most limited use of nuclear weapons would have devastating consequences for the territory on which they were used, and in the context of warfare in Europe widespread doubts exist as to the possibility of containing escalation at levels that would not result in the complete destruction of what was being defended. In response to the political and strategic problems that have resulted from these concerns, two ideas - which though not necessarily linked can nonetheless be seen as complementary - have been suggested as possible ways out of the political and strategic difficulties in which the Alliance finds itself. These are the suggestions that NATO formally declare that it would not be the first to use nuclear weapons, and secondly the suggestion that the Alliance make greater efforts to strengthen its conventional deterrent capabilities. In short, that NATO adopt a posture of no first use and that it rely more on conventional deterrence.

The idea that the nuclear powers should commit themselves not to be the first to use nuclear weapons is by no means a new idea. In one form or another, it has been around since the earliest days of nuclear weapons deployments.[1] In 1964, on the occasion of their first nuclear test, the Chinese declared that they would never be the first to use nuclear weapons; and in 1982, at the Second United Nations Special Session on Disarmament, the Soviet Union also made a unilateral no first use declaration. What is novel about the suggestion that NATO adopt no first use, however, is that unlike earlier suggestions and commitments, it is not, by and large, made as a gesture towards arms control or disarmament. Instead, no first use is advocated as a desirable reform of NATO strategy which would result in a more credible and politically acceptable deterrent posture for NATO.

The best known advocates of a NATO no first use strategy are the so-called 'gang of four' whose views appeared in the spring 1982 issue of Foreign Affairs.[2] These distinguished former American public servants called for study and debate on the proposal that the Alliance make a no first use declaration. Not surprisingly, the initial official response to the proposal was a negative one. Authorities on both sides of the Atlantic were quick to criticise the suggestion, pointing out that given the implications of no first use for the strategy of the Alliance, to adopt it would undermine the essential political consensus underlying that strategy. Nevertheless, no first use serves to focus attention on some of the present and pressing dilemmas of NATO strategy which are already undermining the political consensus on which it rests. If the present strategy is unable to command the necessary degree of support, then changes will be necessary if the Alliance is to retain its political as well as its strategic credibility.

It is not surprising that this initiative should come from American sources. Quite apart from the fact that proposals for change in the Alliance's nuclear policy typically have come from the United States, reflecting the central position of American nuclear forces in alliance strategy, no first use is compatible with long-standing American objectives concerning the military posture of the Alliance. In fact, the American advocates of no first use have reiterated arguments that have been put forward ever since the United States became vulnerable in the 1960s to a significant Soviet retaliatory capability. These arguments have been directed to the problem of making the risks of extending deterrence to its NATO allies acceptable to the United States in a situation of mutual vulnerability and strategic parity, and involve the familiar nostrum of greater conventional defence efforts on the part of the Alliance.

Flexible response was itself a means by which Alliance strategy was adapted to the consequences of American vulnerability, and in the form finally implemented never resulted in the level of conventional forces felt necessary by its advocates. Now, the proponents of no first use place an even greater emphasis on the role of conventional forces in Alliance strategy than did the apostles of flexible response. Even if the kind of conventional balance in Europe envisaged by

McNamara and his advisers had come about, in the declaratory strategy at least, the threat of first use was to be retained. The credibility of this threat was linked to the supposed superiority of American strategic and theatre nuclear forces; but with subsequent changes in the military balance removing any last vestiges of American strategic and theatre superiority, flexible response, with its concomitant threat of first use, is being questioned as an adequate basis for Alliance strategy.

One way in which the loss of strategic and theatre superiority has undermined the promises on which flexible response has been based concerns the ability of the Alliance to exercise what has been termed 'escalation dominance' and 'escalation control'. Given the vulnerability of all the allies to retaliation in the event that NATO initiated the use of nuclear weapons, a crucial underlying premise of the strategic concept of flexible response has been the assumption that after such an action the balance of military and strategic advantage would lie with the Alliance. In other words, that under the United States strategic umbrella, the Alliance possessed theatre nuclear superiority. Whether or not the Alliance in fact has ever enjoyed a meaningful theatre superiority is not by itself crucial to the psychological and political credibility of the Alliance's strategic posture. Until the 1970s, at least on the basis of static indicators, the theatre nuclear balance when coupled to American strategic forces favoured NATO. In these circumstances, the politically important 'myth' of a nuclear deterrent counterbalance to the Warsaw Pact's conventional superiority retained its plausibility. With strategic parity, and with the Soviet Union's build-up and modernisation of its own theatre nuclear capabilities, the credibility of the myth, if not completely undermined has been severely challenged.

A posture of no first use is thus advocated as a recognition of this changed state of affairs. Not only is the NATO posture lacking in credibility, but it is held to invite pre-emption in time of crisis. No first use, then, would be a step towards reinforcing crisis stability. Underlying all the American advocacy of no first use is the view that any use of nuclear weapons in Europe would quickly escalate and would probably involve a central strategic exchange between the United States and Soviet Union. Thus it is no longer in the interest of the United States to support a NATO strategic policy that lacks credibility and that reduces the ability of the United States to practise effective crisis management in the event of a military confrontation in Europe. In short, a first use posture is simply too risky. No first use responds to strategic parity and the loss of theatre nuclear superiority by redefining the nature of the American extended deterrent commitment to Western Europe.

More than anything else, it is the implications of no first use extended deterrence that has aroused opposition to the idea in both the United States and Europe. Alliance authorities have insisted on the continuing deterrent value of the threat of first use. In a situation in which the Alliance must always consider the possibility in the event of conflict of an overwhelming conventional breakthrough, the threat of first use faces the potential attacker with major uncertainties. It is argued that if the attacker could be reasonably certain that NATO would not resort to nuclear weapons, then it would remove a major complication from tactical planning and a major uncertainty concerning the risks attendant upon armed conflict in Europe. American officials in particular have pointed out that an all-encompassing no first use declaration covering all nuclear weapons and all classes of targets, would drastically reduce the flexibility of American nuclear policy. Given the current importance of flexible options in American strategic policy, no first use thus represents a radical challenge to American and Alliance declaratory strategy.[3]

Since flexible response is an escalatory concept, no first use would remove the option of taking the first step in the process of escalation. This of course is the major attraction for those who advocate it, but by linking a no first use posture with increased NATO conventional capabilities, it can be argued that the additional benefit of placing the onus of escalation on the Warsaw Pact would be obtained. In effect, a no first use pledge would shift NATO strategy in Europe from one emphasising deterrence by threat of punishment (the threat of catastrophic nuclear war) to a strategy of deterrence by denial (emphasising effective military resistance to invasion).

Understandably, given their geostrategic position, the Germans have proved most sensitive to the implications of such a shift in NATO strategy. German critics have reiterated a familiar point: that the purpose of Alliance strategy should be the deterrence of any war, whether it be conventional or nuclear. For Germany (as it must be said for the other allies as well), the essence of Alliance strategy is the coupling of conventional defence with nuclear weapons. Ever since the Federal Republic entered the Alliance, the policy of successive governments has been to commit its allies to a policy of forward defence backed by the threat to use nuclear weapons if forward defence should fail. A no first use pledge would be incompatible with this long-standing policy objective, for it would have the effect of weakening, if not entirely breaking, the link between conventional defence and nuclear weapons.[4]

Another point of great sensitivity for the Germans is the impact of a no first use pledge on the sharing of risks in a nuclear alliance. German spokesmen have always stressed that the risks of being defended by nuclear weapons should be shared as equally as possible. Although this is not a principle that the other allies have been willing to endorse without qualification, it has been accepted to some degree as a necessary condition of Alliance persistence. No first use would undoubtedly alter the present balance of risks in the Alliance because such a pledge would alter the terms of the American guarantee. In effect, the formal nuclear guarantee would be limited to reprisal in the event of the Soviet Union initiating nuclear war, thus leaving the territory of the Soviet Union as a sanctuary in any military demonstration against Western Europe short of the use of nuclear weapons. Not only would this affect the balance of risks between the United states and its European allies, but would have also the very important political consequence of underlining the differences between those European allies possessing national nuclear forces and those who do not. Quite apart from the strategic and military consequences of no first use, it is these political implications that help account for the very great wariness with which allied governments have approached the idea.

The implications of a no first use pledge arise within the context of a mutually supporting framework of political and military commitments between the United States and its allies. In so far as no first use limits or redefines the American nuclear guarantee, then in the absence of compensating military and political changes, the Alliance framework of mutual commitments is undermined. In many ways, the no first use proposal is a symptom of the fact that not only is the viability of present NATO strategy being questioned in the light of strategic change, but that no first use is also a symptom of current political stress in the Alliance which, in part, results from the impact of the same strategic changes which challenge the credibility of flexible response. While undue emphasis should not be placed on the latter point, the history of NATO demonstrates clearly that the way in which questions of strategic change are handled is very much affected by the political context in which they occur.

As Leon Sigal, among others, has pointed out, if no first use is seen primarily as an American initiative, then it would be open to interpretation as an American attempt to lessen its own risks in the event of war in Europe.[5] It would be seen also as yet another example of American unilateralism with respect to Alliance strategic doctrine. Together, these considerations highlight a problem that is fundamental to the transatlantic alliance relationship: that as long as European defence rests on the deterrent effect of American nuclear weapons, then ultimately it is the Americans who will determine the terms and scope of their nuclear guarantee. If the credibility of the United States nuclear commitment is perceived as having declined, and if the ability of the United States to extend deterrence through the threat of first use is doubted as well, then the all-important political credibility of the nuclear strategy of the Alliance is challenged. Thus the renewed interest in the role of the Alliance's conventional forces represents not only a search for a way out of NATO's strategic difficulties, but of its political difficulties also.

This interest in de-emphasising the role of nuclear weapons in NATO strategy and of augmenting the Alliance's capabilities for conventional defence, is to be found on both sides of the Atlantic. What might be termed the orthodox view argues that because NATO's ability to offer a 'stalwart' conventional defence against the forces of the Warsaw Pact is now in doubt, the Alliance at present has no option but to rely both for deterrence and defence on the threat to use nuclear weapons early in any conflict. It is thus necessary for the Alliance to augment its conventional forces and to find methods of halting a conventional attack without recourse to nuclear weapons. This can be done without abandoning the Alliance's strategic concept of flexible response and, therefore, without relinquishing the insurance provided by the possibility of resorting to nuclear weapons should conventional defence fail. General Rogers, the Supreme Allied Commander Europe, has reflected this kind of thinking with his suggestion that if the allies were to commit themselves to a 4 per cent *per annum* real increase in defence spending, then an effective conventional defence would be possible.[6]

Essentially, prescriptions of this kind see the solution to the strategic and political problems resulting from the Alliance's reliance on nuclear deterrence in the alleviation of the difficulties facing NATO's military planners. Undoubtedly, improved conventional forces would make the task of planning a NATO conventional defence against a conventional attack much easier; however, whether this would remove the fundamental concerns raised by the NATO threat to use nuclear weapons first is another matter. For the advocates of no first use, conventional defence alone is the only credible way of providing for European security. The only role for nuclear weapons in Alliance strategy should be to deter the threat or use of nuclear weapons by the Soviet Union.

Among the American advocates of no first use, two schools of thought concerning the role of conventional weapons can be distinguished. First, there are those who press for a general Alliance commitment to increased conventional capabilities and what has been termed 'conventional deterrence'. The presumption is, by and large, that the existing distribution of effort in the Alliance would not be much affected. In particular, the leadership role of the United States in the Alliance would be retained. On the other hand, there are those who see no first use as a way of shifting the burden of their defence more onto the Europeans themselves. These range from those who wish to see a straightforward reduction in the size of American forces deployed in Europe to those who favour a radical restructuring of Alliance responsibilities.[7] Whatever the specifics of these various proposals, they do serve as further indication that no first use has far-reaching implications not only for the strategic posture of the Alliance, but for its politics as well.

If no first use is highly controversial, the suggestion that NATO enhance its conventional deterrence capabilities has become an orthodoxy amongst Alliance commentators and would-be reformers. Unfortunately, the notion of conventional deterrence is not without its difficulties and ambiguities. Many who use the term in fact mean no more than the raising of NATO's nuclear threshold by means of augmented conventional capabilities. Beyond this, those who advocate no first use suggest that were NATO to abandon its commitment to first use it would be easier to develop a more effective conventional war-fighting posture. No longer would force planning be affected by the need to integrate conventional forces with the possible use of battlefield and tactical nuclear weapons. The reduction in shorter-range nuclear systems made possible by no first use would release resources for conventional defence and would enable existing resources to be used more effectively. Conventional deterrence would be enhanced, so the argument runs, because the capacity to resist a conventional attack by conventional means would be significantly augmented.

A high degree of confidence in the Alliance's ability to resist and possibly defeat a Warsaw Pact conventional attack would strengthen deterrence by bringing home to the adversary that in order to secure victory it would probably be necessary to initiate nuclear war itself - with all the escalatory risks that would be involved - and which would be incompatible anyway with any objectives that reasonably might be served by victory. In these circumstances of the Soviet Union being forced to contemplate first use, in order to limit the risks of nuclear retaliation, the Soviet Union itself would be faced with the problem of developing a military and strategic posture compatible with the exercise of escalation control.[8]

However, as Samuel Huntington has recently reminded us, more effective defence does not amount necessarily to more effective deterrence. In his view, deterrence requires both a capacity to deny the adversary his objectives and a capacity to retaliate and punish an adversary in the event that denial fails.[9] Historically, NATO has relied on nuclear weapons to provide this retaliatory threat. Now, if the threat of nuclear reprisal in the face of a conventional assault lacks sufficient credibility to be both strategically and politically convincing, then the whole deterrent posture of the Alliance is weakened. Even if the Alliance were to acquire strengthened conventional forces that offered greater confidence in their ability to defeat a Warsaw Pact conventional attack, this would in effect amount to no more than the traditional strategy of denial. What most advocates of a greater conventional emphasis for NATO are suggesting is an augmented capacity for the direct defence of NATO territory; but, according to Huntington a deterrence strategy resting upon denial capabilities only is weaker than one that offers the threat of reprisal as well.[10]

For the Alliance to move away from nuclear deterrence of aggression in the direction of conventional deterrence it would be necessary to add a reprisal component. This would require that NATO adopt a force posture and military plans that would communicate to the potential adversary the intention to put at unacceptable risk values and territory that are important to that adversary. Thus, Huntington suggests that NATO move away from a forward defence designed to meet an attacking force at the border, and instead make provision for a prompt retaliatory offensive into Eastern Europe.[11]

There are, however, at least two major objections to the suggestion that NATO adopt a counter-offensive strategy. In the first place, it is highly questionable whether, within the context of any likely European conventional balance, NATO's ability to threaten conventional reprisals would have anything like the deterrent potential of nuclear weapons. It is indeed the unprecedented capacity of nuclear weapons to hurt and destroy that is the essence of their deterrent effect. Although it might be desirable that the conventional force posture of the Alliance be such as to convince a potential adversary that a conventional war in Europe would be as costly, dangerous and uncertain in its consequences for itself as it would be for NATO, nevertheless, as the historical record demonstrates, there are many examples of the breakdown of conventional deterrence. The European experience in the twentieth century has been disastrous in this respect.

A second objection to a NATO counter-offensive strategy arises from the political implications of such a strategy for both East-West relations and for the allied consensus on the nature of the Alliance. Most, if not all, of the European allies would be extremely reluctant to take any steps that could be interpreted as modifying the character of NATO as anything other than a purely defensive alliance. Quite apart from the political signals that a counter-offensive strategy might give to the Soviet Union and its allies, the restructuring of Alliance forces that such a strategy would require would demand a degree of allied consensus on the direction and need for change that is simply unobtainable in present circumstances.

By and of itself, an increased conventional capability, even though it might adjust the European military balance in favour of NATO, does not solve some of the major problems that arise from the Alliance's strategic circumstances. Stronger and more effective Alliance conventional forces may well raise the threshold at which a decision to use nuclear weapons may have to be faced, but the level of conventional forces by itself will not affect the credibility (or lack of it) of threatening the use of nuclear weapons. Ultimately, one side or the other will have to accept the political consequences of defeat (at least in the sense of failing to secure the objectives for which war was initiated), or of escalating across the nuclear threshold. If the American commitment to initiate the use of nuclear weapons in the face of conventional defeat lacks credibility within the context of the present strategic posture of the Alliance, then raising the nuclear threshold with improved conventional forces will not effect that credibility either. Once the threshold has been reached, there still remains the choice of whether to use nuclear weapons. If the Alliance can no longer exercise escalation dominance, and if the ability to control nuclear escalation once it has occurred is dubious in the light of the strategic and theatre nuclear balance, then augmented conventional forces do not resolve the problems of nuclear deterrence for the Alliance.

Anyway, the very presence of nuclear weapons in Europe casts doubt on the applicability to NATO's strategic circumstances of analyses of purely conventional deterrence. Even if accompanied by unilateral or mutual no first use pledges, the existence of nuclear weapons fundamentally alters the meaning and credibility of the conventional component of a deterrence strategy. It can be accepted that the state of the conventional balance and the interaction of the opposing strategies of the parties to the balance powerfully affect decisions to go to war;[12] but the fact remains that the uncertainties associated with the resort to force are immeasurably increased when nuclear weapons are present. The whole calculus of cost and risk is altered.

By itself, it is very doubtful if conventional deterrence of a conventional attack would be sufficient guarantee for the Europeans to sustain the Alliance in anything like its present form. Virtually since its inception, the military posture of NATO has been premised on the assumption that though an adversary might decide that a military solution to a political problem might be worth the risk if only a conventional response has to be taken into account, the possibility of nuclear weapons being used means that only a clear and immediate threat to national survival would warrant the risks involved in going to war. As articulated in particular by German spokesmen, the justification for theatre nuclear weapons is that when linked to conventional forces war in Europe has been rendered both unwageable and unwinnable. To abandon the threat of first use would be to drastically reduce the effectiveness of the Alliance's present strategy of war prevention.[13]

Of course, most no first use advocates see the imminent threat of nuclear war as fundamental to the efficacy of their preferred strategy. Given the existence of nuclear weapons, there remains the essential possibility that they may be used despite pledges not to be the first to do so. Anyway, nuclear weapons would still have a central place in NATO strategy as a deterrent to the threat of first use by the Soviet Union. Thus the Alliance would still require a credible second-strike capability. Nevertheless, no first use would encourage a substantial reduction in the numbers of weapons deployed, changes in the composition of the nuclear arsenal, and changes in NATO's military plans. No first use, then, would require more than a change in the declaratory strategy of the Alliance; it would require also major changes in conventional and nuclear force posture. In these circumstances it is very doubtful whether the strategic concept of flexible response could be retained in anything like its present form. As already indicated, given the importance of the political functions performed by flexible response, the politically disturbing impact of no first use on flexible response may well be one of the biggest barriers to serious Alliance consideration of a no first use strategy.

In the current debate over NATO strategy, a point that is frequently ignored is the extent to which _de facto_ changes in the Alliance's nuclear posture and, by extension, nuclear strategy have already occurred. First, it should be noted that over the past decade, quite apart from the present reality of the new INF deployments, the Alliance has given considerable attention to the modernisation and composition of its nuclear arsenal. Undoubtedly the 1979 decision to deploy the Pershing II and Ground Launched Cruise Missiles has been the most visible in this respect, but there have been in addition incremental changes of significance too. These have included new artillery warheads, new nuclear munitions for tactical aircraft, new command and control mechanisms and redeployment and improved security for storage sites. Added to this, the withdrawal of 1,000 warheads from Western Europe following the 1979 decision, and the decision taken at the Montebello meeting of the Nuclear Planning Group in October 1983 that a further 1,400 warheads would be withdrawn from the NATO stockpile over the next few years, have together resulted in a substantially altered NATO nuclear arsenal.

When coupled with the renewed interest in more effective conventional defence, it can be suggested that what the recent and planned changes in the Alliance's theatre nuclear arsenal amount to is a move towards a more explicit posture of 'no early first use of nuclear weapons'. Indeed, it is possible to go further, and to suggest that despite its declaratory strategy, NATO already has *de facto* a no first use posture. In the event of conflict, the initial use by the Alliance of short-range battlefield nuclear weapons would seem to be dubious in terms of the benefits that might accrue to the NATO allies; and, on the other hand, the use of the new long-range systems now being deployed would seem to be too great a step on the ladder of escalation, inviting a devastating counter-response by the Soviet Union. The main utility of the changes which have occurred in the Alliance's theatre nuclear arsenal appears to lie more in the area of security against pre-emption. Certainly, one very important characteristic of the modernised INF being deployed in Western Europe is that they are less vulnerable than the systems they are replacing, and so are better suited to being withheld in a reprisal role.[14]

Still, despite arguments that a first use threat now has little credibility, it is by no means clear that the present declaratory strategy of the Alliance has lost most of its utility. As many have argued, even the slightest threat that the Alliance might initiate the use of nuclear weapons in the event of war greatly complicates Warsaw Pact tactical planning, and alters the whole context in which the risks and consequences of war would be calculated. The deterrent value of uncertainty is not to be undervalued, and is a consideration on which much weight had been placed by the European analysts and observers. It is possible to interpret successive changes in Soviet military doctrine and organisation over the years as an attempt by the Soviet Union to lessen the challenge to its own operational plans of a NATO resort to nuclear weapons. Recent developments in Soviet doctrine and organisation governing its conventional forces can be interpreted further as part of a continuing attempt to neutralise the threat posed by NATO's possession of a nuclear option. Certainly Soviet planners have long recognised that the use by NATO of its theatre nuclear forces would be disastrous for any conventional offensive that the Warsaw Pact might mount.[15]

Thus if the argument is accepted that recent changes in the force posture of the Warsaw Pact reveal an acceptance by the Soviet Union of the possibility of a purely conventional conflict with NATO forces, and given that it is not in the interest of the Alliance to facilitate the Warsaw Pact planning process, then it follows that there is still deterrent value in the threat of first use. Improved NATO conventional defences would undoubtedly reinforce a posture of 'no early first use', but the retention of the first use threat serves not only to link conventional defence with nuclear deterrence, but also reinforces the ability of NATO's conventional forces to offer in fact the prospect of a 'stalwart' conventional defence. In other words, the threat of first use can assist in securing the widely shared Alliance objective of building a more effective conventional defence.

For the European allies, in the final resort deterrence rests on the prospect of intolerable losses for all involved, in the event that fighting breaks out. In the European context, this prospect arises for the superpowers, only if nuclear weapons are used and escalation that involves their homelands occurs. If no first use were adopted, for the Russians this risk of escalation would be greatly reduced if not eliminated entirely, whereas for the European allies of the United States the prospect of complete destruction would be very great. It is in the light of considerations such as these, as well as others, that the Soviet Union's no first use declaration should be understood. The simple reality is that neither the Soviet Union's force posture, nor its strategic doctrine, requires a first use threat - a strategic asymmetry which the Soviet Union has not been reluctant to exploit. And, indeed, nuclear modernisation, and the other changes which have occurred in NATO's nuclear arsenal and military posture, can be understood as responses to the adverse implications of this strategic asymmetry in circumstances of nuclear parity and absence of theatre nuclear superiority.

Nevertheless, as Michael Howard cogently reminds us, the security problems of NATO cannot be managed independently of the political context in which they occur. In his view, for broad sections of European opinion, the prospect of nuclear war is seen as being unrelated to the existing political situation and to any security requirements arising out of it. Thus any measures taken to deal with security against the Soviet Union that seem to make nuclear war more likely will be unacceptable and disruptive of the political consensus that supports the Alliance.[16] For Howard, improvements in the mechanism of deterrence such as are attempted by theatre nuclear force modernisation cannot by themselves provide the re-assurance that he sees as the essential political and psychological function of the Alliance. Rather, the plans to deploy new missiles in Western Europe have served instead to arouse very basic fears and anxieties in Western public opinion.

Most observers would agree that these fears and anxieties are unlikely to be allayed simply by the demonstration that new nuclear weapon deployments are necessary if the declared strategy of the Alliance is to be preserved; changes in the strategic posture of the Alliance have to be linked to complementary measures of a political and diplomatic kind. The task of securing and maintaining a strategic consensus will be greatly affected by the state of East-West relations and by Alliance agreement on how those relations should be managed and approached. This in turn means that the task of coalition-building in the Alliance is as essential as the successful management of East-West relations. Once again in the history of the Alliance nuclear strategy has become central to the politics of coalition maintenance. The fact that the credibility of first use has been so widely questioned, and that solutions in the form of conventional deterrence are being so widely assayed, suggests perhaps that the old formulae and compromises will no longer suffice. However, whether no first use and conventional deterrence can provide the basis for a new Alliance strategic compromise must be seen as doubtful. As this paper has pointed out, unless one is prepared to abandon many of the political and strategic assumptions which so far have supported the transatlantic bargain, the military and strategic choices available to the Alliance are limited.

Notes

1. A concise history of no first use proposals can be found in Lawrence D. Weiler, 'No first use: a history', Bulletin of the Atomic Scientists, vol. 39, no. 2, (February, 1983), pp. 28-34.

2. McGeorge Bundy, George F. Kennan, Robert S. McNamara and Gerald Smith, 'Nuclear Weapons and the Atlantic Alliance', Foreign Affairs, vol. 60, no. 4, (Spring, 1982), pp. 753-768.

3. The arguments in favour of NATO retaining a first use posture are well rehearsed in First Use of Nuclear Weapons: Preserving Responsible Control. Hearings before the Sub-committee on International Security and Scientific Affairs of the Committee on International Relations, House of Representatives, March 1976. See testimony of administration officials, pp. 151-183. Testimony to the same hearings by witnesses favouring a no first use position anticipates most of the arguments of more recent advocates.

4. The orthodox German position is restated in Karl Kaiser, George Leber, Alois Mertes and Franz-Josef Schulze, 'Nuclear Weapons and the Preservation of Peace', Foreign Affairs, vol. 60, no. 5, (Summer, 1982), pp. 1157-1170.

5. Leon V. Sigal, 'Political Prospects for No First Use' in John D. Steinbruner & Leon V. Sigal (eds.), Alliance Security: NATO and the No First Use Question, (The Brookings Institution, Washington, D.C., 1983), p. 138.

6. For a comprehensive presentation of the case both for the desirability and possibility of an effective NATO conventional defence see the Report of the European Security Study (ESECS), Strengthening Conventional Deterrence in Europe, (St. Martin's Press, New York, 1983). General Rogers views can be found inter alia in Bernard W. Rogers, 'The Atlantic Alliance: Prescriptions for a Difficult Decade', Foreign Affairs, vol. 60, no. 5, (Summer, 1982), pp. 1145-1156.

7. A useful review of the current debate on United States conventional force posture can be

found in Robert W. Komer, 'Maritime Strategy vs. Coalition Defense', Foreign Affairs, vol. 60, no. 5, (Summer, 1982), pp. 1124-1144. For a radical view questioning the validity of United States extended deterrence see Earl C. Ravenal, 'Counterforce and Alliance: The Ultimate Connection.' International Security, vol. 6, no.4, (Spring, 1982), pp. 26-43.

8. In connection with this point, it is worth noting that although Soviet strategic doctrine has always stressed the importance of surprise and pre-emption, this does not amount necessarily to a posture of threatening first use.

9. Samuel P. Huntington, 'Conventional Deterrence and Conventional Retaliation in Europe', International Security, vol. 8, no. 3, (Winter, 1983-84), pp. 36-37.

10. Ibid., p. 37.

11. Ibid., pp. 40-43. In this emphasis on clearly threatening the Eastern European allies of the Soviet Union, Huntington's suggestions invite comparison with the dissuasion strategy suggested by Kaplan and his associates in 1974. This was designed to provide incentives for the allies of the Soviet Union to stay out of any European conflict. It should be noted, however, that the dissuasion strategy was one that continued to be premised on the threat to use nuclear weapons. Morton A. Kaplan et al, NATO and Dissuasion, (Center for Policy Study, University of Chicago, Chicago, 1974).

12. John J. Mearsheimer, Conventional Deterrence, (Cornell University Press, Ithaca, New York, 1983), pp. 33-62.

13. Karl Kaiser et al, 'Nuclear Weapons and the Preservation of Peace', pp. 1159-1160.

14. Paul Buteux, Strategy, Doctrine and the Politics of Alliance: Theatre Nuclear Force Modernisation in NATO, (Westview Press, Boulder, Colorado, 1983), pp. 78-88 for a fuller discussion of this point.

15. Christopher N. Donnelly, 'Soviet Operational Concepts in the 1980s', Strengthening Conventional Deterrence, pp. 115-121.

16. Michael Howard, 'Reassurance and Deterrence', Foreign Affairs, vol. 61, no. 2, (Winter, 1982/83), pp. 309-324.

Chapter Nine

ARMS CONTROL AND DETERRENCE STRATEGIES

Dan Caldwell*

Deterrence and arms control are two of the most widely used, important and least understood concepts of our time.[1] Sadly, this generalisation applies to theoreticians and practitioners of international relations as well as to members of the public. Part of the difficulty stems from the ambiguity of the lexicon of international relations, for like other concepts in the field such as national security, the balance of power and national interest, deterrence and arms control each have multiple, often contradictory, meanings. The first two sections of this article, therefore, are devoted to the analysis of the various meanings of arms limitation and deterrence. In the third section, the effects of various types of arms control on deterrence are assessed.

Deterrence Strategies

As many observers have pointed out, deterrence is a social concept as old as humanity. For example, parents throughout history have employed deterrence in the raising of their children. International relations scholars have also employed the concept for centuries. In his history of the Peloponnesian Wars, Thucydides noted many instances in which one side or the other attempted to convince its opponent that beginning or expanding a war would not be worth the costs or risks.

The basic meaning of deterrence is relatively simple and widely, even intuitively, understood:

* For their comments on an earlier draft of this article, the author would like to thank Mr. Louie Delvoie, Admiral Robert Falls, Lieutenant Colonel Steve Fought and Dr. Richard Smoke.

Arms Control and Deterrence

'Deterrence is the use of threats of harm to prevent someone from doing something you do not want him to do.'[2] In the context of international relations, deterrence involves the manipulation of one state's or a group of states' behaviour through the use of threat by another state or group of states.

Alexander George and Richard Smoke have noted that by the late 1960s deterrence theory and practice existed on three different levels: the strategic deterrence of the two superpowers, the deterrence of limited war, and the deterrence of threats of conflict below the limited war threshold.[3] Strategic deterrence is defined in the Scowcroft Commission Report as 'a condition in which a strategic power is dissuaded from attack because he believes the potential victim could retaliate effectively'.[4] This article will devote primary attention to strategic deterrence, some attention to the deterrence of limited war through the threat to use nuclear weapons, and very little attention to the deterrence of threats below the level of limited war.

A number of deterrence strategies have evolved since the end of World War II. These strategies constitute a spectrum from non-nuclear deterrence at one end to nuclear war-fighting and damage limitation at the other end. On this spectrum, it is sometimes difficult to differentiate one strategy from another. For example, at what point does a policy of limited nuclear options become a strategy of nuclear war-fighting? This paper will identify and describe four nuclear deterrence strategies and to treat these, following Max Weber, as 'ideal types'. The strategies are: fundamental deterrence, extended deterrence, limited nuclear options and nuclear war-fighting.

Bernard Brodie and his collaborators, who were the first to analyse the political effects of nuclear arms, described them as the 'absolute weapon'. To Brodie and other early strategists nuclear weapons were useful only to deter the use of other nuclear weapons. According to Brodie, 'Thus far the chief purpose of our military establishment has been to win wars. From now on its chief purpose must be to avert them. It can have almost no other useful purpose.' These new weapons stood classical military strategy on its head. One of the major principles of military strategy in the pre-nuclear era was the principle of superiority: the state that had more divisions, ships, artillery and so on was judged to be the superior military power. Classical strategists believed that the offence must possess a ratio of three to one over the defence before launching an attack. Brodie, however, noted: 'If 2,000 bombs in the hands of either party is enough to destroy entirely the economy of the other, the fact that one side has 6,000 and the other 2,000 will be of relatively small significance.'[5]

Brodie's initial thoughts about the significance of nuclear weapons over time evolved into a strategy of nuclear deterrence that came to be called 'minimum' or 'finite' deterrence. During the Kennedy administration, Secretary of Defense McNamara and his systems analysts determined that the United States could be assured of killing 25 per cent of the Soviet population and destroying 50 per cent to 75 per cent of Soviet industry with 400 intercontinental ballistic missiles, the equivalent of 200 deliverable megatons. This strategy of deterrence calls for a single mission for nuclear weapons: to deter the use of other nuclear weapons. The objective is to make sure that no other country will threaten to use or actually use nuclear weapons against the United States or its allies for any purpose other than to deter the use of nuclear weapons. Although this strategy in the past has been called 'minimal', this is not the best descriptive term. A better description is 'fundamental deterrence' because all other strategies of deterrence build on this foundation. Too, there is the possibility that the detonation of as few as 100 megatons could result in a global climatic catastrophe.[6] Even the use of a relatively small number of nuclear weapons could have disastrous consequences. For these reasons, it is better to think of this strategy of deterrence as fundamental rather than minimal or finite.

A second strategy of deterrence asserts that the threat to use nuclear weapons can be 'extended' to deter conventional attacks on the United States and its allies. In an attempt to obtain maximum political influence from American nuclear weapons, the Eisenhower administration adopted the policy of massive retaliation whereby the United States, according to Secretary of State John Foster Dulles, would respond to Soviet aggression by retaliating 'instantly, by means and places of our own choosing'.[7] In essence, this policy was an attempt to translate strategic nuclear power into political-military influence, particularly in Europe. Therefore, although the doctrine of massive retaliation is not often cited as an example of extended deterrence, massive retaliation was criticised on all fronts: Henry Kissinger and William Kaufmann from academia, John Kennedy in the political arena and General Maxwell Taylor from the military standpoint.[8] The basic criticism of massive retaliation was that it simply was not credible; no American President could justify the use of United States strategic nuclear weapons for tactical purposes. Following the election of John Kennedy, United States forces were restructured to provide for flexibility in responding to attacks on the United States or its allies.

A third strategy of nuclear deterrence calls for the capability to exercise limited nuclear options. This strategy is a logical extension of the policy of flexible response to nuclear weapons. American planners had some flexibility in targeting throughout the 1950s and 1960s; however, in 1974 Secretary of Defense James Schlesinger voiced his concern that the United States could be confronted with a situation in which it would not have sufficiently flexible nuclear forces to respond to a Soviet attack on American military targets. Noting that such a Soviet attack would not produce 'anything approximate to a disarming first strike against the United States', Schlesinger noted in his 1975 Report that the growing Soviet counterforce capability could:

> bring into question our ability to respond to attacks in a controlled, selective, and deliberate fashion. It could also give the Soviets a capability that we ourselves would lack, and it could bring into question the sense of equality that the principles of Vladivostok so explicitly endorse. Worst of all, it could arouse precisely the fears and suspicions that our arms control efforts are designed to dispel.[9]

Schlesinger's concern about arousing fears and suspicions of the sort that 'our arms control efforts are designed to dispel' will be addressed in the last section of this article. For the moment, it is sufficient to note that a concern for arms control was one of the principal factors motivating Schlesinger to advocate his limited nuclear options approach.

According to accounts in the press, President Carter and his Secretary of Defense Harold Brown initially were disposed to move away from the counterforce orientation embodied in the Schlesinger Doctrine. In his Inaugural Address, President Carter said that it would be his goal to rid the world of nuclear weapons. In a speech in March 1975, Harold Brown proclaimed that 'only deterrence is feasible' and that nuclear war-winning and coercive strategies employing nuclear weapons were impractical.[10] Once in office, however, Carter and Brown became concerned about the possibility that without some counterforce capability the United States could be put in a position in which uncontrolled escalation or surrender would be the only American options. As a result of these concerns, in August 1977 Carter signed Presidential Directive 18 which re-affirmed the Schlesinger Doctrine. Three years later, Carter signed Presidential Directive 59 which was designed to improve deterrence by improving the United States' capability to fight a limited nuclear war. So, despite their initial misgivings, Carter and Brown accepted the limited nuclear options strategy.

The fourth strategy for maintaining deterrence calls for the capability to fight a prolonged nuclear war. In his book, The Wizards of Armageddon, Fred Kaplan notes that American strategists have thought about means to actually fight a nuclear war for many years. Indeed, Kaplan maintains that this has been a central concern of strategists in the post-World War II period. In order to fight a nuclear war, a country would have to possess the forces needed to wage such a campaign. For many years technological advances in weapons development precluded the United States or the Soviet Union from developing strategic nuclear forces that would be capable of destroying the other side's military forces. For example, the development of ICBMs increased the vulnerability of countries to attack. However, until the late 1970s ICBMs were not sufficiently accurate to be able to effectively destroy the other side's ICBMs. With the degree of accuracy of contemporary ICBMs, land-based missiles are vulnerable to attack.

In his 1983 Report, Secretary of Defense Weinberger notes that the Reagan administration accepted the flexible response policy of the Carter administration. In both doctrinal statements and force posture, however, the Reagan administration went beyond the 'limited nuclear options' strategy toward a nuclear war-fighting posture.

The FY 1983 Five Year Defense Plan called for the United States to develop a strategy and forces for fighting a protracted nuclear war with the Soviet Union,[11] and the strategy outlined in the 1982 defence guidance document called for the United States to develop the ability to destroy Soviet command, control and communications links; in short, to be able to 'decapitate' the Soviet political and military leadership. The defence guidance document issued one year later called for the American military to integrate plans for employing medium and long-range nuclear weapons to enable the United States to fight a war more effectively.[12] Although the rhetoric of the 1983 report was toned down from the year before, the objective was the same: to be able to fight and prevail in a nuclear war.

To support its nuclear war-fighting strategy, the Reagan administration called for the development of counterforce offensive weapons to be able to threaten Soviet hard targets, defensive weapons to limit the damage inflicted on the United States, and improved command, control and communications capabilities. The administration called for the following offensive weapons: (1) 100 MX missiles with a CEP of 300 feet; (2) speeded up development of the D-5 SLBM with a CEP of 400 feet for initial operating capability in 1989; (3) deployment of Tomahawk cruise missiles with 640 operational by 1990; (4) continued deployment of air-launched cruise missiles on B-52 bombers; (5) the development of the new B-1 bomber; (6) the development of an air-launched cruise missile for use at low altitudes against hard targets with a high degree of accuracy; and (7) development of the new single-warhead Midgetman ICBM.[13]

In addition to these offensive forces, President Reagan has called for a massive effort to develop a space-based ballistic missile defence system and the United States began testing an anti-satellite system in January 1984. According to *Aviation Week and Space Technology*, 'One of the main objectives of the five point offensive strategic force modernisation plan of the Reagan Administration is to focus on improvements to enhance survivability of the forces and C^3I elements to withstand a Soviet first strike and effectively retaliate.'[14]

Taken together, the Reagan defence programme must cause Soviet planners to be very concerned about the strategic objectives of the United States. Clearly, there is a significant difference between the strategy for maintaining deterrence pursued by the Reagan administration and the strategies pursued by all previous administrations.

As noted at the outset of this article, it is not difficult to define deterrence. The difficulty comes in deciding how to maintain deterrence. Do we need to possess any nuclear weapons? Would several hundred nuclear weapons suffice to assure deterrence or do we need to be able to fight a nuclear war? There are a host of deterrent strategies and four of the major strategies have been identified and described above.

Arms Limitation Strategies

Like deterrence, arms control has a much longer history than is generally recognised. Isaiah's prophecy comes from the eighth century BC: 'And they shall beat their swords into plowshares, and their spears into pruning hooks; nation shall not lift up sword against nation, neither shall they learn war anymore.' In the sixth century BC, fourteen states in China held a conference to close a seventy-year period of warfare and to reduce the level of armaments.[15] The United States has signed a number of arms control agreements, the oldest of which is the Rush-Bagot Agreement of 1817 which limited the naval forces of the United States and Great Britain on the Great Lakes. In the 1920s and 1930s, the United States and other countries reached several agreements on the most important military forces of that period, capital ships.

The destructiveness of nuclear weapons created added incentive to reach effective limitations on arms, and the United States and Soviet Union each proposed plans for nuclear disarmament in 1946. But neither the United States nor the Soviet Union was willing to accept the other superpower's plan, and, while arms control was discussed at a number of international fora throughout the late 1940s and 1950s, no agreements of significance were concluded until the early 1960s.

During the first years of the sixties, an impressive body of literature on arms control and disarmament was produced by analysts such as Donald Brennan, Hedley Bull, Thomas Schelling and Morton Halperin.[16] These analysts believed that arms control could increase the security of the United States. Arms control, according to Schelling and Halperin, had three major objectives: to reduce the risk of nuclear war, to reduce damage should war occur, and/or to reduce the economic costs of preparing for war. While these early arms control writings were viewed by many policymakers as interesting, they were considered to be somewhat academic and removed from the real world of day-to-day international politics. Nuclear war was viewed as a theoretical possibility with a very, very small probability.

The Cuban missile crisis changed this perception dramatically. During the crisis, both Kennedy and Khrushchev realised that nuclear war was not simply a distant, hypothetical possibility. It really could, and almost did, happen. The Cuban missile crisis served as a catalyst for change, and following the resolution of the crisis, Kennedy and Khrushchev moved to implement some of the ideas of the arms control analysts.

In his book, The Strategy of Conflict, Thomas Schelling pointed out that it was a good idea for conflicting parties to have the capability to communicate with one another.[17] During the Cuban missile crisis, this capability did not exist and nearly resulted in disaster. For example, at one point during the crisis, an American intelligence-gathering plane strayed off course and entered Soviet airspace. There was no immediate means for the Soviets to communicate with American authorities to determine the mission of this plane. As Khrushchev noted in a letter to President Kennedy:

> A even more dangerous case occurred on 28 October, when your reconnaissance aircraft invaded the northern area of the Soviet Union, in the area of the Chukotski Peninsula, and flew over our territory. One asks, Mr. President, how should we regard this? What is this - a provocation? ...an intruding aircraft can easily be taken for a bomber with nuclear weapons, and that can push us toward a fatal step.[18]

Following the resolution of the crisis, the two countries moved quickly to establish a direct communications link, the so-called 'hot line' between Moscow and Washington. This agreement, signed in June 1963, was followed by the signing of the Limited Test Ban Treaty in August. These two agreements marked the first tangible fruits of modern arms control and crisis control efforts.

By the late 1960s, two developments had occurred that literally made possible the negotiation and implementation of a number of arms control agreements. First, the Soviet Union achieved approximate parity with the United States in strategic nuclear weapons. Second, both the United States and Soviet Union deployed reconnaissance satellites enabling them to monitor a number of important weapons-related activities, including the construction of missile silos and missile tests.

During the 1960s and 1970s, a number of arms control agreements were signed. By the end of the 1970s, ten bilateral United States - Soviet Union agreements and ten multilateral arms control agreements had been signed. These twenty agreements covered a remarkable range of subjects from prohibitions on environmental modification to the limitation of offensive and defensive strategic nuclear weapons.

This section will focus on several different types of arms control. The conclusion will turn to a consideration of specific weapons and arms control proposals but before presenting several different types of arms limitation, it is important to note that the 'cosmetic', or 'pseudo-arms control' approach will not be discussed. These terms refer to efforts by policymakers to appear that they are seriously engaged in arms limitation efforts, when they, in fact, have little real interest in achieving meaningful arms control. Two political scientists writing about arms control and disarmament in the 1960s characterised the efforts of the 1950s as essentially 'window dressing' and therefore meaningless.[19] Critics of the Reagan administration have argued that it is simply going through the motions of arms control negotiations in order to placate the voting public that generally favours arms control.

Four types of arms control which will be identified and described are: confidence-building measures, limitations on defensive weapons, limitations on offensive forces, and deep reductions in nuclear arsenals. Although these categories are not mutually exclusive, they can be considered relatively independent of one another.

Confidence-building measures (CBMs) may be defined as 'measures to demonstrate a nation's lack of belligerent or hostile intent, as distinguished from measures which actually reduce military capabilities'.[20] CBMs may be bilateral or multilateral and may involve a wide variety of activities including statements of policy, troop withdrawals, measures to increase communication, and so on. Given this definition, a number of agreements qualify as CBMs. For example the Hot Line Agreement, the 1972 Incidents at Sea Agreement, and the 1973 Agreement on the Prevention of Nuclear War all are examples of confidence-building measures. The final Act of the Helsinki Conference on Security and Co-operation in Europe called for several CBMs including the advance notification of manoeuvers with more than 25,000 ground troops. More recently, CBMs have been discussed at the CSCE Review Conference which met in Madrid in September 1983 and at the Conference on Disarmament in Europe which met in Stockholm in January 1984.[21]

In a recent article, Thomas Schelling noted that 'confidence-building is deadly serious business. It is deadly serious because nothing is more threatening to the nuclear fate of the world than the loss of confidence on each side in the other's restraint, patience, and security.'[22] Schelling believes that the worst characteristic of contemporary strategic weapons is that they provide an incentive to strike first. The principal values of CBMs, then, are to provide confidence and thereby prevent crises and, should crises occur, provide tangible means to manage the crisis without escalation to war.

A second type of arms control places limitations on defensive weapons. The best example of this type of arms control is the 1972 Anti-Ballistic Missile Treaty, which limited the United States and Soviet Union to the deployment of a total of 200 ABM missiles at two sites. In addition, this treaty contained a number of qualitative restrictions on the research and development of ABM missiles and associated equipment such as radars.

Limitation of defensive systems is consistent with the doctrine of assured destruction; by limiting defences, a country leaves itself vulnerable to attack. Given the enormous destructive power of modern nuclear weapons, if only a few nuclear weapons were able to penetrate a state's defensive shield, the destruction would nevertheless be unacceptably high. Bernard Brodie realised this point. Studying the effectiveness of British defences against German V-1 attacks on England, Brodie discovered that the peak effectiveness for the British occurred on August 28, 1944, when 97 out of 101 V-1 rockets were shot down.According to Brodie, 'If those four had been atomic bombs, London survivors would not have considered the record good.'[23]

Several types of defensive weapons could be limited, including anti-submarine warfare, anti-satellite warfare, and anti-ballistic missile defence. Of these three types, ABM or ballistic missile defence is the most important area in which to maintain the controls that have been negotiated to date. Given the political environment of 1984, it is unlikely that controls on BMD will be expanded and it is possible that, as the United States and Soviet Union continue research and development in this area, the limitations on BMD will deteriorate. In the last section of this paper, the effects of such a deterioration on various strategies of deterrence will be examined.

A third type of arms control limits offensive strategic forces. Both the SALT I Interim Agreement and the SALT II Treaty placed various restrictions on Soviet and American strategic offensive forces including ICBMs, SLBMs, and bombers. Generally the approach that has been adopted in the past has been to restrict the aggregate number of the total or particular types of weapons. This approach has led to a great many complicated formulae for trading off various elements of the Soviet and American arsenals. The overriding objective has been to increase the stability of the nuclear balance. In the SALT II Treaty, the objective of reaching quantitative limitations was coupled with an effort to limit the quality of ballistic missiles. The limit on the number of warheads that could be placed on various types of MIRVed ICBMs and SLBMs was perhaps the most significant and least publicly recognised provision of the treaty.

One means of stabilising deterrence in the future would be to limit weapons with clear first-strike characteristics such as fixed, highly accurate, high-yield missiles capable of reaching their targets in a short amount of time. Limitations on this type of weapon would provide the United States and Soviet Union with less incentive to strike first.

A fourth type of arms control calls for deep cuts in the nuclear arsenals of the United States and the Soviet Union. For example, George Kennan has called for 'an immediate across-the-board reduction by 50 per cent of the nuclear arsenals now being maintained by the two superpowers....'[24] Such a reduction, according to Kennan, should apply to all types of nuclear weapons - strategic, medium-range, and tactical - as well as to their means of delivery. The reduction should be implemented at once and should be verified by 'national technical means'. In addition to Kennan, Admiral Noel Gayler has proposed a plan for deep reductions which calls for the dismantling of nuclear weapons and conversion of their fissionable material to fuel for civilian nuclear power plants.[25]

Deterrence-Arms Limitation Linkages

Four strategies of deterrence and four types of arms control have been identified and described in order to address the following questions: (1) What is the effect of arms control on deterrence? (2) How do proponents of each strategy of deterrence evaluate new weapons and contemporary arms control proposals on the stability of deterrence?

Both arms control and 'peace through strength' advocates agree that the principal purpose of arms control should be to reduce the probability that a state will launch a first-strike. As General Brent Scowcroft recently pointed out, '...arms control can reduce the incentive to (launch) a first-strike. Arms control can also increase mutual understanding, which may be of great importance in a crisis.'[26] Reducing the risk of a first-strike is the overriding objective of arms control in assuring that deterrence will not fail. How, then, can the danger of a first-strike be reduced?

There is one type of arms control that helps to strengthen all four strategies of deterrence and to reduce the risk of a first-strike: confidence-building measures. CBMs provide better communication and decrease the probability that a surprise attack can be carried out successfully. In a recent report prepared for the Arms Control and Disarmament Agency, William Ury and Richard Smoke suggest a number of ways that the United States and the Soviet Union can reduce the risk that a crisis will escalate out of control.[27] Ury and Smoke suggest six means by which such a danger can be reduced: (1) reach agreed-upon procedures for handling crises; (2) establish a crisis control centre; (3) following the detonation of one or more nuclear explosions on one's territory, observe an agreed-upon time of reflection and consultation; (4) hold semi-annual meetings between the United States Secretaries of State and Defense and their Soviet counterparts to discuss measures to prevent and control crises; (5) hold briefings and simulations for the President and his advisors on crisis management and prevention; and (6) consider using third parties to mediate in United States - Soviet Union disputes in third areas.[28]

Arms Control and Deterrence

When the effects of arms control efforts other than confidence-building measures on deterrence are considered, there is little agreement among strategists. Proponents of fundamental deterrence favour limitations on offensive (particularly counterforce) and defensive systems. Advocates of extended deterrence favour arms control efforts as long as these do not interfere with the ability to effectively threaten potential aggressors.

Earlier in this article, James Schlesinger was quoted as noting that one of the main reasons for his advocacy of a flexible nuclear options strategy of deterrence was to increase the probability that successful arms control agreements could be negotiated. But to increase this probability, Schlesinger proposed the development and deployment of weapons with first-strike characteristics. Part of Schlesinger's rationale was that the Soviet Union had developed and deployed similar types of weapons. As the United States sought to match Soviet force deployments, Soviet leaders became worried that the United States was seeking strategic superiority. The resulting competition could at best maintain strategic stability and has a possibility of significantly reducing stability.

Proponents of the nuclear war-fighting and damage-limitation strategy of deterrence oppose efforts to limit counterforce weapons and ballistic missile defence. Indeed, the development and deployment of these systems are essential to this approach. Confidence-building measures are the only arms control efforts judged to be capable of strengthening deterrence. Table 1 summarises the perceived effects of various arms limitation approaches on the four deterrence strategies described in this paper.

Up to this point, the article has deliberately dealt with types of arms control and strategies of deterrence in order to assess the broad impact of one upon the other. But what about the impact of new weapons systems and contemporary arms control proposals on deterrence? Tables 2 and 3 list a number of weapons systems and arms control proposals and have indicated whether the particular weapon or proposal strengthens, weakens, or has no effect upon the four strategies of deterrence. In both tables, a plus (+) sign indicates that a particular weapon strengthens the strategy; a minus (-) sign indicates a weakening of the strategy; a question mark indicates a mixed or uncertain relationship; and a zero (0) indicates that there is no impact of the

Table 1: Effects of Arms Control on Deterrence Strategies

Types of Arms Control	DETERRENCE STRATEGIES			
	Fundamental	Extended	Limited Nuclear Options	War-Fighting/Damage Limitation
Confidence-Building Measures	+	+	+	+
Limitations on Ballistic Missile Defence	+	0	-	-
Limitations on Counter-force systems	+	0	-	-
Deep Cuts	+	-	-	-

Key to symbols:

\+ indicates that the arms control measure strengthens the deterrence strategy.

\- indicates that the arms control measure weakens the deterrence strategy.

0 indicates that the arms control measure has no effect.

Table 2: The Impact of New Weapons on Deterrence Strategies

	Fundamental Deterrence	Extended Deterrence	Flexible Nuclear Options	Nuclear War Fighting
Weapons Deployed				
Trident 1 (C-4) SLBM	+	+	+	+
Tactical nuclear weapons	–	+	+	+
Pershing II MRBM	–	+	+	+
Ground-launched cruise missile	–	+	+	+
Conventional force build-up	+	0	?	?
Weapons to be Deployed				
B-1 Bomber	?	0	+	+
MX	–	0	+	+
Trident II (D-5) SLBM	–	?	+	+
Midgetman	?	0	?	?
Ballistic Missile Defence	–	0	0	+
Anti-satellite Weapons	–	0	0	+

Key to symbols: See text.

Table 3: The Impact of Arms Control Proposals on Deterrence Strategies

	Fundamental Deterrence	Extended Deterrence	Flexible Nuclear Options	Nuclear War Fighting
Freeze	+	?	–	–
Comprehensive Test Ban	+	?	–	–
Missile flight Test Ban	+	?	–	–
No first use	+	–	–	–
Deep cut reductions	+	?	–	–
Build-down	?	?	?	?
Current START proposal	–	0	+	+
Current INF proposal	–	?	0	0
Confidence-Building measures	+	+	+	+
Non-proliferation measures	+	+	+	+
Anti-satellite weapons ban	+	+	–	–

Key to symbols: See text.

weapon system or proposal on the deterrence strategy.

Several important conclusions can be drawn from these tables. The number, variety, and power of nuclear weapons required to support each strategy increases as one moves away from fundamental deterrence toward nuclear war-fighting. As can be seen in Table 2, proponents of fundamental deterrence only support a conventional military build-up and the building and deployment of the Trident I (C-4) SLBM, which is the only new weapon system clearly supported by advocates of all four deterrence strategies. In contrast, those who advocate that the United States has the capability to fight and prevail in a nuclear war support the building and deployment of almost all the weapons systems listed.

The similarity in the scoring of the flexible nuclear options and nuclear war-fighting strategies is striking. Perhaps the reason for this similarity lies in the fact that both strategies are based on the same assumption: that the United States must be able to fight a nuclear war. The difference between the two strategies is a matter of degree rather than one of kind, and the military forces developed to provide the President with flexible nuclear options could, in greater numbers, be used to fight a nuclear war.

It is hardly surprising that advocates of fundamental deterrence support a greater number and variety of arms control proposals than proponents of the other three deterrence strategies (see Table 3). There are, however, two arms control measures that proponents of all four strategies support: confidence-building measures and non-proliferation measures.

Because advocates of all four types of deterrence strategies support the negotiation of confidence-building measures, efforts to negotiate CBMs represent the 'lowest common denominator' and are, therefore, the most feasible avenue of pursuing arms limitation. This represents some good news and some bad news. It is good news in that CBMs may provide a point of consensus among advocates of very different types of deterrence. However, CBMs are rather limited measures and may not significantly reduce the risk of nuclear war.

Efforts to reduce nuclear weapons proliferation also represent a point of consensus among advocates of the four deterrence strategies and efforts should be made to capitalise on this.

Arms Control and Deterrence

This article has analysed the relationship between arms control and deterrence in both a general and specific manner. It should now be clear that the effect of arms control on deterrence depends upon what type of arms control and what strategy of deterrence one has in mind.

There is a great need to clarify the meaning of deterrence in the minds of ordinary citizens. In a recent series of public meetings on nuclear weapons and national security, the Public Agenda Foundation found a lack of understanding of deterrence.[29] However, as noted at the beginning of this paper, the concept of deterrence is basic in social relations and intuitively understood by people. What is needed is a return to 'fundamental deterrence', nuclear weapons used only to deter the use of other nuclear weapons. If deterrence was broadly understood in this sense, much of the confusion surrounding deterrence would be removed.

Finally, it is perhaps a mistake to think of deterrence and arms limitation as dichotomous terms. One knowledgable analyst, Patrick Morgan, has argued that deterrence is, in fact, a form of arms control in the sense that the threat to use nuclear weapons has prevented their use since 1945.[30] The contemporary problem, according to Morgan, is that current efforts to try to figure out how to fight nuclear war are in reality efforts to 'design around deterrence' and result in the weakening of deterrence and an increase in the risk of nuclear war. If arms control were perceived as incorporating fundamental deterrence and excluding the limited nuclear options and nuclear war-fighting strategies, then both deterrence and arms control would be strengthened.

Notes

1. Throughout this chapter the terms arms limitation and arms control are used synonymously.
2. Patrick M. Morgan, Deterrence: A Conceptual Analysis, 2nd. edition (Sage Publications, Beverly Hills, 1983), p. 19.
3. Alexander L. George and Richard Smoke, Deterrence in American Foreign Policy: Theory and Practice (Columbia University Press, New York, 1974), pp. 38-45.
4. Brent Scowcroft, Chairman, Report of the President's Commission on Strategic Forces, April 1983, p. 27.
5. Both quotations in this paragraph are from

Arms Control and Deterrence

Bernard Brodie (ed.), The Absolute Weapon: Atomic Power and World Order (Harcourt, Brace and Company, New York, 1946), pp. 76 and 48.

6. Carl Sagan, 'Nuclear War and Climatic Catastrophe: Some Policy Implications', Foreign Affairs, vol. 62, no. 2 (Winter, 1983/84), pp. 257-292.

7. John Foster Dulles, 'Speech to the Council on Foreign Relations', Department of State Bulletin 30 (January 25, 1954), pp. 107-110.

8. William W. Kaufmann, 'The Requirements of Deterrence', Memorandum #7 (Center of International Studies, Princeton, 1954); Henry Kissinger, Nuclear Weapons and Foreign Policy (Harper, New York, 1957); and Maxwell Taylor, The Uncertain Trumpet, (Atlantic Books, Stevens and Sons, London, 1960).

9. Report of Secretary of Defense James Schlesinger to the Congress on the FY 1976 and Transition Budgets, FY 1977 Authorization Request and FY 1978-80 Defense Program, February 5, 1975, pp. 1-16.

10. Fred Kaplan, The Wizards of Armageddon (Simon and Schuster, New York, 1983), p. 382.

11. Richard Halloran, 'Pentagon Draws Up First Strategy for Fighting a Long Nuclear War', New York Times, May 30, 1982.

12. Richard Halloran, 'New Weinberger Directive Refines Military Policy', New York Times, March 22, 1983, p. 18.

13. Clarence A. Robinson, Jr., 'U.S. Spurs Strategic Weapon Advances', Aviation Week and Space Technology (March 12, 1984), pp. 24-25.

14. Ibid., p. 27.

15. Coit D. Blacker and Gloria Duffy (eds.), International Arms Control: Issues and Agreements, 2nd. edition (Stanford University Press, Stanford, 1984).

16. Donald G. Brennan (ed.), Arms Control, Disarmament, and National Security (George Braziller, New York, 1961); Hedley Bull, The Control of the Arms Race: Disarmament and Arms Control in the Missile Age (Praeger, New York, 1961); and Thomas C. Schelling and Morton H. Halperin, Strategy and Arms Control (Twentieth Century Fund, New York, 1961). For a useful review and assessment of this literature, see Steven E. Miller, 'Politics over Promise: Domestic Impediments to Arms Control', International Security, vol. 8, no. 4, (Spring, 1984), pp. 67-90.

17. Thomas C. Schelling, The Strategy of Conflict (Harvard University Press, Cambridge,

1960).

18. 'Letter from Nikita Khrushchev to John F. Kennedy' (official translation), October 28, 1962, in Department of State Bulletin, November 19, 1973, p. 653.

19. John Spanier and Joseph Nogee, The Politics of Disarmament: A Study in Soviet-American Gamesmanship (Praeger, New York, 1962).

20. William H. Kincade and Jeffrey D. Porro (eds.), Negotiating Security: An Arms Control Reader (Carnegie Endowment for International Peace, Washington, D.C., 1979), p. 269.

21. For useful material, see Jonathan Alford (ed.), Confidence Building Measures, Adelphi Paper 149 (International Institute for Strategic Studies, London, 1979); and F. Stephen Larrabee and Dietrich Stobbe (eds.), Confidence-Building Measures in Europe (Institute for East-West Security Studies, New York, 1983).

22. Thomas C. Schelling, 'Confidence in Crisis', International Security, vol. 8, no. 4, (Spring, 1984), pp. 55-66.

23. Kaplan, The Wizards of Armageddon, p. 26.

24. George F. Kennan, The Nuclear Delusion: Soviet American Relations in the Atomic Age (Pantheon Books, New York, 1982), p. 180.

25. Noel Gayler, 'How to Break the Momentum of the Nuclear Arms Race', New York Times Magazine (April 25, 1982).

26. Brent Scowcroft, 'Current Problems in Nuclear Strategy and Arms Control', Essays on Strategy and Diplomacy #1 (The Keck Center for International Strategic Studies, Claremont, California, 1984), p. 9.

27. William Ury and Richard Smoke, Beyond the Hotline: Controlling a Nuclear Crisis, A Report to the United States Arms Control and Disarmament Agency (Nuclear Negotiation Project, Cambridge, MA, 1984).

28. Ibid.

29. Keith Melville, A Report on the Fall 1983 Forums, Prepared for the Domestic Policy Association by the Public Agenda Foundation for a conference on 'The Public and Public Policy', Lyndon B. Johnson Library, March 22, 1984.

30. Patrick M. Morgan, 'Components of a General Theory of Arms Control', Paper presented at the Annual Meeting of the International Studies Association, Atlanta, March 27-31, 1984.

Chapter Ten

THE FUTURE OF DETERRENCE

Part One: DETERRENCE AND THE GENERAL PUBLIC

Robert W. Reford

It is important that the future of deterrence be discussed from the perspective of the attentive publics and non-governmental organisations. Significant segments of the public are concerned about the uneasiness which exists within Western democracies regarding current trends in the evolution of deterrence, given nuclear war-fighting doctrines and enhanced counterforce nuclear capabilities. Specialists in strategic studies must remember that a wide range of opinion exists within the various peace movements of the West. The views in this paper are not necessarily representative of the peace movement as there are groups and individuals who would express views that are considerably more radical.

At the outset it should be noted that perceptions must be taken into account as they can be as important as facts. Perceptions become facts in their own right. The public is becoming increasingly concerned about many aspects of nuclear policy. The officials and the experts try to explain that policy, but the public does not always accept official explanations. In the case of Canada Prime Minister Trudeau argued that:

> The experts would have us believe that the issues of nuclear war have become too complex for all but themselves. We are asked to entrust our fate to a handful of high priests of nuclear strategy and to the scientists who have taken us from atom bombs to thermonuclear warheads, from missiles with one warhead to missiles with ten or more, from weapons that deter to weapons that threaten the existence of us all.
>
> Canadians, and people everywhere, believe

> their security has been diminished, not enhanced, by a generation of work spent on perfecting the theories and instruments of human annihilation.[1]

However, government officials and non-governmental strategists have generally recognised and accepted that there is growing public concern over deterrence - perhaps even a disillusionment over deterrence as it is now practised and its future prospects. There has been a serious erosion in their ability to re-assure the public about the prevention of nuclear war. The link between deterrence and re-assurance has been clearly set out by Michael Howard.[2]

In terms of the problems there are three factors involved:

1. A concern about numbers: We have far more than enough of both delivery systems and warheads for adequate deterrence.
2. A concern about theory: While Mutual Assured Destruction (MAD) may not have been a very satisfactory approach, it was relatively easy to understand. We seem to have moved to arcane theories and scenarios which, from the public's perspective, are perceived as being at least as likely to start a war as to prevent one.
3. A concern regarding morality: If it is wrong to use nuclear weapons, can it be right to threaten the use of them?

The <u>numbers</u> can be dealt with fairly easily. No one is quite sure how many nuclear weapons (or warheads) are required to provide deterrence. The figure 200 has been suggested. But what we do know is that it must be far less than the 2,250 strategic offensive delivery systems permitted under SALT II or the 7,300 warheads on American ICBMs and SLBMs.[3]

Overkill is overkill, and the man in the street is not satisfied with the explanation of why so many weapons and warheads are needed. People believe that the more weapons there are, the greater the danger of something going wrong - of a spontaneous explosion, of a microchip failing, of a teenager breaking the computer code, of the proverbial mad major or crazy commissar. These fears are genuine, and people do not know what they can do. Nor are they satisfied that new gadgets will necessarily make things safer.

The public is also worried about the new theories of deterrence. They do not understand things like 'extended deterrence', 'escalation dominance', or 'flexible response'. The one phrase that is clear is the most disturbing of all - 'war-fighting'. To the man in the street, the two superpowers are looking for some justification to build more weapons and/or new weapons - and for profit, as some people put it.

A group of Canadian church leaders expressed this concern in a submission made to the Prime Minister in December, 1983:

> Both the United States and the Soviet Union continue to develop and deploy nuclear weapons systems whose main function is not confined to threatening retaliation to nuclear attack, but is to demonstrate to the other that it has the technical capacity and the political will to actually engage in nuclear battle.[4]

This problem has been discussed in many circles. Dr. Don G. Bates, a professor of history of medicine at McGill University and founder of the McGill Study Group for Peace and Disarmament, for example, argued that deterrence is the fundamental reason why the public tolerates an otherwise intolerable weapon. Because the stakes are nothing short of the survival of mankind, we must be sure that the case for deterrence is sound. He then expressed serious doubts, on the grounds that the concept has changed. Originally, the purpose was self-defence. The strategy of flexible response began to shift this to intimidation, with threats not confined to the NATO area. Dr. Bates then assessed the consequences of deploying Pershing IIs, including the short warning time and the consequent danger of switching to a launch-on-warning policy, and concluded:

> What the 37 years since the first atom bomb should teach us, then, is that what we may have been living with is not a "pax plutonium" but a metamorphosis. Out of the cocoon of nuclear deterrence is emerging a monster: the nuclear incentive to initiate war, to get on with the final conflict while there is still a chance to salvage something.[5]

There is a fine line between deterrence and war-fighting, and many people are worried that if it has not been crossed already, it will be very soon.

The moral issue has been clearly stated in the brief presented by the Canadian church leaders to the Prime Minister. In their view,

> Ultimately, human loyalty is owed only to God and when defence of human institutions undermines the abundant life of God's people and threatens His earth, then we must regard it as contrary to the will of God.
>
> This has particular implications for our attitude towards nuclear weapons, and we must say without reservation that nuclear weapons are ultimately unacceptable as agents of national security. We can conceive of no circumstances under which the use of nuclear weapons could be justified and consistent with the will of God, and we must therefore conclude that nuclear weapons must also be rejected as means of threat or deterrence.
>
> In other words, it is wrong to threaten what it is wrong to do.[6]

The church leaders acknowledge that nuclear weapons exist, that they are central to the security systems of the major powers, including Canada's allies. Thus, while the objective is the elimination of nuclear weapons from national security systems, they call for carefully planned muiltilateral steps to achieve this. Their proposals 'acknowledge but do not condone' the presence of nuclear weapons.

The Roman Catholic bishops of the United States seem to have reached the conclusion that nuclear deterrence is only conditionally moral, the condition being that genuine efforts be made to reduce reliance on nuclear weapons. In short, it can be tolerated but never liked. It is a necessary evil. Because it is necessary, one cannot abandon it carelessly; because it is evil, one must constantly strive to rely on it less.[7]

The bishops have been criticised for stepping out of their proper field of responsibility. Yet surely it is their duty to speak out on issues that are of central concern to mankind, providing guidance and leadership, especially if there is a belief that political leaders are failing to exercise their responsibility.

It remains to ask whether deterrence is practical or whether it is a concept that works well on paper but will not work in practice. Freeman

The Future of Deterrence

Dyson recalls his experience with the RAF's Bomber Command during the Second World War. When German night fighters began shooting down too many bombers, the scientists developed a system called automatic gun-laying turrets (AGLT) which married radar to the machine gun. The results were astonishingly effective on the firing range. But the system could not differentiate between a German night fighter and another British bomber, and it was never introduced for operations. Dyson reaches this conclusion:

> Perhaps the analogy between MX and AGLT goes deeper. AGLT was a small technical folly embedded within the grand technical folly of Bomber Command. MX is a small technical folly embedded within the grand technical folly of nuclear missile forces. Bomber Command had its roots in the Trenchard doctrine, the doctrine that a strategic bomber force operating independently of armies and navies could by itself be a decisive weapon of war. Nuclear missile forces have their origin in the doctrine of deterrence, the doctrine that offensive forces of overwhelming destructive power will preserve our security by deterring our adversaries from hostile actions. The deterrence doctrine is not identical with the Trenchard doctrine, but it grew historically out of the Trenchard doctrine and it has the same basic weakness. Both Trenchard and the theorists of deterrence believed that they could predict the course of history by rational calculation. Hitler and the German night fighters proved Trenchard wrong. The recalcitrance of the MX basing problem has not quite proved the theorists of deterrence wrong, but it has at least thrown serious doubt upon their credibility. If we look at the story of Bomber Command and the story of MX as variations upon a common theme, we are led to ask whether our reliance on the theory of deterrence as a permanent guarantee of our survival may not be the greatest technical folly of all.[8]

And that is what is worrying more and more people.

Notes

1. Canada, House of Commons, Debates, 9 February, 1984.
2. Michael Howard, 'Reassurance and Deterrence: Western Defense in the 1980s', Foreign Affairs, vol. 61, no. 2, (Winter, 1982/83).
3. The International Institute for Strategic Studies, The Military Balance 1983-84, (London, 1984).
4. Reprinted in Ploughshares Monitor, vol. V, no. 1 (March 1984).
5. Don G. Bates, 'Is the Case for Deterrence Sound?', Toronto Globe and Mail, October 8, 1982.
6. Ploughshares Monitor, vol. V, no. 1.
7. National Conference of Catholic Bishops, 'The Pastoral Letter on War and Peace, The Challenge of Peace: God's Promise and Our Response', Origins, vol. 13, no. 1, (May 19, 1983).
8. Freeman Dyson, Weapons and Hope, (Harper and Row, New York, 1984), p. 64.

Part Two: DETERRENCE: POLITICAL-STRATEGIC PERSPECTIVES

de Montigny Marchand

In order to examine how effective the concept of deterrence is, and what role it plays - and will continue to play - in international security, it is necessary to review some of the major developments of the 1980s and how we expect the remainder of the decade will unfold. Three areas that deserve particular attention are relations within the North Atlantic Alliance, the growing problems within Eastern Europe, and the evolving politics of the Third World.

It is not unnatural for any alliance to experience some difficulties. However, in the 1980s some of NATO's problems touched the very cornerstone of the Alliance. Most disturbing is the continued questioning of United States defence and foreign policies. President Reagan's policies in Central America and in the various arms control forums have been the target of criticism in many parts of Western Europe. The result has been a sense of mistrust over the style of American foreign policy, but more importantly over American leadership itself. Europe's mistrust of American leadership has become so entrenched that it will take some time to dissipate. This is partly contingent on the United States changing its method of conducting relations both with the allies and with the East. For the foreseeable future major changes are not likely to occur in United States East-West policy.

Failure to bridge intra-Alliance differences could also have consequences for the general public which is becoming more involved with, and active on, arms control issues. The peace and disarmament movement is only one manifestation of this involvement which has often, unfortunately, been characterised by a decidedly anti-American undertone.

Differences between Alliance members have not been restricted solely to defence-related and East-West concerns. The 1980s have been characterised by recession, trade imbalances and demand for more open markets. This has resulted in some unilateral measures that have included increased trade protectionism. In some instances disagreements over economic policies have led to situations bordering on trade wars. Inevitably, questions of finance and international trade have spilled over into the security arena and the implications will need to be more carefully considered.

For Eastern Europe, the problems plaguing individual nations and the Warsaw Pact as a whole are no less critical. In the last two years, the Soviet Union has gone through two leadership changes. While he is well established now, there is no certainty that the present leader, Konstantin Chernenko, will remain President for any significant length of time. The problems of leadership transition are not new to Moscow but because of the recent rapid changes, consistency in policies and our own ability to assess the future have suffered somewhat.

To complicate matters further, the Soviet Union faces many social problems that can no longer be pushed aside. Prominent among these is the ethnic composition of the Soviet Union itself. People of Russian descent, who traditionally have been in the majority, are being slowly overtaken in total population by the remaining ethnic groups in the Soviet Union. Combined together, the various non-Russian ethnic groups could soon represent the majority with potentially serious consequences for the future leadership of the country and its internal structure. Ethnic changes could also have implications for Moscow's policies towards certain Third World countries. Added to this are the problems of disaffected youth and a sense of social and ideological malaise, to cite but a few examples. These are all severe problems with which Moscow must deal.

Yet these social problems are comparatively minor when assessed against Moscow's perennial difficulties with economic performance. Lower production and ineffective management continue to hamper economic growth in the Soviet Union. There are no signs that the Soviet economy, as it is being managed now, will improve in the near future. The internal workings of Soviet society, particularly in the areas of political leadership, economic performance, social development and demographic evolution, seem to be entering a transitional stage, whether by deliberate choice or by the force of events.

At the same time, there is some growing pressure on the Soviet Union to return to the arms control negotiating table. Economic pressures and international reaction have played some role in this. But angered by United States foreign and defence policies, which the Soviets characterise as responsible for the deterioration in East-West relations, and in no desire to assist President Reagan's re-election, the Soviet Union refrained from making a commitment to resume nuclear arms control negotiations in the immediate future. The recent moderating of East-West rhetoric has, however, helped improve relations between the United States and the Soviet Union, although we should be under no illusion as to the prospects for rapid change.

Thus, events within Western and Eastern Europe, as well as within the developing countries, have helped set the context of the 1980s and the framework into which deterrence has to fit. More and more, there has been a questioning of the relevance of deterrence. Yet, despite the changes in the areas just noted, some observers have argued that there is no alternative to the present concept of deterrence. Deterrence has already been buffeted by numerous changes within the international system and has remained relatively intact as a basic strategy, which must fulfil both political and military imperatives. It can safely be argued that deterrence has stood the test of time. Admittedly, the concept of deterrence needs to be refined in certain areas, to take account of technological and political developments. But its essential elements remain valid now as they did when first introduced in the 1960s. It may be less than perfect, but until such time as an alternative is found - through East-West dialogue and concrete agreements - there is no realistic alternative to deterrence.

If deterrence is to remain one of the successful cornerstones of Western security, it has to be accompanied by political prerequisites. To remain effective, deterrence must be bolstered by a substantial degree of Western unity. The Western 'consensus' must be developed and renewed constantly, not only in the area of defence, but also in social and economic terms. In an Alliance of sovereign, democratic nations, each with a role in the decision-making process, these issues cannot be separated.

After all, there are economic and social sides to deterrence which are no less important to the viability of the deterrence concept. It could be argued that deterrence ultimately is predicated on the certainty of a social contract between the people and the leaders of a government. In recent years confidence in the continued validity of this social contract has been shaken, in part by the debate over new intermediate-range nuclear systems.

In the future, there has to be better understanding between government and the general public and publics must be convinced their governments have control over key collective policies and decisions affecting their interests. If this means public authorities having to explain and to 'sell' a controversial policy, so be it. Governments must often lead, not just follow public sentiment. Much can be learned from the recent cruise missile testing issue in Canada and from the current INF deployment saga in the Netherlands.

For deterrence to continue to be effective in the years ahead, it must be believable in both political and military terms. There has to be some form of multilateralisation of links with Eastern Europe to create East-West political stability - the context for deterrence or strategic stability. This is a critical component for deterrence which envisages, in part, an expansion of trade and social contacts with Eastern Europe. To ensure the continued effectiveness of deterrence in the future, we should be guided by the following six principles:

1. We must preserve the overall political and

social unity of the North Atlantic Community.

2. We must ensure, as far as possible, NATO's ability to provide effective dissuasion against aggression, particularly in the European Central Front.
3. We must avoid any developments that might be interpreted as indicative of overtly aggressive intentions, particularly from the viewpoint of the Soviet Union, and we must increase public awareness of NATO policies and objectives. In this way, the public would not only better understand NATO's defensive character, but the possibilities of public demonstrations against NATO plans would be reduced.
4. We must negotiate concrete and verifiable military confidence-building measures that would make military manoeuvers and deployments more predictable. This 'transparency' would lead to a more stable balance in Europe.
5. We must ensure arms control efforts address the impact of new technology on deterrence and strategic stability.
6. We must ensure arms control negotiations, at some point, encompass the five nuclear powers as well as find ways of avoiding accidents or miscalculation that could lead to a nuclear conflict.

These six guidelines should help move Western policies towards concrete objectives that ought to include the following:

1. To develop policies that will not necessarily eliminate, but certainly stabilise, competition with the Soviet Union. These policies must take account of the fact that both the United States and the Soviet Union have interests outside the European geographic area.
2. To reduce East-West tension by dampening harsh rhetoric and the need to refrain from the use of 'megaphone' diplomacy.
3. To establish a common agenda of interests between East and West focusing on the highest priority political and security issues.
4. To recognise that mutual East-West trade can be beneficial, and should be judged

more on its commercial base than on the nature of East-West relations, as long as our security interests are not jeopardised.

5. To ensure that human rights are protected and enhanced everywhere.
6. To no longer treat Eastern Europe, in contrast to the past, as a monolithic bloc of satellites subservient to the Soviet Union, but as individual nations with particular interests.
7. To promote greater political and economic links between Eastern and Western Europe.

Part Three: DETERRENCE: MILITARY-STRATEGIC PERSPECTIVES

General G.C.E. Theriault

There are no uniform views regarding deterrence and its future. Some observers have argued in support of deterrence while others have called it into question. Some strategists believe that deterrence has a future, while others contend that it has outlived its usefulness. With respect to the Western Alliance we have been advised that NATO should re-think its strategy and explore possible alternatives. However, the debate has been inconclusive and thus it is incumbent to elucidate some points by examining the military and strategic factors affecting the concept of deterrence.

Deterrence and its strategy of flexible response and forward defence have always been a subject of controversy. From its inception there have been doubts as to whether it rested on sound military principles. These criticisms, however, should take cognisance of the fact that the present strategy of deterrence has worked since 1967 and that no viable alternatives have been proposed to present a legitimate challenge.

Yet for deterrence to continue as a viable strategy, principles must be agreed upon and certain requirements must be met. Most important is that deterrence must be acceptable to all participants of the NATO Alliance and that policy differences can be arbitrated by a higher authority (the North Atlantic Council). Within this framework, individual national strategies must somehow be accommodated.

Another principle is that, unlike classical strategies which have victory as an objective, NATO's strategy must be defensive in nature. Its main purpose must be to deter aggression and not hold out a promise of victory to the opponent. Furthermore, the strategy of deterrence must be consistent with the conduct of peacetime diplomacy. But above all, the strategy must be credible in order to effectively deter aggression.

In designing NATO's strategy of deterrence, it has always been necessary to obtain a balance of extremes. For example, two of the central features of NATO strategy involve the balancing of risks and burden-sharing between the United States and Europe. As well, there is the need to properly balance nuclear weapons with conventional forces. Needless to say, whatever balance is arrived at, there are inevitably political costs and implications which should be made acceptable to the public.

To make a deterrence strategy workable the balance that is achieved should demonstrate a reasonable degree of credibility and probability. This could be done only if NATO could make war appear as apocalyptic as possible and that NATO's resort to nuclear weapons - if necessary - would be entirely within the realm of possibility. The catastrophe that we would confront as a result of a nuclear war, however, also compels us to devise strategies to limit or contain conflicts. This in turn, drives us to seek conventional alternatives.

There are many elements that need to be considered in a balanced strategy and because of their divergent characteristics, they are also controversial. To elaborate, let us examine the concept of flexible response and NATO's strategy of forward defence. Forward defence has been criticised on military grounds which compounds the inherent disadvantages of a defensive posture which concedes to the aggressor the time, place and manner of attack. In the case of an attack, flexible response lacks the adequate conventional forces to implement the strategy and instead has to rely on nuclear weapons of which is no less problematic against an opponent who also possess nuclear weapons.

It is further argued that even if the above situation could somehow be ameliorated the allies still cannot count on the Warsaw Pact being deterred unless the public is also re-assured. The Soviet Union will not be convinced that the NATO governments are determined to resist aggression unless they enjoy the support of their publics. It is agreed that to a certain extent there has been some loss of re-assurance. This is the result of a basic belief that nothing will deter, and fear of a war in which nuclear weapons will inevitably be used. While fear of war is healthy, public opinion that says deterrence cannot be effective is a counsel of despair.

It is also said that Western publics lack confidence in a doctrine which appears to be highly dependent on the early use of nuclear weapons. This proposition is to misunderstand the doctrine. The necessity to resort to first use is directly proportional to the unevenness of the conventional balance. This should not be a criticism of the doctrine itself but of the means or lack of means to implement it.

Finally, the major criticism against flexible response has been its lack of credibility in providing extended deterrence in an age of strategic parity.

All of these criticisms have some validity; the real question is the degree to which the problems impair adequate defence and the extent to which viable alternatives exist.

In theory, at least, five alternatives deserve consideration. The first is a return to the old concept of massive retaliation. The problem with massive retaliation is that it is effective only when one side has a nuclear monopoly or clear nuclear superiority. In an age of obvious strategic balance, the massive retaliation concept is no longer credible. Furthermore, massive retaliation does not distribute equally among the NATO Alliance members the burden of deterring Soviet aggression. Because of its formidable strategic nuclear forces, the United States would be asked to carry the burden entirely by itself. The concept was discarded in the 1960s because it had lost credibility.

Conventional defence is another alternative - one that has been debated extensively in recent years. There are many problems with conventional defence not the least of which is its enormous cost. At a time when the economies of the industrialised world have not fully recovered from the last global recession, there are some doubts as to whether this alternative is acceptable to the NATO governments. Even if the cost factor could be overcome, conventional defence remains problematic given the fact that the Soviet Union could resort to theatre nuclear weapons.

If conventional defence is to play the

prominent role in deterrence there is also the problem of an implied withdrawal of American nuclear forces from Europe. This might achieve the Soviet objective of decoupling Western Europe from American central strategic forces, a situation which would not be entirely welcomed by Western European countries. More importantly, the implied withdrawing of the American nuclear umbrella could have a destabilising effect.

In military terms there is a technical problem of adopting a conventional defence in the Central Front. The length and the depth of the battlefield limits the full extent to which conventional defence could be executed. Added to this is the fact that the aggressor has the initiative which gives rise to doubts regarding the usefulness of conventional defence. History has also proven that conventional forces have failed to deter a determined enemy, an example of which could be found in France and Britain's inability to deter Hitler's Germany in 1939 despite superior force.

The third alternative is tactical nuclear defence. Given current public opposition to nuclear weapons, it would be politically impossible to implement. In addition, there are some doubts whether tactical nuclear defence is workable. Such a defence may be effective against the enemy, but could also be disadvantageous to our own forces because of electromagnetic pulse from tactical nuclear weapons. In short if flexible response is flawed, this strategy is doubly so.

A resort to pre-emptive strikes is no less difficult. Even before considering the strategic advantages of this fourth option, there is a prior question that has to be answered. Is a pre-emptive attack really a strategy or a reaction to a strategy that has failed? Militarily there are some probable advantages to a pre-emptive option, but this is counter-balanced by other no less important considerations. Politically such an option is untenable. There are also constraints of an ethical and moral nature that foreclose any serious consideration of adopting pre-emptive strike as a primary strategy.

Finally, national nuclear forces are an often discussed alternative. For both political and military reasons this alternative cannot be a proper or effective substitute for the current strategy of flexible response.

If these alternatives are not more viable than the existing strategy, what will be the future of deterrence? There is little question that, in the absence of a viable alternative, NATO will continue to rely on a combination of nuclear and conventional weapons for the defence of Western Europe. This implies that the strategy of flexible response remains a valid strategy because it is able to subsume a number of other strategies. This would include massive retaliation, tactical nuclear war and conventional defence. The important feature of flexible response, however, is that it does not prematurely commit NATO to adopt a particular strategy. This helps to maintain a necessary ambiguity in Soviet military planning. Forward defence will also remain a prominent element of NATO's strategy primarily, but not exclusively, because of the need to satisfy West German interests.

In other words, NATO strategy will not change in any fundamental way. This is not to exclude changes, but where changes are necessary they will be more of a shifting of emphasis within the strategy and in its implementation. For example, in the 1970s there was a movement away from theatre nuclear forces towards greater emphasis on conventional forces. Given the increased lethality and array of weapons of this kind, this movement will likely continue for some time. NATO's nuclear forces will continue to serve the role of deterring Soviet theatre nuclear forces and of linking Europe to the central strategic forces of the United States. However, NATO believes that enhancing conventional capabilities is critical in order to achieve a posture where conventional aggression can be met with conventional forces. Thus General Bernard Rogers has exhorted NATO nations to build a more capable conventional structure given that the current strategy is 'one which is still appropriate today if adequate forces are made available.'[1]

If I am to offer a conclusion it is simply that not only does deterrence have a future, but in foreseeable circumstances it is the only viable basis for the military strategy of the Alliance. At the same time, efforts must be mobilised to adjust East-West problems and to achieve a more satisfactory _modus vivendi_.

Note

1. Bernard W. Rogers, 'The Atlantic Alliance: Prescriptions for a Difficult Decade', _Foreign Affairs_, vol. 60, no. 5, (Summer, 1982), p. 1150.

Part Four: DETERRENCE AND THE REAGAN ADMINISTRATION

Helmut Sonnenfeltd

Despite some concerns to the contrary, the Reagan administration's view of deterrence is not substantially different compared with previous administrations. This can be seen in the Reagan administration's formal statements. For instance, the Annual Report to the Congress: Fiscal Year 1985 (Executive Summary) of Defense Secretary Caspar Weinberger states:

> While the world we face is complex and rapidly changing, the ultimate goal of American defence policy remains constant: the preservation of peace with freedom. The growing threat to our interests, the changing global environment, and the evolution of military technology dictate modifications in our military posture and capabilities. But the three underlying principles of our policy to maintain peace remain unchanged - our commitment to deterrence, our defensive orientation, and our determination, should deterrence fail, to fight to restore peace on favorable terms.[1]

As in previous administrations, deterrence remains the 'cornerstone' of the Reagan defence policy. The central goal of 'credible deterrence' continues to be the acquisition of sufficient conventional and nuclear capabilities that any potential adversary would see the costs of aggression easily outweighing any potential gains. However, as the President's Commission on Strategic Forces - the so-called Scowcroft Commission - noted:

> Deterrence is not an abstract notion amenable to simple quantification. Still less is it a mirror image of what would deter ourselves. Deterrence is the set of beliefs in the minds of the Soviet leaders, given their own values and attitudes, about our capabilities and our will. It requires us to determine, as best we can, what would deter them from considering aggression, even in a crisis - not to determine what would deter us.[2]

Thus, successful deterrence requires constant force adjustments and a clear idea about what will best deter the Soviet Union. Nevertheless, the deterrence policy of the United States retains the same basic character as it has had for decades, including its concern with what to do if deterrence should fail. Although there is now a clearer public declaration that the United States must be prepared to fight in order to 'restore peace on favourable terms' in the event of deterrence failing the fundamental American posture remains a defensive one.

The Reagan administration has been quite explicit in addressing a serious and continuing problem for American defence policy - the reputed Soviet interest in 'war-fighting'. Noting that Soviet military writings, exercises and deployments indicate a belief that 'under certain circumstances war with the United States, even nuclear war, may be fought and won', the Annual Report to the Congress: Fiscal Year 1985 (Executive Summary) states that 'If the Soviets recognise that our forces can and will deny them their objectives at whatever level of conflict they contemplate, then deterrence remains effective and the risk of war is diminished.'[3] This, of course, imposes substantial burdens on the American defence budget, requiring adequate forces to guarantee deterrence at both the nuclear and conventional level.

Successful deterrence, in the Reagan administration's view, will depend upon substantial increases in both conventional military and strategic nuclear force capabilities. Conventional deterrence in particular has assumed a somewhat more prominent role in current American thinking. The Reagan administration has recognised that the successful deterrence of Soviet aggression in Europe, South Asia (including the Persian Gulf), and the Pacific Rim is clearly beyond the means of the United States alone. America's allies must participate more fully for deterrence to function effectively. It is clear that this is true in Europe where conventional deterrence is seen to be not only increasingly necessary but also feasible, albeit with nuclear deterrence continuing as well. Implicit in current American thinking is the view that deterrence is not only a matter of restraining a potential aggressor. It also entails resisting the efforts of an adversary to deter resistance. This is quite evident in Europe where the Soviet policy of 'counter deterrence' has been designed to undermine European will and the basic premises of NATO's defence posture.

The pursuit of successful strategic nuclear

deterrence involves the same basic policies as have guided past administrations. The Reagan administration, however, has adopted a more vigorous approach to these policies, including a concerted effort to 'rebuild' the American strategic triad. This 'Deterrence through Diversity', with its emphasis on strategic modernisation (the MX, the Small ICBM, the B-1B, the 'Stealth' ATB bomber, and Trident I and II as well as improved C^3I), is simply a continuation of existing programmes, if on a somewhat accelerated and expanded scale. The Reagan administration's more vocal attention to 'war-fighting plans' (should deterrence fail) and various defensive schemes (civil and ballistic missile defence) also reflect variations in emphasis rather than new directions in American policy.

Having said this, however, there does appear to be a genuine interest on the part of the current administration in somehow escaping from or side-stepping the nuclear predicament. This can be seen in two policy areas discussed briefly earlier. It appears to be the case, for instance, that the Reagan administration is seriously interested in relying less upon nuclear weapons for successful deterrence in Europe. This is evident in some of the statements made by General Rogers as well as in recent shifts in American conventional force policy. The promise of new conventional technologies and tactics (ideas such as 'deep attack') may allow, in the American view, a raised nuclear threshold. It is far from clear, however, whether or not many Europeans share this view. Many may fear that this shift will make fighting a war in Europe much more 'thinkable'.

The eventual decoupling of American strategic nuclear guarantees - no matter how incredible they may currently seem - will certainly tend to diminish the credibility of theatre and tactical nuclear deterrent guarantees. The non-nuclear approach to deterrence in Europe will also be extremely costly - so costly, in fact, that neither the Europeans nor the Americans may be prepared to pay for it. The non-nuclear approach may also increase the chance of conflict as the decoupling of conventional and nuclear forces raises the nuclear threshold in Europe. An increased reliance on new conventional military technology may also have serious transnational industrial implications, if the United States is reluctant to share technological advances with European manufacturers and equally reluctant to buy European equipment. This increased American emphasis on conventional deterrence in Europe is thus not without its drawbacks. But then no strategy is without difficulties.

An associated feature of the Reagan administration's deterrence policies has been the idea of 'horizontal escalation' - the threat that Soviet aggression in one area of the world would precipitate American responses elsewhere within or in different theatres. These responses, nuclear and/or conventional, would be intended to limit the scope, duration and intensity of any conflict. This represents a method of adding deterrent credibility through offensive capacities to the otherwise largely defensive posture of the United States. The overall aim of this shift has been to respond to assessments of what the Soviet Union might do if there was a conflict. The notion of 'horizontal escalation' may not have been a soundly articulated policy given its seeming provocativeness and its resource demands. Perhaps as a consequence of the extensive capabilities such a policy demands, it appears to be a receding feature in present American declaratory policy. In practice, locales for 'horizontal escalation' are hard to identify, apart from Cuba.

Administration interest in various forms of ballistic missile defence (BMD) reflects an earnest desire to explore ways to change the 'rules of the nuclear game' and this type of enhanced interest does constitute a fairly significant departure from most previous official American thinking on this issue. As Secretary Weinberger noted:

> an effective defense against ballistic missiles can have far-reaching implications for enhanced deterrence, greater stability, and improved opportunities for arms control. Our efforts do not seek to replace proven policies for maintaining peace, but to strengthen their effectiveness in the face of a growing Soviet threat. The essential objective of the strategic defense initiative is to provide for a better way to prevent nuclear war in the decades to come. In the President's most apt phrase, "Would it not be better to save lives than to avenge them?"[4]

Despite the extensive nature of the Strategic Defense Initiative's research and policy implications, current administration spokesmen are using very modest terms to describe the aims of the defence initiative. This is likely in response to concerns about costs, technological feasibility and the destabilising potential of massive space-based BMD systems. In addition, there has been no formal response to the idea of linking space defence with extended deterrent guarantees. The longer term consequences of the Strategic Defense Initiative are, at this point, difficult to evaluate.

Although the Reagan administration is serious about arms control - that is, it does want 'equitable, stabilising, verifiable arms reduction' - the practical realities of the contemporary international environment do not appear to offer much real scope for significant arms control, either in the conventional or the nuclear sphere. It seems most unlikely that a comprehensive strategic nuclear arms control agreement can soon be negotiated and ratified. Vast technical difficulties, on-going Soviet-American political competition, differing Soviet and American strategic outlooks and strong contending domestic political pressures from both the 'left' and the 'right' have effectively doomed any comprehensive accord. Because of these cross-cutting pressures and concerns, it is increasingly unlikely that any significant issue will prove to be negotiable. Arms control negotiations, instead, will have to focus on small, substantive issues, seeking accord on individual matters of joint Soviet-American concern. Few, if any, of this type of agreement will be likely to have any real impact on stability or on major weapons programmes. Unfortunately, it now seems likely that no far-reaching anti-satellite (ASAT) accord will be possible. Definitional, verification and compliance issues, in my view, effectively preclude such an agreement. There is a serious possibility that many other 'controllable' systems may slip by the point where they, too, might be controlled. 'Stealth technology' is one good example. In these areas, too, limited concrete steps may be the most sensible to aim at.

While this circumstance is not encouraging, it is well to recall that Soviet-American relations, much like New York City, may be intrinsically 'ungovernable'. Being ungovernable, however, does not mean that nothing can be done to smooth out day-to-day affairs. Filling pot holes, to pursue the metaphor, can help even if it does not actually change the 'governability' of things. So too may discrete, substantively oriented arms control accords smooth the way somewhat for Soviet-American affairs.

Political leaders find it difficult not to hold out grand visions of lasting peace and ultimate disarmament. The Reagan administration is no exception. Indeed, if anything, it has been more insistent than some of its predecessors that arms control agreements must really be effective in reducing the risk of war. Ironically, its ambitious proposals for dramatic offensive weapons reductions have been called insincere because they would impose excessive burdens on the Soviets. 'Negotiability' is the best test of sincerity even if it means that proposals based on what is thought to be negotiable produce ineffective agreements.

Would we not all be better off if political leaders candidly acknowledged that arms control can at best affect the margins of military power, if that, and that security must ultimately rest on what we do unilaterally with our military forces and programmes - combined, where possible, with dialogue and negotiation but without illusion and with the realisation that the nuclear age will not be repealed.

Notes

1. Caspar W. Weinberger, Secretary of Defense, Annual Report to the Congress: Fiscal Year 1985 (Executive Summary), February 1984, p. 7. Cited as Weinberger Report.
2. United States, Report of the President's Commission on Strategic Forces, April 1983, p. 3.
3. Weinberger Report, p. 8.
4. Ibid, p. 30.

LIST OF CONTRIBUTORS

BUTEUX, Paul
Associate Professor
University of Manitoba
Winnipeg, Manitoba

BYERS, R.B.
Director,
Research Programme in Strategic Studies
York University
Toronto, Ontario

CALDWELL, Dan
Associate Professor
Department of Political Science
Pepperdine University
Malibu, California

HAGEN, Lawrence S.
Research Director
Canadian Centre for Arms Control
and Disarmament
Ottawa, Ontario

LEONARD, James
Director, East-West Project
Aspen Institute for Humanistic Studies
Washington, D.C.

MARCHAND, de Montigny
Deputy Minister (Foreign Policy)
Department of External Affairs
Ottawa, Ontario

QUESTER, George
Professor
Department of Government and Politics
University of Maryland
College Park, Maryland

RATHJENS, George
Professor
Department of Political Science
Massachusetts Institute of Technology
Boston, Massachusetts

REFORD, Robert
President
Reford-McCandless International Consultants
Toronto, Ontario

List of Contributors

SIGAL, Leon V.
Visiting Scholar
The Brookings Institution
Washington, D.C. and
Department of Political Science
Wesleyan University
Middletown, Connecticut

SONNENFELTD, Helmut
Guest Scholar
The Brookings Institution
Washington, D.C.

STEIN, Janice Gross
Associate Professor
Department of Political Science
University of Toronto
Toronto, Ontario

THERIAULT, G.C.E.
General, Chief of Defence Staff
Department of National Defence
Ottawa, Ontario

CONFERENCE PARTICIPANTS*

ANDERSON, John
Assistant Deputy Minister, Policy
Department of National Defence
Ottawa, Ontario

BECKETT, W.M.
Director
Nuclear and Arms Control Policy
Department of National Defence
Ottawa, Ontario

BEHRENDS, W.
Ambassador to Canada
Federal Republic of Germany
Ottawa, Ontario

BELL, G.G.
President
Canadian Institute of Strategic Studies
Toronto, Ontario

CAMERON, Robert
Visiting Foreign Service Officer
Department of External Affairs
York University and the
University of Toronto
Toronto, Ontario

DELVOIE, Louie
Director General
International Security and Arms Control Bureau
Department of External Affairs
Ottawa, Ontario

DEWITT, D.W.
Co-ordinator, Regional Conflict
and Conflict Resolution
Research Programme in Strategic Studies
York University, Toronto, Ontario

FALLS, Robert
Past Chairman NATO Military
Committee and Board of Directors, Canadian
Centre for Arms Control and Disarmament
Ottawa, Ontario

* Contributors to this volume, with the exception of George Rathjens, attended the York Deterrence Conference

Conference Participants

GARIGUE, Philippe
Professor
Department of Political Science
Glendon College, York University
Toronto, Ontario

GEORGE, James
Former Co-ordinator NGOs
Independent Commission on
Disarmament and Security Issues
(Palme Commission)

GRIFFITHS, Franklyn
Professor
Department of Political Science
University of Toronto
Toronto, Ontario

HALSTEAD, John
Adjunct Professor
School of Foreign Service
Georgetown University
Washington, D.C.

HERMAN, Brian
Head
NATO Policy Co-ordination Section
Department of External Affairs
Ottawa, Ontario

HOLMES, J.W.
Counsellor
Canadian Institute of International Affairs
Toronto, Ontario

ING, S.C.M.
Research Associate
Research Programme in Strategic Studies
York University
Toronto, Ontario

KIRSCHBAUM, S.
Associate Professor
Department of Political Science
Glendon College, York University
Toronto, Ontario

LEYTON-BROWN, David
Associate Director
Research Programme in Strategic Studies
York University, Toronto, Ontario

Conference Participants

LINDSEY, George
Chief, Operational Research and
Analysis Establishment
Department of National Defence
Ottawa, Ontario

MacDONALD, Brian
Executive Director
Canadian Institute of Strategic Studies
Toronto, Ontario

MACINTOSH, James
Research Associate
Research Programme in Strategic Studies
York University
Toronto, Ontario

MATHEWSON, A de W.
Chief, Policy Planning
Department of National Defence
Ottawa, Ontario

NIXON, R.
Former Deputy Minister
Department of National Defence
Ottawa, Ontario

OLSON, Theodore
Co-ordinator
Alternative Strategic Studies
Research Programme in Strategic Studies
York University, Toronto, Ontario

ORVIK, Nils
Director
Centre for International Relations
Queen's University
Kingston, Ontario

PAUL, Derek
Professor
Department of Physics
University of Toronto and Research Director
Science for Peace
Toronto, Ontario

RIEKHOFF, H. Von
Professor
Department of Political Science
Carleton University
Ottawa, Ontario

Conference Participants

ROSS, Douglas
Research Associate
Institute of International Relations
University of British Columbia
Vancouver, British Columbia

RUINA, Jack
Professor of Electrical Engineering and
Director, Arms Control and Disarmament
Programme
Massachusetts Institute of Technology
Boston, Massachusetts

SLACK, Michael
Research Co-ordinator
Research Programme in Strategic Studies
York University
Toronto, Ontario

SPENCER, Robert
Director
Centre for International Studies
University of Toronto
Toronto, Ontario

TREVERTON, G.
Assistant Professor
Kennedy School of Government
Harvard University
Boston, Massachusetts

TUCKER, Michael
Associate Professor
Department of Political Science
Mount Allison University,
Sackville, New Brunswick

WRIGHT, Gerald
President
Atlantic Council of Canada
Toronto, Ontario

INDEX

Index